FROM CASES

TO COMPOSITION

Linda Woodson

University of Texas, San Antonio

Scott, Foresman and Company

Glenview, Illinois

Dallas, Tex.   Oakland, N.J.   Palo Alto, Cal.   Tucker, Ga.   London, England

An Instructor's Manual is available. It may be obtained through a local Scott, Foresman representative or by writing to English Editor, College Division, Scott, Foresman and Company, 1900 E. Lake Avenue, Glenview, IL 60025.

Library of Congress Cataloging in Publication Data.

Woodson, Linda, 1943-
    From cases to composition.

    1. English language—Rhetoric.   I. Title.
PE1408.W675   808'.042   81-9385
ISBN 0-673-15448-3 (pbk.)   AACR2
1 2 3 4 5 6—KPF- 86 85 84 83 82 81

Acknowledgments

Chapter One

Reprinted by permission of G. P. Putnam's Sons from "Hurts Rent-A-Gun" from *I Never Danced at the White House* by Art Buchwald. Copyright © 1971, 1972, 1973 by Art Buchwald.

Excerpt from *Against Civil Disarmament*, by Don B. Kates, Jr. Copyright © 1978 by Harper's Magazine. All rights reserved. Reprinted from the September 1978 issue by special permission.

Excerpt from "Let the Great Head Count Begin" in *Time*, Vol. 115, No. 13, March 31, 1980. Copyright Time Inc. 1980. Reprinted by permission from *Time*, The Weekly Newsmagazine.

From "Energy" by Garrett De Bell in *The Environmental Handbook,* edited by Garrett De Bell. Copyright © 1970 by Garrett De Bell. Reprinted by permission of Ballantine Books, a division of Random House, Inc.

All other literary credits appear on pages 273-277, which constitute a legal extension of the copyright page.

Preface

In composition classes we try to overcome the artificiality of the situation by finding topics that will help students avoid "writing for the teacher." We admit, however, that this approach often results in few papers in which students have discovered a purpose for their writing, few papers that achieve that middle ground between the painfully personal and the starchily impersonal. The disappointing result of this approach has led me to embrace with enthusiasm writing assignments designed as cases.

A *case* is an extended statement of a writing situation that might be encountered in life. The *case method* assumes that writers write best when they have a sense of purpose and audience, and control of pre-writing processes. The context of a case assignment provides a purpose, an audience, and a set of problems to be solved. Such an assignment fulfills the requirements of a good writing situation. A specific situation from, for example, student life, social issues, or careers can enable students to write from personal experience, from information they are given, or from information they find through research. In every case, students must consider the three parts of the communication triangle: writer, message, audience.

The first part of this book provides basic instruction in the rhetorical principles necessary for good writing. Chapter 1 explains the elements of any writing situation: writer, message, and audience. Chapter 2 analyzes possible audiences and gives instruction in writing for universal and particular audiences. Chapters 3-9 explore the traditional rhetorical modes of development as ways of thinking about and analyzing the world around us. Chapter 10 examines various writers' voices and how to achieve them.

Each of these ten chapters contains three cases with writing assignments that increase in difficulty and highlight the focus of the chapter. Discussion questions are provided to promote pre-writing by exploring the problems raised in each case. The assignments help students improve their writing and communication skills in an interesting and informative way.

Chapter 11 provides basic information for doing research. A special feature is a *researched case,* which can be used as another approach to the traditional research paper.

The second part of the book consists of 15 additional cases, varying in difficulty, that may be used as supplements to reinforce those skills students have developed from the first part. Finally, a brief handbook gives basic grammatical information.

The accompanying Instructor's Manual provides answers to the exercises and discussion questions, as well as information on how to use the additional cases.

This book, then, is designed to be flexible. It is intended for instructors and students who believe as I do that good writing *can* be learned.

My debt is great to scholars, colleagues, and friends. Among the many scholars in composition and rhetoric that I have borrowed from, I owe much to James Kinneavy, Frank D'Angelo, Richard Larson, Jim W. Corder, William Labov, Lawrence D. Green, Charles Kneupper, and Walker Gibson. I would also like to thank my reviewers—David Goslee (University of Tennessee), Jeffrey Gross (University of Mississippi), Eugene Hammond (University of Maryland), Richard L. Harp (University of Nevada), Francis Hubbard (California State University, Sacramento), Robert S. Rudolf (University of Toledo), Joseph Trimmer (Ball State University), and Leonora Woodman (Purdue University).

Many have helped in the actual preparation of the book. My thanks go first to Marilyn Cooper, who cheerfully agreed to serve as developmental editor and then, I'm sure, discovered it to be twice the task she anticipated. Her wisdom, wit, and grace are on every page. Harriett Prentiss thoughtfully guided the development of the book in its early stages. Amanda Clark carried it through to completion and proved once again that she is one of the best editors around. Andrea Berg carefully edited the manuscript and turned it into a readable book.

Finally, Jim said, "Don't get discouraged," as often as was necessary, and Rachel's love kept me sane.

My thanks to all.

Linda Woodson

Contents

4 Writing Description and Using Examples   72

5 Making Comparisons and Drawing Analogies   90

More Cases   231

A Brief Guide to Correctness   260

INTRODUCTION TO STUDENTS

A part of writing that is rarely discussed is the anxiety of finding something to say. The teacher in a writing class gives a writing assignment and tells you it's due in a week. Only you know what you go through during that week. You face a blank sheet of paper, your mind just as blank. You make attempt after agonizing attempt at starting. You crumple these attempts and fill your waste basket with wads. Your palms get sweaty when you think about the fact that you have only three days left, and you've written nothing. You're just plain miserable. Then somehow on the due date there sits everyone, including you, calmly handing in a finished paper. Another writing assignment is finished with never a word about what each person went through to produce that paper. Yet that process is perhaps the most important part of the whole writing assignment.

This book is intended to stay with you during that week as you find what you've got to say, whom you will say it to, and how you will say it. This book consists of cases, that is, writing situations that help you encounter the problems of writing, including what to write about. These cases will enable you to discover some things about the writing process and your role in it that you can apply to all kinds of writing situations.

Cases put you into writing situations; you learn by experience some of the writing principles discussed in the chapters. Through your class discussions of the cases you will learn what to concentrate on in your writing, what is important and what is not, and what your role can be in each situation. By the time you have worked through the beginning cases, you will bring much of your own knowledge to the problems of finding what to say and how to say it, and you should be more confident of your ability to perform these tasks.

In the process, I hope you will discover some things about what writing can be that will help ease some of the anxiety I mentioned earlier. (I suspect it is impossible to get rid of all the anxiety, and perhaps that anxiety, in part, helps us do better. I know I suffered some sweaty palms trying to write this.) Writing can be fun, or at least pleasurable. Writing is something you will be called upon to do on occasion. Finding out what you think about a subject through writing and sharing those thoughts with someone else *can* make a difference.

CHAPTER 1

THE ELEMENTS OF A CASE

After reading this chapter, you should be able to:

identify the elements of any writing situation;

see that the first step in writing effectively is to recognize what sort of case you are dealing with;

formulate problems and questions concerning a subject and an audience.

You have been a writer since the first time your mother made you sit down and write a letter to thank Aunt Ruth for that ugly blue sweater she sent you for Christmas. In writing that letter to Aunt Ruth, you had the makings of a case. You had an audience—Aunt Ruth—whose feelings you would not hurt if you could help it. You had a message to send—you were grateful to her for remembering you on Christmas. And you had an extra problem—you couldn't come out and say, "I hate the sweater you sent me." You didn't want to lie and pretend to be thrilled with it. You had to decide what you could safely say to Aunt Ruth that would convince her of your gratitude without compromising the truth. You probably settled on some statements like, "Thank you for the sweater you sent me for Christmas. Blue is one of my favorite colors, and the sweater will be so warm for those upcoming January days. It was kind of you to remember me." Or, if you were very young, those statements might have been, "Thanks for the sweater. I like blue." Regardless of the actual words, you emphasized the sweater's color and didn't mention its ugly style so that Aunt Ruth would see you were grateful. You accomplished your purpose.

Every piece of writing you do is, in a sense, embedded in a case or situation. Your success with that writing depends in large part on how successfully you can recognize what sort of situation you are in. A *case* is simply a focused, extended statement of a writing situation that you might encounter in your present or future life. In a case, you write in the context of a specified situation.

Sometimes your situation dictates what you will write. You will be asked to write a report or recommendation, you will need to write a letter of complaint to an individual or company, or you will have a thank-you letter to write. Your task will be specified. On other occasions, you will feel a need or a desire to write, to express your opinions, to explore your thoughts. But even on those occasions, you will still be in a situation with all of the elements of a case.

What are those elements? The elements of a communicative situation have been constant since long before Aristotle identified them as *writer, message,* and *audience.* If you think about any situation in which you must write, realize that you have three things to consider. First, you, as the *writer,* have an attitude toward both your subject matter and toward your audience. Second, you have a subject that you want to say something about for some reason—a *message.* Third, you want to affect your *audience* in a way depending upon your purpose—to convince, to persuade, to interest, to gratify, to charm, to inform.

Each of these elements—writer, message, and audience— will be explored more fully in subsequent chapters. But now let us look at them briefly. Notice that you have already begun asking and answering questions about them in your previous writing assignments.

The Writer

As a writer, you will want to be heard. In the chapter on "Persona" we will explore how to insure that you are listened to. Here, however, we will identify some of the things that will persuade your audience that you are worth hearing. *Persona* is the voice or created character with which you speak, and it is chosen for a particular situation. Because there are many writing situations, many personas are possible. Generally, in order to persuade your audience that they are listening to a voice worth hearing, writers need to show evidence that they are fair, logical, humane, reasonable, and good. They should be fair in investigating both sides of an issue and logical in drawing conclusions from appropriate premises. They should be humane in caring for the well-being of others, reasonable in listening to different thoughts and opinions, and good in wishing the best for the greatest number of people.

In Lewis Mumford's appeal for better national highway planning, notice first that he is fair and logical in recognizing that there is no easy solution to the problem of the nation's highways. He is reasonable in understanding the magnitude of the problem. And having established a reliable persona, he then defines the scope of the problem and his solution for creating a better environment for the "care and culture of men."

> There is no purely local engineering solution to the problems of transportation in our age; nothing like a stable solution is possible without giving due weight to all the necessary elements in transportation—private motorcars, railroads, airplanes, and helicopters, mass transportation services by trolley and bus, even ferry-boats, and finally, not least, the pedestrian. To achieve the necessary over-all pattern, not merely must there be effective city and regional planning, before new routes or services are planned; we also need eventually—and the sooner the better—an adequate system of federated urban government on a regional scale.
>
> Until these necessary tools of control have been created, most of our planning will be empirical and blundering; and the more we do, on our present premises, the more disastrous will be the results. In short we cannot have an efficient form for our transportation system until we can envisage a better permanent structure for our cities. And the first lesson we have to learn is that a city exists, not for the constant passage of motorcars, but for the care and culture of men.—*The Highway and the City*

Each time you write, consider what image you want to convey. Decide how much of your personality and your reactions to include, or whether to include them at all. The decisions that you make about yourself as a writer are part of the context of a case or of any piece of writing.

As a writer you will also have an attitude toward your subject. You may be completely caught up in your subject, bubbling over with enthusiasm for it and eager to share it with your audience. Or you may be called upon to write about something for which you have no interest or enthusiasm, and the writing that you do as a result may have little meaning for you, although it may be quite meaningful to your audience. Winston Weathers and Otis Winchester identified some of the attitudes that are possible when discussing a subject: confident, judicious, quiet, imperative, impassioned, compassionate, critical, angry, and absurd. All of these can form a part of your message. Any of the attitudes is a possibility when you write. Although your attitude toward your subject will be determined, in part, by the purpose you are trying to achieve, you will probably have a personal attitude toward your subject as well.

Both of the following pieces of writing concern legislation controlling gun prohibition. In the first, Art Buchwald takes an absurd attitude toward his subject. He advocates gun control by describing a possible, though unbelievable, result of no gun control laws:

The Senate recently passed a new gun-control bill, which some observers consider worse than no bill at all. Any serious attempt at handgun registration was gutted, and Senate gun lovers even managed to repeal a 1968 gun law controlling the purchase of .22 rimfire ammunition.

After the Senate got finished with its work on the gun-control bill, I received a telephone call from my friend Bromly Hurts, who told me he had a business proposition to discuss with me. I met him for lunch at a pistol range in Maryland.

"I think I've got a fantastic idea," he said. "I want to start a new business called Hurts Rent-A-Gun."

"There are a lot of people in this country who only use a handgun once or twice a year, and they don't want to go to all the expense of buying one. So we'll rent them a gun for a day or two. By leasing a firearm from us, they won't have to tie up all their money."

In the second piece of writing, Don Kates' attitude toward the subject of gun control is confident and imperative. He supports his case against it with facts:

It is certainly true that only a little more than 30 percent of murders are committed by robbers, rapists, or burglars, while 45 percent are committed among relatives or between lovers. (The rest are a miscellany of contract killings, drug wars, and "circumstances unknown.") But it is highly misleading to conclude from this that the murderer is, in any sense, an average gun owner. For the most part, murderers are disturbed, aberrant individuals with long records of criminal violence that often include several felony convictions. In terms of endangering his fellow citizen, the irresponsible drinker is far more representative of all drinkers than is the irresponsible handgunner of all handgunners. It is not my intention here to defend the character of the average American handgun owner against, say, that of the average Swiss whose government not only allows, but requires, him to keep a machine gun at home. Rather it is to show how unrealistic it is to think that we could radically decrease homicide by radically reducing the number of civilian firearms. Study after study has shown that even if the *average* gun owner complied with a ban, the one handgun owner out of 3,000 who murders (much less the one in 500 who steals) is not going to give up his guns. Nor would taking guns away from the murderer make much difference in murder rates, since a sociopath with a long history of murderous assault is not too squeamish to kill with a butcher knife, ice pick, razor, or bottle. As for the extraordinary murderers—assassins, terrorists, hit men—proponents of gun bans themselves concede that the law cannot disarm such people any more than it can disarm professional robbers.*

As a writer, you will also have an attitude toward those who will read what you write—your audience. This attitude will affect both the information that you stress and the language that you choose. If, for example, you are explaining why you failed a math test in a letter to a friend at another college and in another letter to your parents, it is possible that you would emphasize your lack of study in the letter to the friend. But in your letter to your parents you might emphasize the difficulty of the material or the fact that the questions were not the ones you had expected.

Exercise

Write a letter to a friend at another college explaining why you want to take off from school for six months and drive around the country with a friend. Then write a letter to your parents explaining the same desire.

The Message

The shape of your message will be determined by your attitude toward your subject, your relationship to your audience, and your purpose in writing. Some of the elements determined by purpose are the following:

— how much information you will or will not include;
— how straightforwardly you will present that information;
— how much of your own observation and opinion will be represented;
— how much exploring you will do in the course of your writing;
— how assured or tentative you will be in your attitude toward your message.

To illustrate the influence that purpose has on the amount of information included and the attitude toward the subject, here are two excerpts from letters from college students to their parents concerning the same subject, unexpected expenditures. In the first letter, the student has a single purpose —to persuade his parents to send more money quickly.

Student fees have gone up sharply this year, and I didn't have enough money in my account to pay my full bill at registration. I still owe $130.00. The cashier said that if I didn't pay the money by Friday, I would be dropped from my classes and would have to go through late registration which would cost an extra $30. Please deposit the amount into my college account as soon as possible and call me to let me know it's OK to write the check.

Notice that the student does not give any of the details or reasons for the increase in student fees. His purpose is urgent—to receive additional money before he is dropped from his classes.

In the following excerpt, the student is writing in a more leisurely way. She is in no hurry, but her purpose is to lay the groundwork for suggesting that she and her parents consider her transfer to another school at the end of the academic year. She gives many more details to support her case.

> Registration was a mess, as usual. And when I got to the cashier's desk, I could hardly believe the bill. Student fees have doubled since last year. When I asked the lady what was the cause, she said that because of inflation the cost of providing student services had practically tripled. Health care services, transcript duplicating services, and other services that the university could formerly provide at minimal cost have soared in cost. Since this is a private university, she said they had to make up the difference from student fees.
>
> Maybe we should think again about my transferring to State next year. The cost to you would be so much less, and they have a better program in my major anyway.

In the second letter, the student made use of the increased fees to reinforce her argument for transferring to a state-supported university. She may have left out some of her other major reasons for wanting to transfer, such as the fact that her new boyfriend goes to State. Instead, she emphasized her concern for the increased financial burden on her parents that her attendance at the private university was becoming. This burden probably is a real concern to her, and from her parents' point of view it is probably the best reason for considering a transfer.

Your *message* is what you write. The specific purpose in writing is probably as varied as the number of times you write. But, broadly, certain purposes can be identified that repeat themselves again and again. Let us take a look at some of these purposes.

Informative Purpose

The purpose of some of the writing we do is to inform. We have a body of knowledge that we want to make available to another person. We do not wish to use the information to accomplish another purpose, unlike the writers of the two letters above who presented factual information about increased student fees in order to persuade their parents to send money or agree to a transfer. We, therefore, present the information clearly, logically, and in a straightforward manner. You can recognize this informative purpose in textbooks, in pamphlets and brochures that help you understand a specific subject, and in many business letters.

Notice in the example that follows the writer is mainly concerned with presenting factual information about the enormous task of taking the census. The facts are presented straightforwardly, and their staggering numbers get across what the writer wanted to tell us. But notice that the writer also emphasizes the point by using suggestive words—such as *avalanche* and *army.*

> Using 120 million forms, 5,000 tons of paper and 85 tons of ink, the survey will amass and tabulate more than 3 billion answers and record them on 5,000 miles of microfilm. To process this avalanche of data, the Census Bureau has had to design (and patent) special scanning equipment that will be plugged into a giant UNIVAC 1100 computer around the clock for months. Meanwhile, an army of 250,000 census takers, or "enumerators," and 15,000 office workers are being recruited; they will earn $4 to $5 an hour and work from four to eight weeks. The cost of the entire exercise: more than $1 billion, compared with $221.6 million in 1970 and an estimated $44,000 in 1790.—*Time*

You will often decide to present the information at hand in a clear, straightforward manner. Emphasize the message itself by presenting it as clearly and objectively as you can. Try not to communicate your feelings about the subject, nor produce any reaction in your audience other than their understanding it.

Expressive Purpose

Sometimes when you write, your purpose will be to express your feelings or emotions, and you will be concerned with expressing those emotions as candidly and honestly as you can. The emphasis will be on you as a writer rather than the subject you address or on the response your audience will make to what you are saying. You may be describing your feelings about marriage, choosing a career, or your high school. You are not concerned with treating your subject objectively or with whether or not your audience agrees with you.

This type of writing provides a way of exploring your thoughts, feelings, and emotions, as well as providing a record of them. But expressive writing can also show your audience how you felt at a particular moment. It can help your audience understand the particular path you followed in arriving at ideas and attitudes. Finally, it can provide a common ground for shared feelings and emotions for you and your audience.

In the paragraphs that follow, Sylvia Ashton-Warner explains her own emotions during a "trough" or emotional lowpoint during the day, when she finds she cannot teach:

> 1 P.M. There are times when I can't teach and this is one of them. There are troughs in effort as well as peaks and this is one of them. There's a lot of noise, a lot of coloured chalk, a lot of music, a lot of reading, some singing and laughing, but a trough nevertheless it is for me.
>
> I'm not one of those souls like drifting rain—wraiths out of touch with the essence of life, looking backward through thick tears at some moment departed and weeping that life is not worthwhile. I use those moments. At each of those times I saw the meaning of life and knew that I saw it. True, I knew that inevitably there would be many deep troughs to follow. But every time I reached those heights I said, "All my life before and my life after is justified by the wonder of this moment." Many of those moments I have forgotten now but I haven't forgotten what I said. And I trust myself. Whatever comes my way now, I know already that it has been worth being alive. Even in troughs like this.—*Teacher*

Warner records her feelings at a particular moment during the day, a particular moment that has occurred often in her lifetime. She does not attempt to record the moment factually as far as the exact circumstances are concerned, although she does give us an exact time and tells of the surrounding activity. What she attempts to record is what happens to her in a "trough," or lowpoint in her day; at those points she takes the time to reaffirm the pleasures and rewards of living. To us, the passage has value in that it explores a human emotion in a unique way, and, if we have experienced a similar emotion, the passage helps us recognize a common human experience.

Persuasive Purpose

Sometimes you will be concerned that your audience not only understands you but also agrees with you. Your purpose will be to persuade that audience to adopt the same attitude toward the subject that you hold, or at least to broaden their own existing attitudes. You may desire a very direct change in behavior. For example, you may attempt to persuade someone to vote for a particular political candidate, or you may implore a professor to change a grade that you consider unfair. Or, you may want your audience to develop a special way of seeing your subject. If, for example, you are writing a letter of recommendation, you want your audience to see the person you are writing about in the same way that you do. Or, if you were writing to the city streets department trying to convince the officials to preserve a one-hundred year old pepper tree on a new street, you would try to help the officials see the value and beauty of the tree as you do. In writing with a persuasive purpose, your special emphasis will be upon your audience.

Notice how, in the following passage, Simone de Beauvoir attempts to persuade us to look at the process of aging in a special way:

> There is only one solution if old age is not to be an absurd parody of our former life, and that is to go on pursuing ends that give our existence a meaning—devotion to individuals, to groups or to causes, social, political, intellectual or creative work. In spite of the moralists' opinion to the contrary, in old age we should wish still to have passions strong enough to prevent us turning in upon ourselves. One's life has value so long as one attributes value to the life of others, by means of love, friendship, indignation, compassion. When this is so, then there are still valid reasons for activity or speech. People are often advised to 'prepare' for old age. But if this merely applies to setting aside money, choosing the place for retirement and laying on hobbies, we shall not be much the better for it when the day comes. It is far better not to think

about it too much, but to live a fairly committed, fairly justified life so that one may go on in the same path even when all illusions have vanished and one's zeal for life has died away.—*The Coming of Age*

Simone de Beauvoir's argument may *indirectly* change behavior—we may decide to act differently or to plan our retirements differently—but her main purpose is to get us to agree that getting old doesn't mean giving up active involvement in life.

Here's an example of a writer, Garrett de Bell, whose purpose is to change his audience's behavior.

The term "standard of living" as used by utility spokesmen in the United States today generally means abundant luxuries, such as the following, for the affluent: electric blenders, toothbrushes and can openers, power saws, toys and mowers, dune buggies, luxury cars and golf carts, electric clothes dryers and garbage grinders, air conditioners, electric blankets and hair dryers.

Are these necessary for a high quality of life? We must realize that a decision made to purchase one of the "conveniences" is also a decision to accept the environmental deterioration that results from the production, use and disposal of the "convenience." Hand-operated blenders, toothbrushes, can openers and saws, clotheslines, blankets, bicycles, and feet produce much less pollution than the powered equivalents.

We can make the ecologically sensible decision to reject the concept of increasing perpetually the "standard of living" regardless of the human or ecological consequences. We can replace the outmoded industrial imperative—the "standard of living" concept—by the more human "quality of life" concept.—"Energy" from *The Environmental Handbook*

In this essay, the writer is urging us to stop using "energy-using" devices that we consider "energy-saving." He asks us to redefine our idea of "standard of living," basing it not on the number of luxury devices we own but instead on the quality of our environment. If we change our definition, he reasons, we will stop using so much energy, and there will be enough energy for everyone.

The purpose that you have for writing will determine the way that you organize your subject matter. Many of the following chapters explore identifiable patterns of thought that you can use to your advantage. The important thing to remember as you work through the cases in those chapters is that elements of all patterns may appear in a variety of combinations in any single piece of writing. If you think of the patterns as resources to be called upon whenever you write, you have a much more realistic idea of their usefulness in accomplishing your purposes.

Exercise

Look at the following short paragraphs and try to determine the author's purpose in writing. What in the paragraphs helps you identify the writers' purposes?

a. Hardness is another property that is governed by the internal atomic arrangement of minerals. Again, graphite and diamond come to mind, because they represent different arrangements of atoms of Carbon. Yet graphite is one of the softest minerals known and diamond is the hardest.—L. Don Leet and Sheldon Judson, *Physical Geology*.

b. Love and knowledge, so far as they were possible, led upward toward the heavens. But always pity brought me back to earth. Echoes of cries of pain reverberate in my heart. Children in famine, victims tortured by oppressors, helpless old people a hated burden to their sons, and the whole world of loneliness, poverty, and pain make a mockery of what human life should be. I long to alleviate the evil, but I cannot, and I too suffer.—Bertrand Russell, "What I Have Lived For," *The Autobiography of Bertrand Russell 1872-1914*.

c. But let's be fair: Is your faculty, by and large, any more uninspired, boring and dull than, say, your classmates? (Don't mistake adolescent agitations for sublime inspiration.) Does not youth always think most adults uninspired and unimaginative? And are there enough competent, intriguing teachers to go around? (Where are they hiding?) And does not your most "uninspired, boring, dull" teacher know more about the course he is teaching than you do? I think it fair to say: "Few persons invent algebra on their own."—Leo Rosten, "To An Angry Young Man," *A Trumpet for Reason.*

d. In the long history of the world, only a few generations have been granted the role of defending freedom in its hour of maximum danger. I do not shrink from this responsibility; I welcome it. I do not believe that any of us would exchange places with any other people or any other generation. The energy, the faith, the devotion which we bring to this endeavor will light our country and all who serve it, and the glow from that fire can truly light the world.—John F. Kennedy, "Inaugural Address," *The Kennedy Reader,* ed. Jay David.

e. In Paris, where the plague lasted through 1349, the reported death rate was 800 a day, in Pisa 500, in Vienna 500 to 600. The total dead in Paris numbered 50,000 or half the population. Florence, weakened by the famine of 1347, lost three to four fifths of its citizens, Venice two thirds, Hamburg and Bremen, though smaller in size, about the same proportion. Cities, as centers of transportation, were more likely to be affected than villages, although once a village was infected, its death rate was equally high. At Givry, a prosperous village in Burgundy of 1,200 to 1,500 people, the parish register records 615 deaths in the space of fourteen weeks, compared to an average of thirty deaths a year in the previous decade. In three villages of Cambridgeshire, manorial records show a death rate of 47 percent, 57 percent, and in one case 70 percent. When the last survivors, too few to carry on, moved away, a deserted village sank back into the wilderness and disappeared from the map altogether, leaving only a grass-covered ghostly outline to show where mortals once had lived.—Barbara W. Tuchman, *A Distant Mirror.*

The Audience

There is an audience for every piece of writing you do. Even in writing in a diary or a journal, you, the writer, are the audience. Writing probably fails more often than not because of writers either failing to consider the audience or failing to understand the audience they hope to appeal to. You don't have as much control over the audience of your writing as you do over the other elements, but there are certain questions about your audience that determine in part how you write:

1. Who is my intended audience for this piece of writing?
2. What do they already know about my subject?
3. What attitudes do they already hold about my subject?

Obviously a variety of results can occur after someone has read what you have written. The audience may walk away from your writing completely unconvinced, holding on to former beliefs, attitudes, or values, even feeling very hostile toward you for attempting to alter those attitudes. Or, the audience may walk away from your writing holding on to former attitudes, but equally assured of your right as a writer to your own beliefs and values. Or, the audience may be transformed in the process of reading your writing and actually modify, expand, or incorporate your expressed attitudes. Finally, the audience may be completely convinced by what you have said and completely change attitudes, beliefs, or values. The last three outcomes are, of course, much more desirable than the first. Chapter Two will explore how best to achieve them.

Exercise

Look again at the short paragraphs in the exercise on pp. 14-15. Describe the intended audience for each.

Summary

Writing as an activity begins with your first awareness of an occasion for writing and continues until you have made the last comma correction, reread your writing for the last time, and sent it on its way. When you approach a case, ask the same questions, make the same choices, as with any other writing you will ever do. Those questions will always be about writer, message, and audience. Somehow, however, thinking of your writing as a case makes it a less formidable task. Identifying the kind of case you are in helps you identify your options and make decisions.

The following is a list of questions that you should ask before you start to write. The questions are asked in the first stage of writing called *pre-writing*. Pre-writing may be defined as the mental activity before you write, activity in which you evoke, design, and plan your ideas for writing. You may do some writing in this stage—notes, thoughts, rough outlines—but only as an aid to thinking about what you want to do and say in your writing. Pre-writing, in fact, may be the most crucial stage of all writing. But you will also ask the same questions again and again as you write, and your answers to those questions will continue to modify what you say and how you say it in the second stage, *writing*. Finally, those same questions will help you in the third stage of writing—your *rewriting*. In this last stage, you will rework and redesign your ideas using those questions as guides to accomplish your purpose more successfully. Your honest answers to those questions and your appraisal of your writing in light of those answers will help you decide when you have done your best.

Questions to ask while writing
1. What kind of person do I want to be in my writing? How much do I want to involve myself in my writing?
2. What attitudes toward my subject and toward my audience should I adopt?
3. What purpose am I trying to accomplish?
4. Who is my intended audience? What do they already know about my subject? What attitudes do they already hold about my subject?

Service Station Rip-Off

You are a commuter, driving each day from the town where you live to the nearby city—a distance of forty miles each way. Your car's condition is important to you. You have an Arrow Oil credit card, and so you regularly go to the two Arrow-owned gas stations conveniently located in your town.

About a month ago, you stopped at one of them to get gas on your way home from work. The attendant, Fred, was always eager to talk; that day he went on and on about his bad luck fishing yesterday, which was his day off. Tired, you responded politely, but you were glad when you could sign the credit slip and finally head home. When you pulled into your driveway and got out of your car, you saw immediately that Fred had forgotten to replace your gas cap. The next morning, you left for work early to go by the station. You were hoping that Fred had found your gas cap and put it away for you. As you drove up to the station, you saw your gas cap lying on the side of the street. When you picked it up, you found that it had been run over. You went inside the station and told Fred what had happened. He laughed and said, "I must be getting forgetful in my old age." Then, without apologizing, he took out a box of miscellaneous gas caps (he had obviously done this before) and went out to your car, where he spent twenty minutes trying out caps. The one he settled on filled the hole but was about half an inch smaller than the original—it stayed on, but not too securely. Since you were already late for work, you didn't protest.

You listened to it rattle for two days, eighty miles a day, then went to your dealer to get a replacement. The parts man informed you that they were presently out of gas caps for your model but to come back in a week. That meant four hundred more miles with a rattling gas cap.

A second incident happened last week. Driving home on the busy freeway, you had a flat. Fortunately, because you were in the slow lane, you were able to get safely to the side of the road and put on the spare. Because the tire was only six months old, you took it to the store where you bought it to get them to check what was wrong. The man returned almost immediately: "This is what's wrong." He was holding up an inner tube marked with big red letters "Do not put in radial tire." "This isn't the tube we put in when we mounted your tire." You were puzzled—then you remembered. Four months ago you had discovered a roofing nail in the tire and took it to the other Arrow station in town for repair. They had obviously not had a correct tube, and to save going out for one they put in one they had. It saved them time, but it risked your life!

Today was the last straw. On the way to work this morning

you stopped for gas at the first Arrow station. Fortunately, it was Fred's day off, and the new attendant, Judy, remembered to replace your gas cap. You asked her to check the oil and water, and after a quick look under the hood, she told you they were fine. But just as you got off the freeway on your way home from work, you noticed your engine was overheating. You pulled over to a phone booth and called your auto club. When they came, they quickly diagnosed and fixed the problem—you had no water in the cooling system at all. The auto club man told you that you were lucky to notice the overheating before it damaged your engine.

Home at last, you sit down at your desk to write a letter of complaint to the Arrow Oil Company. As you pull out a piece of paper, the company's ad comes over your radio: "You can trust us with your car and your life." You mutter to yourself that you haven't been able to trust their local stations with either.

Assignment
Write a letter to Arrow Oil Company complaining about the incidents.

For class discussion
1. What attitude will be most effective in this letter?
2. Which details of the incidents should you include?
3. Who is your audience? What can you assume about that audience?
4. What is your purpose in writing?

Anita Ford

You are sitting in the porch swing reading the Sunday newspaper when Anita Ford walks up the street and joins you. Anita has been your five-year-old daughter's babysitter for the three years that you have lived in this community.

Anita is sixteen and is applying for her first "real" job as a teacher's aide at a nearby day-care center. She needs a letter of recommendation—a character recommendation. She has come to you because she feels that if you trust your daughter to her, you will probably give her a good recommendation.

You agree to write the recommendation. After Anita leaves, you wonder what the letter should say. Your only reservation in recommending Anita is that she is not particularly punctual. In fact, last month you missed fifteen minutes of a play because she was late for babysitting.

You can remember a number of incidents that verify Anita's good judgment. One summer evening when your daughter Beth was three, you left her with Anita while you attended an art lecture at the museum. At about 7:45, you received a message to call home. Anita told you that your daughter had been running in the hall and had fallen, banging her head against the corner of a floor-type air-conditioning grate. Anita said that she thought stitches might be needed. When you arrived home, Anita had used ice to stop the bleeding. Beth was lying on the couch, and Anita was sitting beside her, reading a story. Later, at the hospital, the doctor said that because you had come so quickly to get stitches, your daughter would be left with only a tiny scar on her forehead. You were grateful to Anita for calling you and for handling the problem the way she did.

On another occasion, you left Beth with Anita while you did some Christmas shopping. Beth had been playing outside when a boy from around the corner came over and started throwing rocks at the smaller children. Anita went outside and sent him away, but he came back in just a few minutes saying that he wasn't afraid of a babysitter. Anita called his parents and explained the problem to them, and they came to your house and took the boy home. Later when you talked to the parents at the grocery store, they remarked about the extreme tact Anita had used in the situation.

In addition to incidents like these two, you know that Anita always does her best to respect the rules you have for your daughter's behavior, and she has never, to your knowledge, had a friend over or spent an inordinate amount of time on the phone while she is supposed to be babysitting.

Assignment

Write the letter of recommendation. Include the specific examples of Anita's good judgment.

For class discussion
1. What points in the examples should you emphasize to support Anita's job application? How will you emphasize them?
2. Should you mention Anita's lack of punctuality? If so, how should you word that part of the letter?

High School Impressions

A letter came last week from the yearbook editor at your former high school:

Dear Former Student:

In an effort to create a new image for the high school yearbook, we are adding some features that we hope will make the yearbook more interesting to all. One of the features will be called "My Lasting Impression," and we hope to include representative impressions of our high school written by both present students and recent graduates, as well as graduates who have been away from the high school for several years. I would like to ask you to be one of the representatives for the class of 19___ . If you agree to do this, we would like a specific kind of account from you. To make the entries as varied as possible, we are asking each contributor to focus on a particular kind of impression. Yours is to be "My Worst Day at _____ High." Because of space limitations, we must ask you to keep this to a maximum of 600 words. We would like for you to be as candid as possible.

Thank you for your time, and we hope, for your participation. We would like to have your contribution by one month from today. If you are unable to participate, please let us know as soon as possible so we may contact another member of your class.

Sincerely,

Greg Smitten, Editor

You are flattered to have been selected and eager to participate. You certainly suffered through more than one bad day in high school, so you'll have lots of material to choose from.

Assignment 1

On Saturday morning you sit down at your desk to begin your impression. As you consider what to say, you are soon lost in reverie. You think about the harmless pranks you and your classmates participated in, and you remember getting caught, too. You remember the athletic events. You remember your favorite teacher and the one you hated most. You remember the school dances and dating—and its problems. You remember your best friend (a person you haven't seen or heard from for years). Finally, you decide on which day was your worst. Spend some time getting all of your memories of that day on paper. Don't worry about complete sentences, connecting ideas, or organization. All of that will come later.

For class discussion

1. Who will be the audience for this piece of writing in its finished form?
2. What sort of organization would be useful for this piece of writing?
3. What is your purpose in writing?

Assignment 2

Write your contribution for "My Lasting Impression."

CHAPTER 2

KNOW YOUR AUDIENCE

After reading this chapter, you should be able to:

identify your audience whether particular or universal;

approach your audience, whether sympathetic, hostile, or indifferent, in such a way that you will be heard and your purpose accomplished.

Imagine yourself in the snack bar with a group of friends discussing the professors that you have this semester. The conversation might go something like this:

"Professor Jackson is the best professor I've had on this campus."

"Why?"

"She gives fair grades, and she makes the class interesting."

"You mean easy?"

"No, fair. She's pretty good about judging your work and giving you what you deserve. And she grades on progress."

"Does she lecture all period?"

"Yeah, but she always has a funny story to tell that keeps you awake."

This conversation contains several elements common in many speaking situations. You make a statement such as "Professor Jackson is the best professor I've had on this campus." Your audience asks you to clarify points that are not understood: In what ways is Professor Jackson the best? Is she easy? Does she lecture all period? Your gestures, tone of voice, eye movements, all play a part in whether or not your audience understands and believes you.

Writing is different. As a writer, you usually will not be there to explain what you meant if your audience says, "I don't get it." Your writing should always consider what questions your audience might have, what problems they might have in understanding, and what connections between ideas they need to make. You try to anticipate the questions your audience might have.

Assume that instead of talking about Professor Jackson to your friends, you are writing about her to a high school friend who is coming to your university in the fall. You want to convince your friend to take a class from Professor Jackson. You need to anticipate what questions she might have about Professor Jackson and to answer those questions for her. You might write something like this:

> When you get here next fall, you really ought to try to get into Professor Jackson's art history class. She's the best professor I've had on this campus. She seems to be really fair in her grading practices, and she can make an otherwise boring class interesting with a funny story. I know it sounds like I'm saying she's easy, but that's not what I mean. Her tests and assignments are as hard as anyone's. But in her grading she's pretty good about judging your work, and she grades on progress in your outside essays because she says it takes a while to learn to write about paintings with any insight. Like most of the professors on campus, she lectures all period, but her funny stories keep you awake.

Of course, it is possible that after you consider what questions a particular audience would ask, a different audience might read what you wrote. Maybe the audience does not know as much about the subject as you anticipated they knew. Or maybe they know a great deal more! They might have different questions and concerns than the ones you assumed they would have. And they might have prejudices and opinions that were impossible for you to anticipate. You can't expect your writing to succeed with all possible audiences. But if you want to succeed with any audience, consider their expectations. This does not mean, though, that you should change what you believe fits a particular audience, or say only what you think they want to hear.

A Particular Audience

A *particular audience* is a person or group of persons whom you know in a personal way or about whom you know certain things. Writing to a particular audience may be much easier than writing to a universal audience because you have much more information about your readers. On the other hand, you also have to take more things into consideration when you write for a particular audience. For example, consider the mood of your audience, the established opinions regarding the issue, more specific values and beliefs held, and particular experiences with the issue that your audience may have had.

In analyzing your particular audience, begin by asking yourself what your audience feels and knows about your subject. To illustrate, let's analyze the particular audience addressed in the following case.

After-Fivers

As a young, enterprising assistant manager in the largest supermarket in town, you discover that a large segment of your store's customers is being overlooked by the store manager. These are the "after-fivers," the customers who shop for groceries after five P.M. From reading your trade journal you know that these people have an average income of $21,100, they are usually under 30, and they are almost always rushed; they spend about 25 minutes on the average in the store. Three-fourths of them have full-time jobs, and they stop at the market on their way home from work. The "after-fivers" like to be able to purchase everything they need (including cleaning and personal care items) at one place. They purchase mostly convenience and frozen foods, and their average purchase amounts to $19.89.

Since this group of customers represents a substantial source of profits, you realize that your store might do well to offer some attractive services to this group. Some of the ideas you have come up with are extending store hours and opening extra express lanes. Just the other day you overheard a customer complain, "If one more person comes up to me and says, 'Can I get in ahead of you? I only have these three items,' I'm going to punch him in the mouth." You also think these customers would be attracted by longer hours for the deli and bakery, free coffee, easy-to-prepare menus and recipes, and a charge system for purchases. You write up your proposal for your manager, and it is approved. To announce your "after-fiver" program to the public, your manager asks you to prepare a flier to be distributed to all apartment dwellers in the store's neighborhood.

Valid Assumptions About Your Audience

In this case, you know and can infer a great deal about your audience's values and knowledge.

What does your audience value?
1. Quick, efficient service (they're always in a rush).
2. One-stop shopping.
3. A large and varied inventory of convenience foods.
4. Convenience over low prices (they have plenty of money and their full-time jobs don't leave them much time for shopping or cooking).

What does your audience know?
1. When the store is open.
2. What items the store stocks and where they are to be found.
3. The hours and inventories of other stores in the neighborhood.

What you cannot assume
1. They know exactly when the store is open.
2. They are completely familiar with the store's inventory and layout.
3. They are completely familiar with the store's services and policies.
4. They know in detail how the store compares in convenience with other stores in the neighborhood.

When you are writing to a particular audience, it is often helpful to ask what information will provide "surprise value" for that audience. Depending upon the age, interests, and attitudes of your audience, certain elements of information will be "surprising" to them, whereas those same elements might not be surprising to a different audience. For example, in this case it might be surprising to the after-fivers that the store carries such household items as wastebaskets, brooms, and hibachis. The after-fivers may race into the store, go directly to the area where what they need is kept, and never become fully acquainted with the store. Those who shop in a more leisurely fashion, on the other hand, may not be surprised by the fact that the store carries household items.

Exercise

Write the text for the flier to be sent to the after-fivers audience.

For class discussion
1. What services would after-fivers appreciate most, and why?
2. Describe a typical day for these successful under-30 shoppers.
3. What foods and products are these people likely to be attracted to and why?

A Universal Audience

In some of your writing, your audience is relatively unknown to you. If you were writing a letter to the editor of your local newspaper, for instance, your readership would be large, and it would be impossible to pinpoint its exact characteristics. Your audience might include oil-company executives as well as farmers, people with high school educations as well as people with advanced degrees, and rich people as well as poor people. You can not pin down specific characteristics of your audience as you can when you are writing to one person or to a small group of persons you know. But there are some assumptions you can make even about this type of audience that will enable you to make decisions regarding the style and tone of your writing and the type and quantity of information you will include.

The universal audience is made up of reasonably intelligent adults. All people have certain expectations of you as a writer; they expect you to have a purpose and to try to fulfill that purpose. For example, to convince your audience that the state of California should regulate pesticides more strictly, they expect you to give them valid and compelling reasons why this should be done. They are busy, and you have to give them an important reason for taking time to read what you write. They expect you to treat them intelligently, honestly, and fairly, and to respect their ideas and values. If you live up to these expectations, you can be confident they will hear you out, whether or not they finally agree with you.

You might try an experiment with some of your friends. Write a sentence that you believe is a simple statement. Hand it to your friends and ask them to list all of the questions that sentence brings to mind. You will be astonished at the number of questions that can be asked about a subject. Where, then, do you begin with the information you will give to a universal audience?

The simplest answer to that question is to set reasonable limits for yourself regarding how much you can cover *well* in the amount of time and space you have to write. Assume that your audience has a general knowledge of your subject. Anticipate questions that your audience might have regarding your subject, and limit the ones you will answer to the number that you can cover in the time or space allotted. Arrange the questions you have decided to answer into a logical order and indicate early in your writing precisely what aspects of your subject you will cover. By using this procedure, you have said to your readers, "I will do just this much," and when you have done that well, they will feel satisfied.

The following passage by René Dubos is written for a universal audience.

> Killing is a behavioral trait common to all predator animal species. This does not justify the assumption, however, that aggressiveness *per se* is a fundamental instinct which drives man to kill man. Early man was very sparse in numbers and most of his efforts must have been directed to food getting rather than to engaging in conflict with his own kind. Judging from the people who still live today in a Stone Age culture, the kind of "mutual aid" that the Russian

anarchist Prince Kropotkin (1842-1921) observed among animals in the wild is a more characteristic attitude of primitive human life than is destructive conflict. From the beginning, human behavior was characterized by long-continued care of the young and by other altruistic qualities. Furthermore, mankind seems to have been remarkably peaceful for thousands of years during the early Neolithic period that preceded the establishment of cities and of social power structures. Even during modern times, several primitive tribes exhibit little evidence of violent conflicts. Biological aggressiveness commonly finds ample outlet in hunting, ritualized conflict, and in the patterns of retributive justice. In their intragroup relationships, the Australian aborigines seem to have successfully channeled most of their aggressiveness into socially useful behavior. Even between groups, conflict is often limited by cultural canons such as equality of chance and limitations on permissible casualties.—*A God Within*

Dubos' writing does not contain highly technical language and does not depend on specialized knowledge of anthropology, but at the same time it is not condescending. The audience is considered to consist of reasonably intelligent adults, who know that killing and aggressiveness are related and that human behavior is in many ways like animal behavior. In the second sentence, Dubos brings up and rejects an assumption probably held by many in his audience, the assumption that "aggressiveness *per se* is a fundamental instinct which drives man to kill man." He then offers reasons and facts to support his contention, thus anticipating his audience's question, Why should I believe that man is not by nature aggressive?

Let's look at a case and discuss how you would go about analyzing a universal audience.

Campus Pub

For several years now there has been a controversy over an on-campus pub. There is not a pub now, and many people would like to see one opened. Recently the Student Association polled student opinion and the controversy was revived. Here is the student newspaper's report of the poll.

Poll Shows Slight Majority Favor Pub

By a majority of only 108 to 97, participants in the recent poll conducted by the Student Association supported the sale of beer by the drink at a campus pub.

Almost all of the respondents to the poll, 195 out of 205, said that they did drink alcoholic beverages. Eighty-seven of those who drink said that alcohol should not be sold on campus.

Those who favored the on-campus pub said that they would go to the Student Center more often if there were a pub there.

Beth Sanders supported the pub idea: "Just because there is no pub on campus doesn't mean students don't drink. They even bring alcohol on campus, though it has to be done in a sneaky fashion now."

Bob Johnson agreed: "Five other colleges in this state have pubs on campus, and they don't have any additional reported problems because of those pubs."

Other reasons given for supporting the pub were the profit to the college from the sales, a better atmosphere than is found in local clubs, and a decrease in off-campus automobile accidents because students would be drinking on campus instead.

Johnny Boswell disagreed, "Students are going to drink regardless, but without a pub a student goes off campus for that drink, and any discipline problems that occur don't reflect on the university."

Joe Washington also disagreed with the idea of a pub: "Students would be coming to class drunk, and the quality of education would go right down the tubes."

Bill Pinkerton, Director of the Student Center, opposed the pub on campus saying that a college exists for the purpose of education and that everything that is done on campus should support that education. He added that policy is made on campus by the board of trustees and not by the students.

Fred Gray, Director of Student Life, favored the idea of a campus pub: "Our office receives two or three complaints a week from local club owners complaining of vandalism in their clubs done by drunken students. A pub on campus would help us oversee the drinking of many of these students and create better relations with local merchants. Last year two drunken students in a car ran into another car, killing a mother and her little girl and injuring two other children. Accidents like that one might be prevented by the presence of an on-campus pub."

The student newspaper has invited a number of "guest editorials" about the pub issue, and you have been asked to write one.

Valid Assumptions About Your Audience

The audience that you will be writing to qualifies as a universal audience. Many will be students, but the student body at your university is varied. It includes eighteen-year-olds just out of high school, working adults attending school part time, retired military personnel, foreign students, and older persons returning to school after many years of being away. In addition to students, the paper is read by faculty members, administration officials, staff members, and anyone else who happens to pick it up. It is best, then, to make only the assumptions about this audience that you could make about a universal audience.

What does your audience value
1. They will look at a campus as a place of work and study.
2. Most will value education.
3. If the sample in the poll accurately reflects the whole campus population, most will be drinkers.

What does your audience know
1. A pub does not now exist on campus.
2. The results of the campus newspaper poll are known.
3. The majority of college students drink.
4. The sale of alcohol on campus is currently prohibited.

What you cannot assume
1. Your audience remembers the details of the poll.
2. All of your audience are drinkers.
3. All who are against the pub are also against drinking.
4. Those who are against the pub have only moral or religious reasons.
5. All of your audience will be affected equally or care equally about a pub on campus.

Exercise

Write a "guest editorial" stating and explaining your position on this issue. Don't neglect the prewriting stage of writing; begin by making some notes about the various issues and arguments connected with the controversy.

For class discussion
1. Which of the arguments presented in the newspaper account will a universal audience find most convincing? Which are least convincing? Why?
2. How could you counter the arguments that do not support your position?
3. How can you tie your position to your audience's values and ideas?

A Hostile Audience

Occasionally you will find yourself writing to an audience that may not be very reasonable, at least from your perspective. In fact, they may be hostile toward the beliefs, opinions, judgments, or values that you are expressing. Your audience may have access to the same facts and figures that you have and may have reached a different conclusion. For example, you might draft a plea for the preservation of an historic building to be sent to a group of city government officials who can only see the increased revenue a convention hotel in its place would bring to your city. Or, you might represent female athletes seeking financial support before a group of male coaches whose budgets would be cut as a consequence. In both of these instances, the audience would be hostile because they would see your position as contrary to their best interests. When facing a hostile audience, you will need to demonstrate that your position will be of greater benefit to them than their own. Show the city officials in the example above that preservation of the historic building would increase the value of the city as an attractive location for conventions. Show the male coaches that a strong women's athletic program will build the prestige of the university and attract endowments and gifts.

Sometimes an audience is hostile because your position contradicts their own values or beliefs. People are sometimes persuaded to a different point of view, but this change rarely occurs in any kind of enduring way under duress or force. Instead, differing positions must be somehow linked to shared values. In other words, you will need to make this hostile audience see that you understand their point of view as well as they do and that your position is a logical extension of theirs. You will want to ask yourself:

1. If they know what I know about this issue, why does their opinion differ so markedly from mine?
2. What *do* they, in fact, know about this issue?
3. What might they not know that would make a difference in how they think about the issue?

After you have answered these questions, there are certain useful strategies for approaching a hostile audience:

1. Establish your credentials early. Detail your relevant experiences and sources of knowledge, and acknowledge your limited experience with the subject, if that is the case.
2. Use a tone and language that will let your audience know that you consider them intelligent and informed.
3. Present all of the evidence that you have found, including that which might hurt your case. The audience would consider an evasion of that evidence a sign of weakness in your argument.
4. Make sure your conclusions follow logically from stated premises.

In the passage that follows, Archibald Cox, representing Harvard University, is attempting to quiet the audience at a teach-in on Indochina on March 26, 1971. The audience, primarily against the war in Vietnam, was preventing a speaker from talking in support of that war by shouting him down.

Disruptive tactics seem to say, "We are scared to let others speak for fear that the listeners will believe them and not us." Disruptive tactics, even by noise alone, start us on the road to more and more disruption, and then to violence and more violence, because each group will come prepared the next time with greater numbers and ready to use a little more force until in the end, as in Hitler's Germany, all that counts is brute power.

And so I cling to the hope that those of you who started to prevent the speakers from being heard will desist. You have the power to disrupt the meeting, I am quite sure. The disciplinary action that will surely follow is not likely to deter you. But I hope that your good sense and courage in doing what's right will cause you to change your minds—to refrain from doing grievous and perhaps irretrievable harm to liberty.

Answer what is said here with more teach-ins and more truth, but let the speakers be heard.

As a well-known lawyer, Cox need not explicitly mention his familiarity with the subject of freedom of speech; the students will believe he knows what he's talking about. Note that he does not berate the students. He does mention the disciplinary action that might occur if the students continue with their disruptive tactics, and he shows that he understands their position by acknowledging its uselessness as a threat. He appeals to their good sense and attempts to show the students that taking away the "freedom of speech" of another endangers the very existence of that freedom. Cox speaks to the students as equals not in the condescending tone of a superior member of the establishment to a group of powerless students.

Exercise

Write a brief statement countering Archibald Cox's argument above.

Summary

Writers write to people. Your ability to determine what an audience is like, what they will want to know about your subject, and how they will react to what you say will play a large role in the success of your writing. Your audience will hear a written voice speaking to them from the page. If you speak to your audience condescendingly, or tell them too much or too little, or fail to show reasons why you should be believed, then no matter how well you write in other respects, your message will have little impact.

In one sense, you determine who your audience will be. You decide who you want to talk to and you create them in your mind. You determine what about your subject they already know, what they believe about your subject, and what their attitudes are toward the subject. You decide what they will want and need to learn. If you remember that your audience in some ways will be pretty much like yourself, thoughtful and caring, then your job should not be difficult.

As a student, your most common audience will be your teachers. Think of them as a particular audience about whom you know a great deal. Many teachers explain their expectations about student papers and projects, and both in and out of class they reveal a lot about their values, knowledge, and interests. As you write for your classes, keep in mind that the more you can observe and learn about a particular audience, the more successful and informed your writing will be.

Exercise

Identify the audiences in the following paragraphs. Tell whether the audiences are universal or particular, and list as many characteristics as you can of the audience the author seems to be addressing.

a. The absence of any solvent shifts in the spectra of the carbonium ions considered herein is a surprising and significant result in view of the apparent high degree of solvation of superacid media. Although a general and comprehensive treatment of solvent effects on spectra have been given by Bayliss and McRae, they do not consider any examples where a charge is present. It is expected that an electronic excitation would be accompanied by a change in the effective ion radius as well as a shift in the charge distribution. Both of these effects cause a change in the solvation energetics and would likely result in a blue shift. The absence of such a shift may be due to a cancellation of effects.—B. S. Freiser and J. L. Beauchamp, "Photochemistry of Organic Ions in the Gas Phase, Comparison of the Gas Phase Photodissociation and Solution Absorption Spectra of Benzoyl Cation, Protonated Benzene, and Protonated Mesitylene."

b. Oppressed people cannot remain oppressed forever. The urge for freedom will eventually come. This is what has happened to the American Negro. Something within has reminded him of his birthright of freedom; unconsciously, he has been swept in by what the Germans call the *Zeitgeist*, and with his black brothers of Africa, and his brown and yellow brothers of Asia, South America, and the Caribbean, he is moving with a sense of cosmic urgency toward the promised land of racial justice. Recognizing this vital urge that has engulfed the Negro community, one should readily understand public demonstrations. The Negro has many pent-up resentments and latent frustrations. He has to get them out. So let him march sometime; let him have his prayer pilgrimages to the city hall; understand why he must have sit-ins and freedom rides. If his repressed emotions do not come out in these nonviolent ways, they will come out in ominous expressions of violence. This is not a threat; it is a fact of history. But I have tried to say that this normal and healthy discontent can be channeled through the creative outlet of nonviolent direct action. Now this approach is being dismissed as extremist. I must admit that I was initially disappointed in being so categorized.—Martin Luther King, Jr., "Letter from Birmingham Jail."

c. It is surely discreditable, under the age of thirty, not to be shy. Self-assurance in the young betokens a lack of sensibility: the boy or girl who is not shy at twenty-two will at forty-two become a bore. "I may be wrong, of course"—thus will he or she gabble at forty-two, "but what I always say is . . ."

No, let us educate the younger generation to be shy in and out of season: to edge behind the furniture: to say spasmodic and ill-digested things: to twist their feet round the protective feet of sofas and armchairs; to feel that their hands belong to someone else—that they are objects, which they long to put down on some table away from themselves.—Harold Nicolson, "A Defence of Shyness."

Consumer Affairs

In an effort to keep students from getting "ripped-off" by local merchants, the Student Association on your campus has formed a consumer commission composed of seven members who will investigate student complaints about local businesses. The commission will keep a file of the investigations that turn out to be legitimate and refer students to student legal counsel for further help. The commission was formed as a result of numerous recent student complaints about local merchants and landlords. Landlords have been accused of failing to make necessary repairs and unjustly keeping deposits, merchants have reportedly refused to extend credit to students with good credit ratings, and auto repairmen have reportedly charged students exorbitant prices.

As a marketing major, you were chosen for the commission on the recommendation of the professor from whom you took a course called "Advertising Methods and Media," in which you studied fair business practices. As news about the commission began to spread, you received a call from the Better Business Bureau asking you to share with them any information you receive about unfair practices of businesses in the area. The first complaint letter arrived today.

Dear Commission:

I would like to acquaint you with the unfair practices of Maxi-Sound Stereo Systems. I recently responded to an ad they had in the local newspaper that sounded too good to be true. It apparently was! The ad said that between the hours of 12:00–1:00 on Saturday, September 25, the Maxi AM–FM cassette recorder system for automobiles would be sold for $52. The ad said nothing about limited quantities. That was the system that I had been wanting for a long time, but I knew that I could never afford the $84.50 it usually costs. I marked my calendar with a big X.

On Saturday, I arrived at Maxi-Sound Stereo at 12:05 to be told that they had already sold out of all of the advertised systems, but that I could buy an eight-track system for the same price. I had looked at both systems the week before, and the eight-track was just not as good. I told them, "No, thank you," and pretended to leave. On a hunch, however, I went behind the shelves of record albums and browsed. My hunch was right. Every customer that came in for the cassette recorder was given the same line, and almost every one of them settled for the lower quality system.

I think that since college students buy so much stereo equipment, they should be cautioned about these practices.

Sincerely,
Bill Bates

This letter interests you because you are one of the college students who buy a considerable amount of stereo equipment, and you ask to take on the investigation. Your first step is to call the manager at Maxi-Sound Stereo Systems, John Bailin. You explain the complaint to Mr. Bailin, and he informs you that the incident to which the student is referring is an unusual occurrence. The store had a limited number of systems, 25 in all, and as unbelievable as it sounds, twenty-eight people were lined up outside the door at exactly 12:00 that day.

It *does* sound unbelievable. If Bill Bates had gotten there at 12:05 as he says, how could they have finished making all the twenty-five sales? When you ask Mr. Bailin that very question, he replies that Bill Bates must be mistaken about what time he arrived.

You see that there will be only one way to get to the truth in this matter. You will have to wait until the store runs another similar advertisement and pretend to be a customer.

Assignment 1
Write a letter to Bill Bates explaining the situation.

For class discussion
1. What should you tell Bill about the investigation?
2. What attitude should you express toward Bill?

Assignment 2

A similar Maxi-Sound ad appears in the paper two weeks later, a system offered at a large discount for one hour on Saturday with no mention of limited quantities. You make sure that you are in the store at exactly the appointed hour. You observe a salesman sell five of the advertised systems. When the sixth customer walks in, she receives the same story that Bill Bates received before.

Returning to your dorm room, you get down your advertising methods textbook and look up government regulation of advertising. There you find the information that you think you can use in a letter to the store owner that will convince him either to live up to the advertising promise or to change the advertisement. Although some "trade puffery" is within the law, the advertising that Maxi-Sound is doing seems to fall under the federal, state, and local truth-in-advertising laws based upon the Printers' Ink Model Statute of 1911 which makes guilty of a misdemeanor any person, firm, or corporation placing before the public an advertisement that contains untrue, deceptive, or misleading facts, assertions, or representations.

Because laws governing advertising vary so much from state to state, you may want to call your Better Business Bureau or do some investigation in the library about your state's particular laws. Write to the store owner explaining the results of your investigation and threaten to pursue the case through the Campus Legal Office if he does not stop the deceptive advertising.

For class discussion

What attitude should you take in your letter to John Bailin in order to be most successful? Should it be angry? Should it be polite? Should it be simply informative?

Assignment 3

Find and investigate an example of local advertising that you believe contains untrue or deceptive statements. Write a letter to the company responsible for the advertisement. Then write a report of your investigation and its results for your local newspaper.

Human Services For Older Persons

You have been working as a paralegal in the legal aid office of a multipurpose Senior Center in a large metropolitan city. Most of your assignments so far have been routine—drafting wills and helping clients fill out complex forms for Social Security and insurance.

Last week you received a call from one of your former clients for whom you wrote a will, Mr. David Greene. Mr. Greene told you that recently he had had extensive work done to his home to help cut down on the amount of heating fuel he used. This weatherization included weatherstripping the windows and doors. The advertisement for the weatherizing service in the local newspaper had said, "We will eliminate all leaks and drafts from your home." Two weeks ago the first cool spell of the season blew in, and temperatures dropped overnight from 70 degrees to 42 degrees. Mr. Greene discovered a draft around his front door. He called Winter Tight, Inc., who installed the weatherstripping, but the serviceman replied that with an old home like Mr. Greene's, it was almost impossible to stop all the drafts and that there was nothing that they could do about it. Mr. Greene requested that they refund some of his money since the weatherization was not effective. The employee at the company rudely replied, "Not a chance," and hung up.

Interested in the case because you had found Mr. Greene one of your more likeable clients, you promise to come over to his house and see how serious the draft is and then to help him get some results. When you arrive at Mr. Greene's, you inspect the front door and find that there are gaps in the weatherstripping where the hinges hold the door to the frame. If those gaps were eliminated the draft would disappear.

Assignment 1

Write a letter to Winter Tight asking them to complete the job or refund some of Mr. Greene's money.

For class discussion

Knowing that Winter Tight has already refused Mr. Greene's request to make the necessary adjustments, what would be the most effective tone for getting results?

Assignment 2

Your persuasive letter and your paralegal title impelled Winter Tight to fix the weatherstripping to Mr. Greene's satisfaction. As you think back over the Greene case, you realize that many of the older persons at the Center probably are unaware of how much money they could save from weatherizing their homes. Also, since older persons are more sensitive to cold, they would be especially interested in ways to weatherize their homes. You call a local storm window firm (not Winter Tight) and learn from the employee that good weatherization could result in from $65 to $320 a year saved in heating costs. You ask the employee to send you a brochure with the details. From the brochure you get the following information:

Checkpoints: windows, doors, heating system, attic, walls, floors

Types of materials:

Weatherstripping—spring metal (expensive, durable)
tubular vinyl gasket (for outside)
felt (inexpensive, less durable)
self-adhesive strips (expensive, easy to install)

Caulking—oil-base (inexpensive, suitable for narrow cracks around windows and door frames)
rubber (metal to masonry where parts of house are joined, around outside of pipes)
latex (expensive, long-lasting)
silicone (superior)

Storm windows and doors—Storm doors of safety-tempered glass over doors frequently opened
Storm windows permanent, aluminum, maintenance free

Insulation—batt and blanket (mineral wool, most commonly used in attics, exterior walls, storage areas)
loose-fill (particles of cellulose fibers, mineral wool, or vermiculite; poured or blown into place; for inaccessible spaces)

insulation boards (plastic foam, for walls, edges
of floors)
foamed-in-place (urea formaldehyde injected
into outside walls through small drilled holes)
Savings on heating bills: Weatherstripping—33%
Caulking, storm windows and
doors, or insulation—up to 30%
Checking heating system—10%
—*McCalls' Magazine*

On the basis of this information, you decide to write a brief
article (500 words) for the monthly newsletter put out by the
Senior Center encouraging the members to consider weatherizing their homes. You cannot figure out how much
weatherizing will cost individual homeowners, for each house
is different. But because most of the readers are on fixed
monthly incomes, you will want to help them evaluate
whether weatherizing is worth the initial cost.

For class discussion
1. What might you do at the start of the article to catch the
casual reader's attention?
2. What do you know about older persons that will help you
decide how best to appeal to them?
3. What can you tell your audience that will help them
evaluate whether weatherizing their homes will be worth
it?

You Are What You Eat

You are a nutritionist working for the local office of Public
Health. Your job includes helping welfare families achieve
better nutrition, advising school cafeterias, and informing the
public about good nutrition. Shortly after coming to the office,
you surveyed the pamphlets that the office was distributing to
the public at school programs, booths at fairs, and in other
public places. These pamphlets are hopelessly outdated and
old-fashioned; there is not a chance of their competing with
the slick, fast food and cold cereal commercials that the public

sees every day on T.V. You decide that updating these pamphlets can be one important service you can provide to the
department.

You pick up one of the worst offenders entitled "Fiber
Consumption." This one's really awful. On the cover is a
1950's family straight out of "Leave It to Beaver." The mother
is standing by the stove stirring something in a pot. She is
wearing a tailored blue dress with a white collar. The father, in
a dress suit, is seated at the head of the table. To his left is a boy
about fifteen, and to his right is a girl about thirteen. The
father and the two teenagers are eating bowls of cereal. The
pamphlet is obviously aimed at teenagers. The opening
paragraph of the text is as follows:

> As your teenage body goes through the changes of puberty, you
> must be increasingly aware of your nutritional needs. The
> temptation is great at this time of your life to hang around with
> the gang at the local drugstore and to eat only junk foods like
> potato chips, candy, and soft drinks. Your body needs more
> nutrition than these junk foods supply. One important considera-
> tion is the amount of fiber that you consume each day.

You are appalled by the naive approach of this pamphlet.
What teenager would read past the first sentence, if he or she
got that far? Does anyone really hang around at a local
drugstore anymore? And the rest of the paragraph sounds like
nagging.

Then, you notice the author of the pamphlet—your supervisor! Fred Grimes, a man of about forty-eight, has been
employed at the Public Health office for seventeen years. He
has been supervisor for the last eight years. He apparently
wrote the pamphlet when he had the very job that you now
hold. You have found him a patient and reasonable employer.
He is, however, extremely sensitive to any criticism.

Assignment 1
Write a memorandum to Fred Grimes explaining the need for
updating the pamphlet and asking for permission to do so.
Word your request in such a way that Grimes will not be
offended, since he is the author of the outdated pamphlet.

For class discussion
1. What's wrong with the pamphlet?
2. What points should you emphasize that will help Fred Grimes see the need for updating the pamphlet without being offended?
3. Because the Public Health office gives the pamphlets away and makes no profit on them, what would be the best approach to use to convince your supervisor that updating the pamphlets would be worth the extra expense?

Assignment 2
You have been given permission to update the pamphlet on fiber consumption. Teenagers are your primary audience. Knowing that your appeal for good nutrition must compete with the appeals made by advertising agency experts who spend millions of dollars in marketing surveys, you decide to run your own experiment to see which appeals cause people to buy different kinds of food. As a nutritionist, you regularly enter the homes of families to do case studies. That would provide a good opportunity for you to find out what advertising appeals work best with teenagers. You decide to conduct this survey as simply as possible. You will show teenagers in the families some sample food advertisements that rely on different appeals (convenience, health, attractive packaging, good taste). You will ask them which product they would be most likely to buy and why. Choose some advertisements and devise questions that will give you the kind of answers you need. Survey a representative sample of teenagers—friends, your family, or other acquaintances—using your list of questions. Write a summary of your findings.

Assignment 3
Write the text for a brief (no more than three hundred words) pamphlet to replace the old fiber consumption pamphlet. Your audience is teenagers, so use what you learned from your survey to make your pamphlet appeal to them. Here is some information you might want to use:

Crude fiber—residue left over after boiling plant foods in acid and then in alkali; composed of lignin and part of the cellulose.

Dietary fiber—that part of the residue that reaches colon.

Fiber of starchy plants such as cereals and tubers more effective than fruits and vegetables.

Modern diet is high in: Fats and proteins
 White flour
 Sugar

Diseases caused by fiber lack: Constipation, appendicitis, hemorrhoids, varicose veins, hernia, possibly diabetes.

Positive benefits of eating fiber: Absence of above diseases; unrefined carbohydrates not fattening.

Foods to eat: Whole wheat bread, high-fiber cereals, wheat, barley, oats, rice, corn, bran.

Foods to avoid: Sugar, white bread, low fiber cereals, raw celery, bananas, cooked oatmeal, and iceberg lettuce actually low in fiber.

—Nutrition Today

For class discussion
1. What do you know about the eating habits of teenagers that probably ought to be considered when preparing the pamphlet?
2. Why do people resist making changes in their dietary habits?
3. Which of the health reasons given for fiber consumption should probably be stressed?
4. What interests of teenagers could be used to attract them to the pamphlet?

Assignment 4
Your first pamphlet is such a success that your supervisor gives you permission to develop another one. Create your own subject for this one; choose the audience, find the material that you will need, and write the text for the pamphlet. This one will be approximately the same length as the first.

CHAPTER 3

CASES AS PROBLEMS TO SOLVE AND QUESTIONS TO ANSWER

After reading this chapter, you should be able to:

define problems that can be solved and ask questions that can be answered;

devise remedies for problems and answers for questions;

decide which remedies or answers lead most directly to a solution and devise a course of action for achieving the solution.

At various times, all of us feel uneasy about something. You read that women's salaries are lower than men's, and you wonder why. You notice that many tasks are duplicated in your office, and you think better communication among employees is needed. You learn that whales are an endangered species, and you think about how they could be saved. All of these are problems. All of them can be solved—though perhaps not overnight.

Recognizing questions that need answering and problems that need solving is the first step toward making changes, toward creating a better world. And it's often the first step in writing. We have to recognize something as a problem before we devote our creative energy to its solution. Much of the writing that you do begins with a question you want an answer to or a problem you want to solve. Sometimes the questions will require direct, simple answers. A credit company writes to you saying, "We have not received your monthly payment. Is there some cause for the delay?"

And you reply, "I have not received my monthly bill yet. Please send me a duplicate, and I will promptly pay it."

But most of the time in writing, the problems will not be so easy. Your clear definition of the problem to be solved, and your concise understanding of the question to be answered may determine your success. Let's work through a case together to see how writing is a problem-solving activity.

The Counseling Problem

It's the middle of your second semester at the U and you're beginning to discover that you made a big mistake. You thought you had the complexities of requirements and scheduling all figured out. When you went to register in January, you blithely got the dean's secretary to stamp the counseling slip you'd filled out for yourself. You didn't need to bother your counselor, you thought. Anyway, he'd been distracted and not much help when you saw him for ten minutes in the fall. But now you're beginning to wish you'd had someone— anyone—check over your schedule.

"I'm sinking," you complain to your roommate. "I'm carrying six credits more than anyone I know, I'm getting a D in Expressionist Art because I didn't notice that you're supposed to take Intro. Art first, and what's worse, only one course I'm taking meets my major requirements, at least that's what this School of Technology bulletin says." As you collapse melodramatically into a chair, your roommate doesn't help matters.

"And all you ever talk about is studying," she observes. "If I'd known you were like that, I'd never have . . . oh, well. Why don't you drop a couple of courses?" she suggests.

"I can't," you reply. "It's too late to get my money back."

"Problems, problems," she sighs as she picks up a notebook and saunters off to Spanish class.

"Problems for sure," you mumble. Which reminds you of what you have to do tonight—start a paper for your composition class, the only class you're taking that *does* fulfill a requirement. The assignment is to examine some aspect of college life that bothers you. Your lack of counseling sure bothers you right now. And as you think about it, you realize that you're not the only one with this problem. Several of your friends have complained about not being able to get appointments to see their counselors, being scheduled for two classes that meet at the same time, and not knowing which classes fulfill what requirements. You grab a pen and paper and start to write down some of these complaints. Half an hour later, you read over the list. You've got lots of angry accusations and frustrated questions. But what do you do next?

Steps in Problem-Solving

As you work through this case, remember that problem-solving can be tackled as a step-by-step procedure. The following steps in problem-solving are based on an article by Richard L. Larson entitled "Problem-Solving, Composing, and Liberal Education."

Defining a Problem

The first step in solving a problem or answering a question is to define or state the problem or question as clearly and concisely as possible. If you understand the exact dimensions of the problem, you will be able to explore the dimensions of the solution more efficiently. To say that your problem is "counseling" is not very helpful. You really don't want to do a detailed study of all the procedures for counseling and all of the kinds of counseling being done. What you want to do is to find out what's wrong with counseling. You might state your question more completely as: "Why and in what ways does the counseling students receive fail to help them plan their academic careers?"

As you think about that question, you see that a number of other, more specific questions underlie it:

1. Are all students receiving counseling?
2. How often are students counseled?
3. Are counselors adequately informed about all areas of the academic program?
4. How are counselors chosen?
5. Are there alternatives to the present system of counseling that would be more effective?

Thinking up questions is a problem-solving procedure that helps you identify what aspects of your subject you need to explore. Answering the questions you have devised will generate subject matter to use as you write. And by organizing information in a way related to your problem, the questions help you organize the presentation of your problem and solution. They serve both as a way of exploring your subject and as a way of organizing your writing.

Exercise

What situation or fact have you encountered recently that makes you feel uneasy or bothers you in some way? Define your uneasy feeling as a problem—state it in terms of a question, and list the more specific questions that underlie it.

Determining the Causes of the Problem

After clearly defining your problem and devising questions that underlie it, your next step is to determine the causes of a problem. By reflecting on your own experience and by doing some research, you begin to find answers to the questions you asked as you defined the problem.

1. Are all students receiving counseling? Some students do not know who their counselors are. Some students have never been assigned a counselor. Except in the college of business administration, there is no established procedure for being sure that each student has a counselor.

2. How often are students counseled? Students are required to show a counseling slip once a semester at registration; however, in many instances these have been filled out by the student and stamped by a dean's secretary.

3. Are counselors adequately informed about all areas of the school program? Counselors are full-time faculty members with full class loads, research duties, and private family lives. They cannot be expected to stay abreast of all areas of the academic program. You talked to several who are unaware of requirements outside their own departments.

4. How are counselors chosen? Full-time faculty members have counseling duties "dumped" on them by their department chairpersons. Counseling duties are rotated, so an individual faculty member only has to counsel students one year in five.

These four questions have helped identify why counseling is a problem at your college—inadequate checks to insure that each student is being counseled and overworked faculty counselors who simply cannot stay informed about all aspects of the academic program. In one sense, you have solved your problem—you have found out what causes it. Sometimes that's all you want to do. But often you want to remedy the problem situation—how can students get better counseling? What you have found out about the causes of the problem will help you devise solutions.

Exercise

Determine the causes of the problem you defined in the exercise above.

Determining Remedies

The third step in solving a problem is to look for aspects of the situation that could be changed. Looking over our notes on the causes of the counseling problem, we might come up with this list of changes:

1. Establish a system that makes sure every student has a counselor and knows who the counselor is.

2. Rule that counseling slips can be signed only by counselors.
3. Set up training programs for counselors so they will be adequately informed.
4. Devise a better system of choosing counselors so they will be more interested and informed.

All of these remedies could help solve the problem. But which are the most workable, and which would help students most? The first two simply establish more regulations, and regulations are notoriously hard to enforce. The third would help, but a whole new set of counselors would have to be trained each year, and overworked faculty members are not likely to want to attend training meetings. The fourth remedy seems to have the best chance of working. And if counselors were chosen who were interested in helping students and had enough time to prepare for and do their jobs, the other remedies would not be necessary. Dedicated counselors would keep track of their students, check their counseling slips carefully, and keep themselves informed about programs and requirements.

Once a remedy has been identified, the obvious next step is to decide how to develop it as a complete solution. In the case of the counseling problem, you might decide to take a careful look at the counseling procedures of the school of business administration since it is the one school where adequate counseling is being done. You discover that the business school employs two full-time counselors for their 500 students. Since the main problem with faculty counselors is that they haven't enough time to do their job adequately, this is a reasonable and workable solution. You decide to propose that the present system of counseling be replaced by full-time counselors in every department, the number of advisors dependent on the number of students majoring in each department.

Exercise

Again, take the problem you've been working on the previous exercises, and devise some remedies. What in the situation could be changed? Which remedy is the most workable?

Weighing the Consequences

After devising a course of action, you need to look ahead and predict what the consequences of that action will be. Such a prediction may help you revise your solution and avoid unpleasant consequences. It may also help you foresee some of the objections to your plan of action.

Looking ahead to the possible consequences of hiring full-time counselors in every department, we can readily see the positive benefits. Students will know who the counselors are for each department. The counselors will be in their offices from eight to five; therefore, students will be able to see them no matter what time schedules they have. Counselors will have no other duties and can spend their time becoming acquainted with the school's academic programs. The one concern of the counselors will be that students are counseled properly. Only one negative consequence seems apparent; departments will have to provide extra money to hire these counselors. The cost seems justified, however, since the goal of the college is to serve the students in the best way possible. Also, some of the cost will be balanced by savings from eliminating costly errors. And faculty members will have more time for their teaching and research.

Exercise

What are the consequences of the remedy you chose in the previous exercise?

Devising a Course of Action

Now that you've come up with a workable solution, how do you turn your solution into a reality? The questions to ask are:

— who is responsible for the area my solution addresses?
— who is most likely to be receptive to my solution?
— what format will I use to present my solution?

In the counseling case, you might decide that since students are most affected by the problem, you will present your solution in a letter to the Vice President of Academic Affairs.

Exercise

What could you do with the solution you developed in the exercises in this chapter?

Some Problem-Solving Procedures

The sets of questions that you create to solve problems can be determined in a more systematic way than relying on what pops into your head. For years journalists have been using the questions *Who? What? When? Where? Why?* and *How?* as a systematic way to explore their subjects. If you add to that list *Which?* you have the beginning of almost all the questions you can generate.

— Who is responsible for the decision? Who created the problem? Who is involved in the problem?
— What are the major issues to be dealt with? What is causing the problem?
— When did the problem first occur? When did you first become aware of the problem? When is the problem most severe?
— Where is the problem located? Where can you turn for a solution to the problem?
— Why is the problem a problem? Why do the conditions exist that are creating the problem? Why has the problem not been solved before?
— How can the problem be solved? How can you see the problem more clearly?
— Which is the best solution to the problem?

Asking these questions systematically can help you discover all that needs to be said about your problem. Just as the journalist attempts to answer the questions in the first few paragraphs of the story, so you can use the questions as a way of organizing your writing about a problem—tackling the questions one at a time.

Notice how in the following excerpt about the Cuban refugee problem, the questions are answered very quickly.

When?   *Still they come,* although no longer are the arrivals welcomed to the U.S. with "open heart and open arms," in Jimmy Carter's memorable phrase of May. Even so, *Cubans continue to set sail from their* **What?** *homeland* and *arrive on the shores of* **Where?** *Florida.* Some 185 disembarked at Key West on a single day last week.

Who?

      Still they come, despite a dismaying

Why?   fact: the passage of *time has not helped* the U.S. to absorb *the 120,000 Cuban* **Who?** *refugees* who have poured in *since April.* **When?** The problem endures stubbornly, disrupting life in *Miami and southern Florida* **Where?** in particular, posing *special difficulties of* **What?**   *assimilation* that have baffled and enraged local, state and federal *officials.* **Who?**

                                       —*Time*

We see the journalist working through the questions again and again as he explores the problem of the Cuban refugees. You can use the questions as you work through a problem in the same way.

The Unsolvable Problem

Some problems simply cannot be solved. This isn't to say that they will never be solved, but given the limitations of the moment, some problems are unsolvable.

When writing you should remember that asking a question or defining a problem leads your audience to expect a solution. If your problem or question is so broad that you cannot satisfactorily solve or answer it, you will leave your audience unfulfilled. Is there a Loch Ness monster? Some people claim to have seen it; others say it's a hoax. Unless you're prepared to spend a few years in Scotland gathering new evidence, there's little you can say on this question that would fulfill your audience's expectations. Sometimes it is worthwhile to define an unsolvable problem; if you can at least determine its causes, perhaps your analysis will lead someone else to a solution. Why is the United States automobile industry in such a decline? News magazines see no good solution to the problem, but they have offered detailed analyses of how the situation came about. In general you should be sure that the problem you define is one that you can solve. The rule to follow is, give your audience what you have led them to expect they'll get.

Summary

Writing is a special way of thinking. It is the activity of answering questions and solving problems. Your success in defining clearly and concisely the problem you want to solve will determine the success of your writing.

The steps to follow in problem-solving are as follows:

1. Define your problem.
2. Determine why the problem exists.
3. Determine remedies and find a solution.
4. Weigh the consequences of your solution.
5. Devise a course of action to realize your solution.

A systematic set of questions can be used to define a problem. The questions Who? What? When? Where? Why? How? and Which? can be successful questions for exploring your problem.

Ideally, the problems you address should be solvable ones. In writing, defining a problem too broadly can only frustrate you and your readers. In all writing, you have certain limitations of space and time. Keep those limitations in mind when you set about solving a problem.

Exercise

The following is a long example of a writer solving a problem. Identify the problem that the writer is attempting to solve. Find the exact place where the writer states that problem or asks the problem as a question. Then try to find evidence of the writer following the problem-solving procedures presented by this chapter.

Order in the Classroom

William O'Connor, who is unknown to me in a personal way, was once a member of the Boston School Committee, in which capacity he made the following remark: "We have no inferior education in our schools. What we have been getting is an inferior type of student."

The remark is easy to ridicule, and I have had some fun with it in the past. But there are a couple of senses in which it is perfectly sound.

In the first place, a classroom is a technique for the achievement of certain kinds of learning. It is a workable technique provided that both the teacher and the student have the skills and, particularly, the attitudes that are fundamental to it. Among these, from the student's point of view, are tolerance for delayed gratification, a certain measure of respect for and fear of authority, and a willingness to accommodate one's individual desires to the interests of group cohesion and purpose. These attitudes cannot be taught easily in school because they are a necessary component of the teaching situation itself. The problem is not unlike trying to find out how to spell a word by looking it up in the dictionary. If you do not know how a word is spelled, it is hard to look it up. In the same way, little can be taught in school unless these attitudes are present. And if they are not, to teach them is difficult.

Obviously, such attitudes must be learned during the years before a child starts school; that is, in the home. This is the real meaning of the phrase "pre-school education." If a child is not made ready at home for the classroom experience, he or she usually cannot benefit from any normal school program. Just as important, the school is defenseless against such a child, who, typically, is a source of disorder in a situation that requires order. I raise this issue because education reform is impossible without order in the classroom. Without the attitudes that lead to order, the classroom is an entirely impotent technique. Therefore, one possible translation of Mr. O'Connor's remark is, "We have a useful technique for educating youth but too many of them have not been provided at home with the attitudes necessary for the technique to work." There is nothing nonsensical about such an observation. In fact, it calls to mind several historical instances when some magnificent technology was conceived, only to remain undeveloped because the conditions for its creative use did not exist. The Aztecs, for example, invented the wheel, but applied it only to children's toys because the terrain on which they lived made it useless. In other words, the classroom—even the traditional classroom—is not to be abandoned because some children have not learned to use it.

In still another way Mr. O'Connor's remark makes plain sense. The electronic media, with their emphasis on visual imagery, immediacy, non-linearity, and fragmentation, do not give support to the attitudes that are fundamental to the classroom; that is, Mr. O'Connor's remark can be translated as, "We would not have an inferior education if it were the nineteenth century. Our problem is that we have been getting students who are products of the twentieth century." But there is nothing nonsensical about this, either. The nineteenth century had much to recommend it, and we certainly may be permitted to allow it to exert an influence on the twentieth. The classroom is a nineteenth-century invention, and we ought to prize what it has to offer. It is one of the few social organizations left to us in which sequence, social order, hierarchy, continuity, and deferred pleasure are important.

The problem of disorder in the classroom is created largely by two factors: a dissolving family structure, out of which come youngsters who are "unfit" for the presuppositions of a classroom; and a radically altered information environment, which undermines the foundations of school. The question, then, is, What should be done about the increasing tendency toward disorder in the classroom?

Liberal reformers, such as Kenneth Keniston, have answers, of a sort. Keniston argues that economic reforms should be made so that the integrity and authority of the family can be restored. He believes that poverty is the main cause of family dissolution, and that by improving the economic situation of families, we may kindle a sense of order and aspiration in the lives of children. Some of the reforms he suggests in his book *All Our Children* seem practical, although they are long-range and offer no immediate response to the problem of present disorder. Some Utopians, such as Ivan Illich, have offered other solutions: for example, dissolving the schools altogether, or so completely restructuring the school environment that its traditional assumptions are rendered irrelevant. To paraphrase Karl Kraus's epigram about psychoanalysis, these proposals are the Utopian disease of which they consider themselves the cure.

One of the best answers comes from Dr. Howard Hurwitz, who is neither a liberal reformer nor a Utopian. It is a good solution, I believe, because it tries to respond to the needs not only of children who are unprepared for school because of parental failure but of children of all backgrounds who are being made strangers to the assumptions of school by the biases of the electronic media.

Until his retirement, Dr. Hurwitz was the principal of Long Island City High School in New York, where he became at once famous and infamous for suspending a disruptive student. Dr. Hurwitz, in his turn, was suspended by the Board of Education for being too quick on the suspension trigger, the board being not exactly slow itself. During the eleven years Dr. Hurwitz was principal at Long Island City High School, the average number of suspensions each year was three, while in many New York City high schools the average runs close to one hundred. Also, during his tenure, not one instance of an assault on a teacher was reported, and daily student attendance averaged better than 90 percent, which in the context of the New York City school scene represents a riot of devotion. The students at Dr. Hurwitz's school are, like youth everywhere, deeply influenced by the biases of the media and many of them come from home backgrounds that do not prepare them well for school. Yet he seems to have solved much better than most the problems of disorder.

Although I consider some of Dr. Hurwitz's curriculum ideas uninspired and even wrong-headed, he understands a few things of overriding importance that many educators of more expansive imagination do not. The first is that educators must devote at least as much attention to the immediate consequences of disorder and to its abstract causes. Whatever the causes of disorder and alienation, the consequences are severe and, if not curbed, result in making the school impotent. At the risk of becoming a symbol of reaction,

Hurwitz ran "a tight ship." He holds to the belief, for example, that a child's right to an education is terminated at the point where the child interferes with the right of other children to have one.

Dr. Hurwitz also understands that disorder expands proportionately to the tolerance for it, and that children of all kinds of home backgrounds can learn, in varying degrees, to function in situations where disorder is not tolerated at all. He does not believe that it is inevitably or only the children of the poor who are disorderly. In spite of what the "revisionist" education historians may say, poor people still regard school as an avenue of social and economic advancement for their children, and do not object in the least to its being an orderly and structured experience.

All this adds up to the common sense view that the school ought not to accommodate itself to disorder, or to the biases of other communication systems. The children of the poor are likely to continue to be with us. Some parents will fail to assume competent responsibility for the preschool education of their children. The media will increase the intensity of their fragmenting influence. Educators must live with these facts. But Dr. Hurwitz believes that as a technique for learning, the classroom can work if students are oriented toward its assumptions, not the other way around. William O'Connor, wherever he is, would probably agree. And so do I. The school is not an extension of the street, the movie theater, a rock concert, or a playground. And it is certainly not an extension of the psychiatric clinic. It is a special environment that requires the enforcement of certain traditional rules of controlled group interaction. The school may be the only remaining public situation in which such rules have any meaning, and it would be a grave mistake to change those rules because some children find them hard or cannot function within them. Children who cannot ought to be removed from the environment in the interests of those who can.

Wholesale suspensions, however, are a symptom of disorder, not a cure for it. And what makes Hurwitz's school noteworthy is the small number of suspensions that have been necessary. This is not the result of his having "good" students or "bad" students. It is the result of his having created an unambiguous, rigorous, and serious attitude—a nineteenth-century attitude, if you will—toward what constitutes acceptable school behavior. In other words, Dr. Hurwitz's school turns out to be a place where children of all backgrounds—fit and unfit—can function, or can learn to function, and where the biases of our information environment are emphatically opposed.

At this point I should like to leave the particulars of Dr. Hurwitz's solution and, retaining their spirit, indicate some particulars of my own.

Let us start, for instance, with the idea of a dress code. A dress code signifies that school is a special place in which special kinds of behavior are required. The way one dresses is an indication of an attitude toward a situation. And the way one is *expected* to dress indicates what that attitude ought to be. You would not wear dungarees and a T-shirt that says "Feel Me" when attending a church wedding. That would be considered an outrage against the tone and meaning of the situation. The school has every right and reason, I believe, to expect the same sort of consideration.

Those who are inclined to think this is a superficial point are probably forgetting that symbols not only reflect our feelings but to some extent create them. One's kneeling in church, for example, reflects a sense of reverence but also engenders reverence. If we want school to *feel* like a special place, we can find no better way to begin than by requiring students to dress in a manner befitting the seriousness of the enterprise and the institution. I should include teachers in this requirement. I know of one high school in which the principal has put forward a dress code of sorts for teachers. (He has not, apparently, had the courage to propose one for the students.) For males the requirement is merely a jacket and tie. One of his teachers bitterly complained to me that such a regulation infringed upon his civil rights. And yet, this teacher will accept without complaint the same regulation when it is enforced by an elegant restaurant. His complaint and his acquiescence tell a great deal about how he values schools and how he values restaurants.

I do not have in mind, for students, uniforms of the type sometimes worn in parochial schools. I am referring here to some reasonable standard of dress which would mark school as a place of dignity and seriousness. And I might add that I do not believe for one moment the argument that poor people would be unable to clothe their children properly if such a code were in force. Furthermore, I do not believe that poor people have advanced that argument. It is an argument that middle-class education critics have made on behalf of the poor.

Another argument advanced in behalf of the poor and oppressed is the students' right to their own language. I have never heard this argument come from parents whose children are not competent to use Standard English. It is an argument, once again, put forward by "liberal" education critics whose children *are* competent in Standard English but who in some curious way wish to express their solidarity with and charity for those who are less capable. It is a case of pure condescension, and I do not think teachers should be taken in by it. Like the mode of dress, the mode of language in school ought to be relatively formal and exemplary, and therefore markedly different from the custom in less rigorous places. It is particularly important that teachers should avoid trying to win their students' affection by adopting the language of youth. Such teachers frequently win only the contempt of their students, who sense that the language of teachers and the language of students ought to be different; that is to say, the world of adults is different from the world of children.

In this connection, it is worth saying that the modern conception of childhood is a product of the sixteenth century, as Philippe Aries has documented in his *The Centuries of Childhood*. Prior to that century, children as young as six and seven were treated in all important respects as if they were adults. Their language, their dress, their legal status, their responsibilities, their labor, were much the same as those of adults. The concept of childhood as an identifiable stage in human growth began to develop in the sixteenth century and has continued into our own times. However, with the emergence of electronic media of communication, a reversal of this trend seems to be taking place. In a culture in which the distribution of information is almost wholly undifferentiated, age categories begin to disappear. Television, in itself, may bring an end to childhood. In truth, there is no such thing as "children's programming," at least not for children over the age of eight or nine. Everyone sees and hears the same things. We have already reached a point where crimes of youth are indistinguishable from those of adults, and we may soon reach a point where the punishments will be the same. Oddly, some of our most advanced social critics have come out in favor of laws that would eliminate many of the distinctions between child and adult in the area of civil rights. This they do in the interests of "liberating" children. The effect would be to help push us rapidly back to the fifteenth century, when children were as liberated as everyone else, and just as unprotected.

I raise this point because the school is one of our few remaining institutions based on firm distinctions between childhood and adulthood, and on the assumption that adults have something of value to teach the young. That is why teachers must avoid emulating in dress and speech the style of the young. It is also why the school ought to be a place for what we might call "manners education": the adults in school ought to be concerned with teaching youth a standard of civilized interaction.

Again, those who are inclined to regard this as superficial may be underestimating the power of media such as television and radio to teach how one is to conduct oneself in public. In a general sense, the media "unprepare" the young for behavior in groups. A young man who goes through the day with a radio affixed to his ear is learning to be indifferent to any shared sound. A young woman who can turn off a television program that does not suit her needs at the moment is learning impatience with any stimulus that is not responsive to her interests.

But school is not a radio station or a television program. It is a social situation requiring the subordination of one's own impulses and interests to those of the group. In a word, manners. As a rule, elementary school teachers will exert considerable effort in teaching manners. I believe they refer to this effort as "socializing the child." But it is astonishing how precipitously this effort is diminished at higher levels. It is certainly neglected in the high schools, and where it is not, there is usually an excessive concern for "bad habits," such as smoking, drinking, and, in some nineteenth-century schools, swearing. But, as William James noted, our virtues are as habitual as our vices. Where is the attention given to the "Good morning" habit, to the "I beg your pardon" habit, to the "Please forgive the interruption" habit?

The most civilized high school class I have ever seen was

one in which students and teacher said "Good morning" to each other and in which the students stood up when they had something to say. The teacher, moreover, thanked each student for any contribution made to the class, did not sit with his feet on the desk, and did not interrupt a student unless he had asked permission to do so. The students, in turn, did not interrupt each other, or chew gum, or read comic books when they were bored. To avoid being a burden to others when one is bored is the essence of civilized behavior.

Of this teacher, I might also say that he made no attempt to entertain his students or model his classroom along the lines of a TV program. He was concerned not only to teach his students manners but to teach them how to attend in a classroom, which is partly a matter of manners but also necessary to their intellectual development. One of the more serious difficulties teachers now face in the classroom results from the fact that their students suffer media-shortened attention spans and have become accustomed, also through intense media exposure, to novelty, variety, and entertainment. Some teachers have made desperate attempts to keep their students "tuned in" by fashioning their classes along the lines of *Sesame Street* or the *Tonight* show. They tell jokes. They change the pace. They show films, play records, and avoid *anything* that would take more than eight minutes. Although their motivation is understandable, this is what their students least need. However difficult it may be, the teacher must try to achieve student attention and even enthusiasm through the attraction of ideas, not razzmatazz. Those who think I am speaking here in favor of "dull" classes may themselves, through media exposure, have lost an understanding of the potential for excitement contained in an idea. The media (one prays) are not so powerful that they can obliterate in the young, particularly in the adolescent, what William James referred to as a "theoretic instinct": a need to know reasons, causes, abstract conceptions. Such an "instinct" can be seen in its earliest stages in what he calls the "sporadic metaphysical inquiries of children as to who made God, and why they have five fingers. . . ." But it takes a more compelling and sustained form in adolescence, and may certainly be developed by teachers if they are willing to stand fast and resist the seductions of our media environment.

I trust that the reader is not misled by what I have been

saying. As I see it, nothing in any of the above leads to the conclusion that I favor a classroom that is authoritarian or coldhearted, or dominated by a teacher insensitive to students and how they learn. I merely want to affirm the importance of the classroom as a special place, aloof from the biases of the media; a place in which the uses of the intellect are given prominence in a setting of elevated language, civilized manners, and respect for social symbols.—*Neil Postman*

Athlete's Dilemma

Jeff Mason, a starting junior this year for the Mavericks, was aware that most of his teammates were being paid by various alumni of his university for work they weren't doing. He personally, however, had not had to face the problem of deciding whether or not to accept the money until this past week, the last week of the summer.

Coming home to the dorm, Jeff, exhausted from practice, fell into bed, closed his eyes, and was immediately asleep. Suddenly he was startled by the phone ringing. Answering in a groggy voice, Jeff took a while to grasp that it was Brad Grayson calling, the Brad Grayson the Grayson Letterman's Room was named after. Grayson interrupted Jeff's thoughts.

"You're bound to know, Jeff, how much we appreciate all you do for the team. I've had my eye on you since the first day you ran out onto that field. I said to myself, 'Now there's a winner.' Coach Oakes tells me you're having a little financial difficulty staying in school."

It was true. Jeff's father left his mother about five years ago, and Jeff had to help out financially at home. None of his brothers and sisters were old enough to work. This summer Jeff worked on an oil drilling rig and managed to earn enough to make up for his not working during the school year. Still, it would be a struggle for his mother to get by until next summer. Knowing how much Jeff loved football, she would never let him give it up. Also, he hoped someday to play pro-ball; then his mother wouldn't have to worry at all.

"Well, as I was saying, I know it's hard for you, Jeff. What I'd like to offer you is a job at my gravel company. It would be a special job. You'd give us five hours of work a week anytime you could squeeze it in. We'd put you on the payroll in a forty-hour-per-week job. What do you say?"

Caught completely off guard, Jeff managed to tell Mr. Grayson that he certainly appreciated the consideration that Mr. Grayson had given to him, but that he'd have to think over the offer for a few days.

"Don't think about it too long, son. Remember, you owe it to your school to be out on that field every Saturday doing your best. You can't be bogged down with worries. Let me know what you decide. And, give 'em hell!"

Assignment 1
You are Jeff. After worrying about your problem for several days, you decide to consult Dave Hutchins, the assistant coach you are most comfortable with. You explain your problem, and Dave tells you to stop worrying—he'll handle it. But he needs the problem in writing. He asks you to write a letter to him explaining your dilemma. Write the letter to Dave.

For class discussion
What is Jeff's problem?

Assignment 2
You are Dave. After talking to Jeff, you realize how big this problem really is. You had known that many of the boys on the team had part-time jobs, but you assumed that they were only being paid for the hours they worked. Shocked at how naive you have been, you realize that not only must several of the boys have these bogus jobs, but also the head coach must be fully aware of the situation. You are offended personally by this dishonesty, but you also realize how damaging this could be to the university if the press got hold of this information.

You call the athletic director and discuss with him the information that you have just learned. He tells you that the problem will have to be handled a step at a time, that he had long suspected the problem, and that now there would be proof for at least one incident. He suggests that the alumni office might deal with the problem quietly by going directly to the alumni who are giving the players bogus jobs. He asks you to write a report explaining the problem to the alumni office. Write the report.

For class discussion
1. What precisely is Dave's problem?
2. How should Dave handle the fact that he suspects his coach knows about the alumnus' offer to Jeff?

Assignment 3
You are the Director of Alumni Affairs. It falls to you to deal with Mr. Grayson. Write the necessary letter to him.

For class discussion
1. What is the alumni director's problem?
2. How can he tactfully explain why Mr. Grayson's offer creates a problem for the university?
3. Although it may be impossible, what can the alumni director do that might keep Mr. Grayson a happy, contributing alumnus?

Betty Beaumont

You sat next to Betty Beaumont in an economics class, occasionally went for a coke with her and on two or three occasions met in the library to study together. After that class Betty invited you to lunch a couple of times and dropped you a card on your birthday. She was nice, but not too ambitious; her only goal was to move back to her hometown. Although you expected your graduation to end your contact with Betty, you received three or four letters during the summer from her at home in Mississippi, and you replied.

In November, you heard from her again by mail. You had landed a job calculating dividends for an insurance company immediately after graduation and were so busy getting your new life started that you didn't realize how long it had been. You settle down with Betty's letter expecting to hear more gossip about her family and childhood friends:

> I'm sorry I haven't written in such a long time, but I've spent the last three months doing everything I could to find a job. The job market here is really tight, and there were almost no jobs available. I wanted so much to move out of my parents' house and get an apartment of my own.

Anyway, I finally got a job as a secretary in an insurance firm. It's not what I want to do the rest of my life, but at least it pays the rent.

The reason I'm writing to you is that I desperately need some advice. You were always the most level-headed person I knew in college, and since you've been working for an insurance company too, I felt like you were the person I should write to. I've been working now for two weeks. The first week everything went fine. My boss, Mr. Grady, was helpful to me in showing me around, and I thought I was really going to like this job. Then on Monday, he asked me out to dinner. Because I knew he was married and because I don't think it's a good idea to get involved with your boss, I turned him down. It turned out I was glad I did! Some of the other women in the building told me he's known as "Groper Grady" and that he's very persistent. So on Tuesday when he asked me again to dinner, I told him no in such a way that he could see I wasn't interested.

That's when the problem started. Now everything I do he complains about, and he yells that I'm stupid and incompetent. I know I'm still learning in the office, and I do make a lot of mistakes, but he yells even when I've done things exactly the way he told me to. Besides that, yesterday he asked me to stop by on my lunch hour and pick up some cologne for his wife's birthday. And then today he laid a stack of claim notes on my desk and told me to write up reports for the file. Those claim reports are his job, and in my interview he said nothing about my having to compose—just typing was mentioned.

I don't know what to do. I need the job to pay my bills. Jobs are so hard to find here I don't dare do anything to lose this one. But I feel like I'm being harrassed.

You were always so smart about these kinds of things. Please write me back and tell me what I should do.

As you try to think about what you should advise Betty to do, you put together all the details you can about her. She has always seemed straightforward and honest, and you've never known her to exaggerate. In fact, she is easygoing about most things. She never became unduly upset over tests, and once or twice when you were angry about an unjust assignment, she just commented, "Well, I guess we'll just have to get it done." Based upon her personality, you decide that she is probably giving you a fairly accurate picture of the situation.

Assignment

Write the letter to Betty telling her what you think she ought to do. In order to be helpful, make your advice to her as specific as you can.

For class discussion

1. What is Betty's problem?
2. What characteristics of Betty's personality will influence the advice you give her?
3. What characteristics of Betty's boss, "Groper" Grady, will influence what you advise her to do?
4. Would it be more effective for Betty to speak to her boss or to write to him? If you decide that she should write to him, what should she say?

Plagiarism Charges and Professor Proudhon

You put down the telephone in astonishment. You can't quite believe the conversation you have just had with Professor Proudhon. You are a junior this spring at Southwestern, and you are majoring in business and minoring in anthropology. You are enrolled in a course taught by Professor Proudhon called "The Tiwi of Australia, A Case Study."

Two weeks ago you turned in your third paper for the course—"Bargaining for Wives Among the Tiwi." You did the paper pretty much like the other two you had done for the course. Professor Proudhon is known as a hard grader, and you received a B– on each of them. While you didn't expect an A on this paper, you thought you would at least maintain your B– average.

When the phone rang and it was Professor Proudhon, you assumed that he was calling about your roommate who had skipped the class for the last three meetings. Instead, however, he asked to speak to you. He said in a matter-of-fact way that he had serious concerns about your paper because a major section of it was identical to a section contained in one of the sources cited, and that this section was inadequately referenced. He said that he could not accept the paper as independent work, and he offered you two options:

1. accept a grade of No Credit
2. accept a grade of Incomplete and write another paper on a
   different topic. This paper would be graded and counted as
   your third paper with no demerit.

In either case, he said, you would be disciplined by having a
letter from him included in your academic file. The letter
would be released only if an individual requested information
relative to your performance and character while a student at
Southwestern.

Shocked and horrified, you replied that there must be some
mistake. He answered that there was no mistake and asked
you to stop by and pick up your paper from his office the next
day. He also asked you to indicate to him in a letter which
option you would like to choose and whether you wish to
appeal the decision. You are to reply within three days. With
that, he said goodby and hung up.

You are glad the next day that Proudhon isn't in his office
when you stop in for your paper. You just can't face him yet.
Up to now, you had had no personal dealings with him. He is
one of those professors who walk into the classroom at the
appointed hour, lecture, and leave after making the assignment. There had been no reason for you to see him in his office
either. His student assistant, who is doing some filing, hands
you your paper.

Back in your dorm room, you sit staring at the passage
marked "Plagiarism."

> The males spent their greatest energies bargaining for new wives.
> "In many nonliterate societies, including most, if not all of the
> mainland Australian tribes, there is a tendency to believe that the
> main purpose in life for a female is to get married," Hart and
> Pilling state.[9]
>
> In a society such as ours, with our emphasis upon equal rights
> for women, we have a hard time understanding the bargaining for
> women that takes place among the Tiwi. It is inconceivable that
> there could be a group of people left in the world who still consider
> human beings as property.
>
> Anthropologists have long been aware that the Australian
> aborigines generally ignored the role of the man in conception and
> believed that a woman becomes pregnant because a spirit has
> entered her body. The Tiwi believed this too, but went a step

further than the mainlanders. Since any female was liable to become pregnant by the spirits, every female should have a husband *all the time* so that if she did become pregnant, the child would always have a father.

Note 9 on your "Notes" page reads:

⁹C. W. M. Hart and Arnold R. Pilling, *The Tiwi of North Australia* (New York: Holt, Rinehart and Winston, 1960), p. 14.

You can't understand what Proudhon means. You gave a footnote for your direct quote, and you are sure that you changed the wording of the paragraph marked "Plagiarism" from the original. You assumed tht the reader would understand that the information after the quote was from the source cited in the note. To doublecheck, you turn to the page cited in the book. The original passage appears as follows:

Anthropologists have long been aware that the Australian aborigines generally (and indeed some of the Melanesians, such as the famous case of the Trobriand Islands) ignored the role of the male in human conception and firmly believed that a woman becomes pregnant because a spirit has entered into her body. The Tiwi were no exception, but went a step further than the mainlanders in dealing with the dangerous situation created by the unpredictability of the spirits. Since any female was liable to be impregnated by a spirit at any time, the sensible step was to insist that every female have a husband *all the time* so that if she did become pregnant, the child would always have a father.

Puzzled that this could be considered plagiarism, you look up the definition of "Plagiarism" in your student handbook:

Plagiarism is stealing or using passages or ideas of another and using them as one's own. It is considered a very serious offense in this university. Plagiarism may result in failure on a paper or test, failure in a course, and in extreme cases, suspension from the university.

Painfully, you conclude that your superficial wording changes probably do not entitle you to use the paragraph as your own. And perhaps you were wrong to assume your professor would understand that you meant the previous footnote to apply to this paragraph too. But you didn't commit plagiarism knowingly and intentionally.

Assignment 1
Write a letter to Professor Proudhon explaining your position regarding the plagiarism charge.

For class discussion
1. What's the student's problem?
2. What options could the student suggest other than those offered by Professor Proudhon?
3. What tone should the student use in the letter?

Assignment 2
There is still that matter of the discipline letter in your file. You call the Dean's office, and he informs you that the letter cannot be removed, but that you would be wise to write a letter concerning the situation from your point of view. Your letter will be included in the file, along with the letter from Professor Proudhon, and will be sent to any individual receiving his letter. Write the letter for your file.

For class discussion
1. What is the student's problem here?
2. What defenses of his conduct could the student offer?
3. What will the audience for the letter infer about the student from each of the possible defenses? Which defense might enhance the student's character most?

CHAPTER **4**

WRITING DESCRIPTION AND USING EXAMPLES

After reading this chapter, you should be able to:

write a verbal description that will enable your readers to picture what you are describing;

use examples to discover and develop ideas;

use examples both inductively and deductively.

The prevalence of expressions like, "I see what you mean," and "Show me," demonstrates the importance of description in expressing meaning. In supporting general statements we make with description, we create for our audiences a picture, a pattern of imagery, that allows them to "see" what we mean and to understand that meaning better. If I say "dog," for example, you may conjure up a picture of your very first dog— short black hair, a white muzzle, short pointed ears, and long tail. I may mean, in fact, an auburn cocker spaniel with long, wavy hair, ears that reach almost to the floor, bobbed tail, and feet that spread out like dust mops. If I want to make sure you understand what I mean when I say "dog," I'd better tell you about the times that the dog's ears flop into his drinking water and come away dripping, or the times that the dog starts yelping, and I look down to discover that I'm standing on the hair spread out around his feet.

Description in writing is the process of creating visual images and sensory impressions through words. Occasionally writers will describe something for the sheer enjoyment of their audience. More often, description is a part of another piece of writing and is used to inform an audience about how something or someone looked or to persuade an audience to see something from the writers' point of view. If writers want to inform their audience about how something or someone looks, they will try to be as *factual* as possible in their descriptions, letting the audience see what they are describing exactly as it looks, smells, tastes, or feels. A restaurant critic might describe the chef's salad he was served as follows: "An eight-inch pottery bowl contained about one cup of slightly wilted head lettuce, one ounce of shredded turkey, one ounce of shredded luncheon meat, two cherry tomatoes, one ripe olive, and a sprinkling of carrot shreds. The dressing tasted a bit rancid but was nicely spiced with basil and pepper." If writers try to persuade their audience to look at something or someone in the same way they do, they may give an *impressionistic* description, emphasizing details that will give their audience a certain dominant impression of what is being described. The restaurant menu might describe that same chef's salad like this: "Generous portions of breast of turkey and smoked Virginia ham, resting on a mound of crisp, farm-fresh lettuce, colorfully garnished with tomatoes, carrots, and Greek olives. Served in an authentic stoneware tureen with our famous herbal dressing."

As with any piece of writing, you need a way of approaching your subject for description, of organizing your subject to provide the best picture for your readers. *Spatial organization* can provide one means of exploring your subject fully. Because what you are describing will exist in space, you can use a spatial arrangement as you write about it. You can move from top to bottom, bottom to top, right to left, left to right, side to side, back to front, front to back, and so on. The important thing is to stay with that arrangement and to give your readers verbal clues that will let them follow your pattern with you. When art critics describe paintings, they use these clues: "in the upper left corner of the painting," "the bottom half," "just to the left of the center." In creating a verbal image, you too will use these clues: "near the window just to the left of the door," "to the left of the road just before you reach the bend leading to the river," "just above her right eyebrow about an eighth of an inch."

In the following example, Oscar Wilde uses clues to locate the position of people and objects in the room. Notice, too, the sensory imagery, especially sound and smell, that makes the passage so effective.

> The studio was filled with the rich odor of roses, and when the light summer wind stirred amid the trees of the garden, there came through the open door the heavy scent of the lilac, or the more delicate perfume of the pink-flowering thorn.
>
> From the corner of the divan of Persian saddlebags on which he was lying, smoking, as was his custom, innumerable cigarettes, Lord Henry Wotton could just catch the gleam of the honey-sweet and honey-colored blossoms of a laburnum, whose tremulous branches seemed hardly able to bear the burden of a beauty so flamelike as theirs; and now and then the fantastic shadows of birds in flight flitted across the long tussore silk curtains that were stretched in front of the huge window, producing a kind of momentary Japanese effect, and making him think of those pallid jade-faced painters of Tokyo who, through the medium of an art that is necessarily immobile, seek to convey the sense of swiftness and motion. The sullen murmur of the bees shouldering their way through the long, unmown grass, or circling with monotonous insistence round the dusty gilt horns of the straggling woodbine, seemed to make the stillness more oppressive. The dim roar of London was like the bourdon note of a distant organ.
>
> In the center of the room, clamped to an upright easel, stood the full-length portrait of a young man of extraordinary personal beauty, and in front of it, some little distance away, was sitting the artist himself, Basil Hallward, whose sudden disappearance some years ago caused, at the time, such public excitement, and gave rise to so many strange conjectures.—*The Picture of Dorian Gray*

The particular position from which you choose to describe your subject spatially is called your *point of view*. Just as when you sit down in a particular chair in a room and look around you, some things appear large, others small, some things appear close and distinct, others far away. So too will your point of view determine what you can see and what you describe for your reader. If you are describing a very large or complex subject, it may be necessary to change your point of view a number of times. The important thing is to be sure your readers know exactly what your point of view is at all times.

Exercise

Sit down in a chair in a room and describe the room as you see it from that position. Now take a deliberately different position. (Be as imaginative as you like—hang your head upside down off the bed if you want.) Describe the room as you see it from your new position.

Another way of organizing your subject for description is in time. Because people, objects, and things are always changing, it is possible to describe those changes chronologically. This kind of description results in the "before-after" or "then-now" kind of writing.

In "Once More to the Lake," E. B. White describes the changes that occur around him during a thunderstorm. He describes the present scene, but he also tells us that the present is much like many scenes in the past he has been a part of:

> One afternoon while we were there at that lake a thunderstorm came up. It was like the revival of an old melodrama that I had seen long ago with childish awe. The second-act climax of the drama of the electrical disturbance over a lake in America had not changed in any important respect. This was the big scene, still the big scene. The whole thing was so familiar, the first feeling of oppression and heat and a general air around camp of not wanting to go very far away. In midafternoon (it was all the same) a curious darkening of the sky, and a lull in everything that had made life tick; and then the way the boats suddenly swung the other way at their moorings with the coming of a breeze out of the new quarter, and the premonitory rumble. Then the kettle drum, then the snare, then the bass drum and cymbals, then crackling light against the dark, and the gods grinning and licking their chops in the hills. Afterward the calm, the rain steadily rustling in the calm lake, the return of light and hope and spirits, and the campers running out in joy and relief to go swimming in the rain, their bright cries perpetuating the deathless joke about how they were getting simply drenched, and the children screaming with delight at the new sensation of bathing in the rain, and the joke about getting drenched linking the generations in a strong indestructible chain. And the comedian who waded in carrying an umbrella.—*Once More to the Lake*

Factual Description

When your purpose is to inform your audience, your description should be as factual as possible. Attempt to remove your own impressions from the description. In a sense, simply transmit an image to your audience that is as close as possible to the way the person or object exists in space and time.

In this kind of description, your choice of words is extremely important. Your ability to find the precise words to fit what you are describing determines the success of your factual description. You will be as specific as possible.

In the following description of the grizzly bear from *Encyclopaedia Britannica*, notice the emphasis is on the audience having a specific image of the subject.

> Grizzly Bear and its close relatives include some of the largest bears. The coat colour is brownish to buff; the hairs are usually pale-tipped, producing a frosted, grizzled effect. A large animal may be nine feet long and weigh over 1,000 lb. and can easily kill and carry a cow. The height of these bears at the shoulders produces a humped appearance. Because of their great bulk and long, straight claws, they seldom climb, even as cubs.

The description above can be universally accepted. It is not an individual writer's way of looking at the grizzly bear.

Impressionistic Description

Sometimes when you write, you want your readers to share your impressions of the subject, as well as see it. We call this kind of writing *impressionistic description*. You deliberately choose certain details and observations, certain kinds of language, to evoke a particular emotion in your readers. Novelists and short story writers often use impressionistic description. Like an impressionist painter, don't be concerned with your audience having a factual image of the subject but with their having the same image as you do.

In this passage, Dylan Thomas wants us to sense the delicious fright of the children singing carols at a large, dark house:

And I remember that we went singing carols once, a night or two before Christmas Eve, when there wasn't the shaving of a moon to light the secret, white-flying streets. At the end of a long road was a drive that led to a large house, and we stumbled up the darkness of the drive that night, each one of us afraid, each one holding a stone in his hand in case, and all of us too brave to say a word. The wind made through the drive-trees noises as of old and unpleasant and maybe web-footed men wheezing in caves. We reached the black bulk of the house.—*Quite Early One Morning*

The description of the dark, snow-silent streets, the huge black house lost in shadows, the eerie noises of the wind, and the cold of the stone makes us as nervous as the children who were actually in the scene.

Character Sketch

When a writer describes a person at length, we call such writing a *character sketch*. In a character sketch you combine physical characteristics, habits, and personality to give your audience a dominant impression of that person.

Here N. Scott Momaday describes his grandmother:

Now that I can have her only in memory, I see my grandmother in the several postures that were peculiar to her: standing at the wood stove on a winter morning and turning meat in a great iron skillet; sitting at the south window, bent above her beadwork, and afterwards, when her vision failed, looking down for a long time to the fold of her hands; going out upon a cane, very slowly as she did when the weight of age came upon her; praying. I remember her most often at prayer. She made long, rambling prayers out of suffering and hope, having seen many things. I was never sure that I had the right to hear, so exclusive were they all of mere custom and company. The last time I saw her she prayed standing by the side of her bed at night, naked to the waist, the light of a kerosene lamp moving upon her dark skin. Her long, black hair, always drawn and braided in the day, lay upon her shoulders and against her breasts like a shawl. I do not speak Kiowa, and I never understood her prayers, but there was something inherently sad in the sound, some merest hesitation upon the syllables of sorrow. She began in a high and descending pitch, exhausting her breath to silence; then again and again—and always the same intensity of effort, of something that is, and is not, like urgency in the human voice. Transported so in the dancing light among the shadows of her room, she seemed beyond the reach of time. But that was illusion; I think I knew then that I should not see her again.—*The Way to Rainy Mountain*

Momaday tells us physical details—long, black hair, dark skin, slow, cane-assisted walk, and so on. But principally he concentrates on his impressions of her. He chooses from his memory various postures to place his grandmother in—bent over her sewing, praying, or cooking. And he interprets her actions for us. Her prayers are long because of the suffering and hope she has experienced. Her sounds are those of sorrow and urgency. She seems "beyond the reach of time."

Exercise

Describe a person that you know as factually as you can. Then rewrite that description to give your audience an impression of that person.

The Language of Description

The language of description relies on sensory details. The verbs may often be the linking verbs—to *be,* to *seem,* to *appear.* The emphasis of description is upon nouns, adverbs, and adjectives that give the audience the most precise image possible. In writing descriptions, you can't settle for the easy or the obvious—they won't give your audience a vivid image of the exact person, place, or thing you're describing. You don't want to describe bottles as just "old," but, as does Wallace Stegner in the following example, as "bottles caked with dirt and filth, half buried, full of cobwebs":

> We hunted old bottles in the dump, bottles caked with dirt and filth, half buried, full of cobwebs, and we washed them out at the horse trough by the elevator, putting in a handful of shot along with the water to knock the dirt loose; and when we had shaken them until our arms were tired, we hauled them off in somebody's coaster wagon and turned them in at Bill Anderson's pool hall,

where the smell of lemon pop was so sweet on the dark pool-hall air that I am sometimes awakened by it in the night, even yet.— *Wolf Willow*

One of the problems with writing description is the great temptation to rely on what we call clichés—expressions that were once original and provocative but are now so common that they no longer communicate an image. If I write, "Her eyes shone like stars in the sky," you have heard the expression so often that it contributes no more to your image of her than "her eyes shone" would. If I write, however, "Her eyes shone like the tiny pinpoints of light in the planetarium sky," you are more likely to actually see the brightness in your mind's eye.

Exercise

Choose a common object, sit down in front of it, and describe it so specifically that anyone would be able to tell that particular running shoe, telephone, or philodendron plant from all others.

Using Examples

Generally, your audience is actively trying to understand what you are telling them. You can help out with particular examples. Of course, even with good examples, your audience may still misunderstand you. But without particular examples your audience may not grasp your meaning at all or may relate your general statements to situations other than those you intended.

To illustrate quickly the value of particular examples, look at this paragraph by Lewis Thomas:

But there is something else about words that gives them the look and feel of living motile beings with minds of their own. This is best experienced by looking them up, preferably in one of the dictionaries that provide all the roots back to the original, hypothetical fossil language of proto-Indo-European, and observing their behavior.

Taken alone, this paragraph permits us to understand that Thomas, if his assertions are to be believed, sees words as alive with "minds of their own." He assures us that all we need for proof is a dictionary that gives us the roots of words. But in what way do words have minds of their own, and how does looking at their roots demonstrate this? Thomas answers these questions by providing examples in the next paragraph:

> Some words started from Indo-European and swarmed into religion over a very large part of the earth. The word *blaghmen*, for example, meant priest. It moved into Latin and Middle English as *flamen*, a pagan word for priest, and into Sanskrit as *brahma*, then "brahman." *Weid*, a word meaning to see, with later connotations of wisdom and wit, entered Germanic as *witan*, and Old English *wis* to "wisdom." It became *videre* in Latin, hence "vision." Finally, in its suffixed form *woid-o*, it became the Sanskrit word *veda.—The Lives of a Cell*

After reading Thomas's examples, we still may not share his enthusiasm for etymology, but we do understand why he says words are alive, and chances are that next time we're in the vicinity of the *Oxford English Dictionary*, we may do a little browsing of our own.

Providing examples not only helps your audience understand your meaning, but also helps you work out exactly what you mean. Examples force you into the kind of precision that makes writing a special way of thinking. If you were writing about a high school teacher whose stern manner made everyone afraid of her, you might add that you suspected that under that stern manner was a warm person. If you go a step further and tell about the time the teacher lent you her car to run an important errand when your car wouldn't start, you could illustrate both to you and to your audience that you had cause for your suspicions. Without the example to support it, your claim remains vague and unclear.

When you use examples, be careful that they are relevant to the general statement they mean to illuminate. If you are writing a script for a film that teaches children the proper care of dogs, your examples will not emphasize particular dogs, but rather particular actions to be carried out with all dogs. In fact, you should be careful that your examples included many types of dogs so that children do not conclude that only auburn cocker spaniels with long ears should be cared for in these ways.

Exercise

Provide particular examples to support the following general-izations:

Saying "no" to a friend is always difficult.
Television talk shows are all alike.

Inductive Reasoning

Examples can be related to general statements in two ways. One way is to first give several examples or one extended example, and then to state your generalization. This process builds the generalization *inductively*. Inductive reasoning allows your audience to think along with you. Once they have seen several examples supporting the concept, they begin to make their own generalizations, and they may be more willing to accept your statement.

In the following paragraphs, Edward T. Hall begins with examples:

Several years ago a magazine published a map of the United States as the average New Yorker sees it. The details of New York were quite clear and the suburbs to the north were also accurately shown. Hollywood appeared in some detail while the space in between New York and Hollywood was almost a total blank. Places like Phoenix, Albuquerque, the Grand Canyon, and Taos, New Mexico, were all crowded into a hopeless jumble. It was easy to see that the average New Yorker knew little and cared less for what went on in the rest of the country. To the geographer the map was a distortion of the worst kind. Yet to the student of culture it was surprisingly accurate. It showed the informal images that many people have of the rest of the country.

As a graduate student I lived in New York, and my landlord was a first-generation American of European extraction who had lived in New York all his life. At the end of the academic year as I was leaving, the landlord came down to watch me load my car. When I said good-by, he remarked, "Well, one of these Sunday after-noons I put my family in the car and we drive out to New Mexico and see you."—*The Silent Language*

From the two examples, Hall then draws the generalization that is the real point of this writing: "The map and the landlord's comment illustrate how Americans treat space as highly personalized. We visualize the relationship between places we know by personal experience. Places which we haven't been to and with which we are not personally identified tend to remain confused."

Regardless of whether we accept Hall's generalization or not, we at least accept his right to make it based upon the truth of his examples. We understand the experience that has led him to believe his general concept.

Deductive Reasoning

The second way of relating examples and generalizations is more straightforward. Asserting a generalization and then supporting that generalization with examples is the process of *deductive reasoning.* The advantage of using deductive reasoning is that your audience knows immediately what point you want to make. In your writing you may want to use a combination of inductive and deductive reasoning. Start with an example to involve your audience in the reasoning process, then make your generalized statement, and then give more examples to support the point you are making. There are many other possible combinations.

The following paragraph by Carl Sagan illustrates clearly the process of making an assertion and then supporting it with an extended example:

> In paranoid thinking a person believes he has detected a conspiracy—that is, a hidden (and malevolent) pattern in the behavior of friends, associates or governments—where in fact no such pattern exists. If there *is* such a conspiracy, the subject may be profoundly anxious, but his thinking is not necessarily paranoid. A famous case involves James Forrestal, the first U.S. Secretary of Defense. At the end of World War II, Forrestal was convinced that Israeli secret agents were following him everywhere. His physicians, equally convinced of the absurdity of this *idée fixe*, diagnosed him as paranoid and confined him to an upper story of Walter Reed Hospital, from which he plunged to his death, partly because of inadequate supervision by hospital

personnel, overly deferential to one of his exalted rank. Later it was discovered that Forrestal was indeed being followed by Israeli agents who were representatives of Arab nations. Forrestal had other problems, but having his valid perception labeled paranoid did not help his condition.—*The Dragons of Eden*

Summary

When you write, you want your audience to have a concrete image of your subject. You want to describe your subject for your audience or to give your audience examples of your meaning. In this way, you help your audience share your world and understand that world as you see it.

Description gives your audience visual images and sensory impressions of your subject. Either describe as factually as possible, or give your audience your impression of the subject. If the purpose is to inform your audience, choose factual description. If the purpose is to entertain or to persuade your audience, then choose *impressionistic description*. A description of a person is called a *character sketch*.

Accurate, relevant *examples* can also help link your generalizations to particular situations that you share with your audience. Your audience may or may not have experienced those situations, but if the chosen situations accurately illustrate your generalizations, then your audience will be more willing to accept those generalizations.

If you present your examples *inductively*, first give several examples, or an extended example, and then draw your conclusion based upon those examples. If you use the *deductive method*, you first state your generalization and then give examples that prove it. In your writing, you will probably use these methods in a variety of combinations.

God's Gift

For several months now Charlie Russell, the D.J. on your favorite radio station KUUL, has been promoting himself in an amusing way. Calling himself "God's Gift to Women," Charlie has appeared on billboards on the freeway and has been featured in short spots on television. But Charlie weighs about 230 pounds, and while he has a very pleasing radio personality, few women would consider him "God's Gift."

As an extension of the ad campaign, the radio station just recently announced a contest: "God's Gift to Men" and "God's Gift to Women." The rules are as follows:

> Write an essay of no more than 600 words in which you present yourself or someone you know as "God's Gift." Give examples that show evidence of that person's charms.

The winner of the contest will receive two free tickets to an upcoming concert and will be the station's guest of honor at dinner with the performing artist before the concert.

You realize that entries could be either serious presentations of someone who really is "God's Gift," or outrageous descriptions of real losers. What will make an entry a winner is the ˌoriginality of the description or the aptness of the examples.

Assignment 1
Write your entry for the contest. Choose either yourself or someone you know, and through your description and examples, make that person appear to be "God's Gift." Since the contest is somewhat "tongue-in-cheek," you may enlarge upon your examples to make them more interesting.

For class discussion
1. Since all the other contestants are likely to use the format, "_____ is God's Gift because . . ." and give some examples, what are some formats you could use that would be more effective in calling attention to your entry?
2. What can you assume about your audience's values that will help you describe your chosen person effectively?

Assignment 2
You spent the whole day last Thursday listening to KUUL because that was the day that they were to announce the contest winner. At 3:30 you were curled up in bed, halfway reading your history assignment and about to doze off, when Charlie with much fanfare said, "This is the moment we've

been waiting for. Yes sir, in just two minutes we'll know exactly who is 'God's Gift,' in addition to me, of course." After explaining the rules of the contest and bringing in the station manager to participate in the announcement, Charlie said, "Now I'm going to call that winner and make the announcement personally." And at that moment your phone began to ring. Astonished, you picked up the receiver, and on the other end was Charlie saying, "Congratulations, you wrote the winning entry."

Completely shocked, you muttered something like, "I just can't believe it," the very words you'd heard a thousand times from other winners. After a bit more conversation, Charlie took your call off the air and put the station manager on the phone. You were given the details about the concert, and then you were asked to do one more piece of writing. The station manager asked for a biographical data report to read on the air about "God's Gift," either you or the person you wrote about. He asked you to restrict it to about two typewritten pages. Write up the biographical data page.

The Backpacking Trip

Because his anger usually subsides quickly, Kenneth Coleman was astonished at how angry he still was. He had just returned from a long-anticipated backpacking trip to Colorado. Two years ago he took the same trip—riding the train from Silverton, getting off way out in nowhere, and hiking up the Needle Creek Trail to Chicago Basin and back. That experience had been wonderful. It was his first backpacking trip by himself, the weather was great, and the scenery was spectacular.

Needle Creek Trail, skirting waterfalls and cliffs, was extremely steep. Although he knew that there were probably fifty people in the basin at the same time he was, Kenneth rarely saw traces of anyone on that first trip. He had a real sense of being alone in the wilderness.

This trip was different. The first thing that shocked Kenneth was the number of people getting off the train at his stop. About twenty people unloaded their gear from the small platform behind the engine and started up the mountain with their packs on their backs. Kenneth waited for a while at the abandoned railroad shack until the others were out of sight. Then, starting up the trail, he had a real shock. Everywhere along the trail was trash. Here are some entries from the journal he always kept on backpacking trips.

> Monday, 10:30 P.M.—Got off train exhilarated. Air brisk and cool. Wispy clouds. Train arrived early enough so I could be halfway up mountain by sundown. Twenty others got off train same time. Trash everywhere on trail—gum wrappers, plastic bags, aluminum foil, cigarette butts, moleskin—you name it. Have to pick out new spot for next year.

> Tuesday, 8:45 P.M.—Went through Columbine Meadow today. Surprised two backpackers stripping branches off aspens. No room to camp in meadow. I had to camp at side of trail. In meadow campsite fire pits full of glass and cans. Where are all those ecology-minded people I used to know?

> Wednesday, 10 P.M.—Camped by Crystal Lake. Went fishing for dinner but caught only a beer can and a tangle of old fishing line. Now "enjoying" a rock concert from group camped across lake. Saw them coming in with large radio at dusk. Before concert heard an owl.

> Thursday, 7:30 P.M.—Just finished putting food sack up tree safe from bears. Took only an hour. Bear cable that was here last year not usable—trees it was attached to blown down. Campsite more open than I like, but only one not surrounded by previous campers' uncovered latrine sites.

> Friday, 10:15 A.M.—Waiting for train. No deer spotted whole trip— and no rangers either. What a bummer.

Although Kenneth had no time to stop when he got back to Silverton, he did write down the address of the Park Ranger Station. Now back home, he felt he had to vent some of his feelings about his spoiled trip.

Assignment 1
You are Kenneth. Write a letter to the Park Ranger Station in Silverton. Be sure to give specific examples that will illustrate the reason for your protest.

For class discussion
1. What problem is Kenneth concerned about?
2. What attitude does Kenneth have toward his subject and toward his audience? How should you, as Kenneth, express it?

Assignment 2
In answer to your first letter you received the following:

> Dear Mr. Coleman:
>
> Thank you for bringing to our attention the daily abuses to our wilderness area along the Needle Creek Trail.
>
> We are grateful for concerned visitors like you. Please be assured that we, too, feel considerable concern for the existing conditions. Unfortunately our hands are tied.
>
> Our staffing is inadequate to supervise correctly the increasing numbers of visitors to our area. We have the same number of personnel that we did five years ago, although the number of visitors up the trail has increased 85 percent.
>
> You would do us a favor by relaying your concerns to the following agency: Department of Environmental Conservation, Washington, D.C.
>
> If enough people like you take the time to voice a complaint, perhaps some action will be taken.
>
> Thank you,
> Robert Reed, Head Ranger

You are Kenneth again. Write the suggested letter to the Washington agency.

For class discussion
1. What are the causes of the condition of the Needle Creek Trail?
2. What remedies can you come up with?
3. What are the consequences of your remedies, and which of them is your audience most likely to accept?

Assignment 3
Still Kenneth, you decide to write an article on the experience for the newsletter put out by the Silverton Outing Society.

Perhaps you can directly reach some of those who are cutting down trees and leaving trash.

Assignment 4
Select a situation concerning a problem that you have witnessed and bring the problem to the attention of the appropriate persons. Give examples of your own experience with the problem.

The Toddle-In Grill

You are a food inspector trainee for the local office of the Department of Health and Welfare in your city. You have been assigned to accompany your supervisor on an inspection of the Toddle-In Grill because the department received a number of reports concerning the conditions there:

July 1—Judith Brown found a piece of glass in her tapioca. When incident reported, manager apologized and brought another bowl.

July 9—Bob Gillis reported seeing dead roaches on kitchen floor.

July 15—Maxine Gilbrey reported that there was no hot water in the women's restroom. Women employees wash there.

August 3—Guadalupe Garcia reported rats in the vicinity of the storerooms. She also reported that there are no screens on the bathroom windows.

You and your supervisor had a hard time making your inspection of the Toddle-In because its owner, Max Toddle, kept following you around offering you a piece of pie or a cup of coffee and distracting you (deliberately) from your work. When you returned to the office and compared your notes with your supervisor's, you were both shocked at how bad conditions are at the Toddle-In.

Assignment 1
You jot down a combined list of notes concerning the Toddle-In, and your supervisor asks you to write a complete report for the files including the reasons for your visit, a description of your observations, and a justification for closing the restaurant. Your notes are below:

Inspection Report—The Toddle-In Grill—August 5

Cooked green beans—stored in jar on counter

Fried chicken in hot-holding device—below 130 degrees.

Worker (with cold) picked up cooked chicken with hands.

No hot water in women's restroom. No soap—men's. Dirty towels on floor.

Dirty kitchen equipment and counters. No-pest strip over pie table.

Outside—garbage piled up. Evidence of rats in storeroom.

Waitresses without hair nets.

Cook smoking in kitchen.

Dirty utensils in storage drawer.

For class discussion
1. How could you organize your description?
2. Should your description be factual or impressionistic?

Assignment 2
Your supervisor asks you to perform your first official capacity for the agency. You are to write a letter to Max Toddle informing him of your report and of your mandatory closing of the restaurant in three days. It will remain closed until all violations have been taken care of. Write the official letter.

For class discussion
1. How many of the specific examples should you cite in your letter to Max?
2. What attitude toward Max should you express?

Assignment 3
Write a factual description of your own school cafeteria, dorm cafeteria, or snack bar, a description that might appear in a government report on educational food facilities.

Assignment 4
Write an impressionistic description of your school cafeteria, dorm cafeteria, or snack bar, a description for an out-of-town friend.

CHAPTER 5

MAKING COMPARISONS AND DRAWING ANALOGIES

After reading this chapter, you should be able to:

use comparisons in a variety of ways to develop your ideas;

use analogies as a major means of understanding and communicating.

Whenever we encounter something new, one of our first reactions is to determine how that object, event, or idea is similar to or different from other objects, events, or ideas. If we see a new model of automobile our first reaction might be to say, "It looks a little like a Mustang, but the front end is different. It has a square body like the four-door Chevrolet, but I think it's a Buick because it has those portholes on the side." In other words, we look for all the features that are similar to and different from automobiles we are familiar with.

This process of looking for similarities and differences is called *comparison*. (Traditionally, *comparison* referred to ways things are alike, and *contrast* referred to ways that things differ, but *comparison* is now used as the general term to refer to both.)

Because writing is a way of thinking, it's not surprising that comparison is also important in writing. By showing your audience the ways in which your subject is similar to and different from something they are more familiar with, they will understand your subject more quickly. The subjects you compare may be very similar, as in, "The game of Indian Ball is like softball, except that the players of Indian Ball do not run the bases." Sometimes you may compare subjects that are very different, but the qualities of one will make the qualities of the other much clearer. For instance, you might say, "My dating habits as a freshman during the first three weeks of school were quite similar to the game of musical chairs. I was always the one left standing."

In addition to helping your audience understand the subject more clearly, you can use comparison to link elements that your audience might not have considered similar, thus heightening the interest of your writing. Good writing often makes use of this kind of comparison every few sentences. Here are some examples:

"Men are like stone jugs—you may lug them where you like by the ears."—Samuel Johnson

"As poor as a church mouse."—English phrase

"Under Marcel too the ground was breaking away like ice in a river."—Barbara W. Tuchman, *A Distant Mirror*

"Art is like religion in many respects. Its development does not consist of new discoveries which strike out the old truths and label them errors (as is apparent in science). Its development consists of sudden illuminations, like lightning, of explosions, which burst like a fireworks in the heavens, strewing a whole 'bouquet' of different shining stars about itself."—Wassily Kandinsky, *Reminiscences*

These brief comparisons are used as efficient ways to clarify ideas. More extended comparisons serve other purposes—to evaluate, to inform, to persuade. For example, you might compare the merits of one shopping center site to another in order to evaluate which would make the best choice for future development. You might then use the same comparison to inform your partner of the merits of each. Finally, you might use the same information to persuade your partner to choose the one you favor.

Organization of Comparisons

There are two standard patterns of organization for extended comparisons. You may list all of the qualities of one thing being compared, and then discuss all the qualities of the other in the same order. Or, you may discuss one quality at a time, comparing the two things as you go. When the things being compared are better understood as a whole, or when a set of qualities on which to base the comparison is not apparent, the first pattern is more useful. When you want to stress the qualities on which to base the comparison is not apparent, the first pattern is more useful. When you want to stress the qualities one at a time, helping your audience evaluate the merits of each member of the comparison concerning each quality, then the second pattern is more useful. Determine your purpose and audience in deciding which to use.

In the following advertisement, the authors have made use of the second pattern:

Puma Meets the Other Family Cars

Compare Puma to the other family cars in its price range, and you will notice the differences right away.

In the front of Puma there's enough room for five adults to ride comfortably all the way to the farthest destination.

Puma's trunk holds 10 suitcases, three tennis rackets, two carry-on bags, and a lady's purse. The other family cars? Well, they do hold 6 suitcases.

Now look under the hood. There's a fuel-injected engine in Puma that goes from 0 to 50 in 8 seconds. The other family cars get there in 12 to 15 seconds.

And at the gas pump? Well, Puma gets 23 miles to the gallon in town, 30 on the highway. Your mileage may vary with driving conditions. The other family cars don't even begin to compare.

With Puma you also get independent suspension, front-wheel drive, rack-and-pinion steering, zippy colors, and European styling.

Which car would you rather put your family into? Do we even need to ask?

This ad focuses on several characteristics of automobiles, then for each characteristic describes first the Puma and then the other family cars. Notice that since the ad is meant to sell Puma automobiles, they are described in more detail than the others. And, in fact, the comparison is incomplete—the other family cars aren't mentioned at all in several characteristics listed.

	Puma	**The Others**
1. Roominess	Holds five adults	Doesn't say
2. Trunk size	Holds 10 suitcases, 3 tennis rackets, 2 carry-on bags, 1 purse	Holds 6 suitcases
3. Fuel-injected engine	0–50 in 8 seconds	12–15 seconds
4. Gasoline mileage	23 in town, 30 on the highway	Doesn't say
5. Extras	Independent suspension, front-wheel drive, rack-and-pinion steering, zippy colors, and European styling	Doesn't say

In the next example, Sylvia Plath contrasts the method of the novelist to the method of the poet. Writing methods are not easily divided into qualities or steps. Plath wants you to understand each method as a whole, so she uses the first organizational pattern.

> How I envy the novelist!
> I imagine him—better say her, for it is the women I look to for a parallel—I imagine her, then, pruning a rosebush with a large pair of shears, adjusting her spectacles, shuffling about among the teacups, humming, arranging ashtrays or babies, absorbing a slant of light, a fresh edge to the weather, and piercing, with a kind of modest, beautiful X-ray vision, the psychic interiors of her neighbors—her neighbors on trains, in the dentist's waiting room, in the corner teashop. To her, this fortunate one, what is there that isn't relevant! Old shoes can be used, doorknobs, air letters, flannel nightgowns, cathedrals, nail varnish, jet planes, rose arbors and budgerigars; little mannerisms—the sucking at a tooth, the

tugging at a hemline—any weird or warty or fine or despicable thing. Not to mention emotions, motivations—those rumbling, thunderous shapes. Her business is Time, the way it shoots forward, shunts back, blooms, decays and double-exposes itself. Her business is people in Time. And she, it seems to me, has all the time in the world. She can take a century if she likes, a generation, a whole summer.

I can take about a minute.

I'm not talking about epic poems. We all know how long they can take. I'm talking about the smallish, unofficial garden-variety poem. How shall I describe it?—a door opens, a door shuts. In between you have had a glimpse: a garden, a person, a rainstorm, a dragonfly, a heart, a city. I think of those round glass Victorian paperweights which I remember, yet can never find—a far cry from the plastic mass-productions which stud the toy counters in Woolworth's. This sort of paperweight is a clear globe, self-complete, very pure, with a forest or village or family group within it. You turn it upside down, then back. It snows. Everything is changed in a minute. It will never be the same in there—not the fir trees, nor the gables, nor the faces.

So a poem takes place.—*A Comparison*

First, Plath tells of the imagined life of the novelist. The novelist can use all of her experiences in a novel and can approach her art in a leisurely way. She can include a lifetime of observations in a novel. But the poet, Plath tells us, has only the small space of a poem to capture a moment in time. If the moment is lost, it will never be the same again. Plath uses the additional comparison of a poem to the round glass Victorian paperweight to show us further what she means about the small space of a poem. Though Plath does not work through a list of characteristics of each method, note that she does describe both in the same terms—in the amount of time and space each writer has available.

When you want to compare two or more things, make some decisions before you start writing. Say, for example, that you have just finished your first semester of college and are writing an article for an issue of your old high school newspaper designed to prepare high school students for the college experience. You've decided to compare high school and college teachers to show that the differences aren't as great as many assume. You know your audience, you have a purpose, and you've hit on a way of developing your ideas—by comparison. What do you do now?

First, choose several qualities on which you want to compare teachers. These qualities may be quite specific, as in the Puma ad, or more general, as in Plath's contrast of novelists and poets. There are many possible qualities of anything, but choose the ones that seem most relevant to your purpose and audience. The teachers could be compared on the basis of sex, dress, marital status, salary, patterns of speech and accent, and geographic, educational, and family backgrounds—but these characteristics would be more relevant in a sociological study of high school and college teachers than in the article you want to write. For your purpose you are more likely to compare the teachers based on grading standards, attitudes toward students, knowledge of subject matter, assignments, and age.

Whatever characteristics you choose, you should discuss each of the things you're comparing in terms of all the characteristics. For some purposes, though, as in the Puma ad, you may wish to discuss one thing in more detail.

Second, choose an organizational pattern appropriate to your audience, purpose, and subject matter. Will you present each item compared separately, or will you present qualities? Which should be presented first? What order should qualities be presented in? In the case of the article on teachers, you might present high school teachers first because the high school students will be more familiar with them. On the other hand, high school students might be more interested in a quality-by-quality comparison than in getting a whole picture of each type of teacher.

Say that you finally chose the second option. You then look at the list of qualities you want to discuss and decide which to start with. You could begin with the one students will be most interested in—grading standards—or you could save it till last, in order to keep their attention. Then, within the discussions of each quality, you'll have to decide whether to describe the more familiar high school teachers first, then link the new information about college teachers to the old or to do it the other way around. Here's a part of the article you might write:

I have had over twenty high school teachers and only four college teachers so far. But I think from what I have experienced and from what my friends have told me about their college teachers, I am qualified to compare the two.

The grading standards of both high school and college teachers seem to be pretty high. In high school my teachers graded hard, but the projects that they assigned stressed a particular skill. Now, in college, my teacher expects me to put all of those skills to use at once. Perhaps that is the reason that my college teacher seems to grade so much harder.

High school and college teachers both seem to have the same attitude toward students—they're there to help. In high school I received a lot of individual help from some of my teachers. I just assumed that all that would change when I got to college. I was wrong. My college English teacher is just as often willing to help. I have been by his office three times and have always felt welcome. . . .

Exercises

1. Read the following paragraphs and tell what the purpose of the comparison is and which pattern of comparison the author is using:

a. "The tipi is much better to live in; always clean, warm in winter, cool in summer; easy to move. The white man builds big house, cost much money, like big cage, shut out sun, can never move; always sick. Indians and animals know better how to live than white man; nobody can be in good health if he does not have all the time fresh air, sunshine and good water."—Chief Flying Hawk, a Sioux Indian, quoted in *Touch the Earth,* compiled by T. C. McLuhan.

b.   "There's no other dog food like it.
   Ken-L Ration Special Cuts.
   It's more nutritious than prime beef.
   Dogs prefer it over burger dog food.
   It's a cut above beef. When it comes to nutrition, Special Cuts is actually better for your dog than a butcher's best beef. It has all the nutrition dogs need every day.
   It's a cut above burger dog food. When it comes to good

taste, dogs prefer Special Cuts over the leading burger dog food. We proved it with tests in homes like yours.

Special Cuts really is something special.

A cut above burger.

A cut above beef."

—Advertisement for Ken-L Ration Special Cuts.

c. "A body of research is evolving that describes a dramatic distinction between the functions of the two hemispheres of the brain.

The left cerebral hemisphere works like a computer. By stringing together linear messages into a logical chain of thought and filtering out sensory messages that don't directly apply to solving the problem at hand, it acts as an abstract deduction center.

The right cerebral hemisphere operates intuitively. It allows a person to link external and internal qualities so that the self can be experienced as interrelated to nature, to others, to the chain of existence. It has the capacity to fantasize, which makes possible leaps of imagination and invention."—Gail Sheehy, *Passages.*

2. Based upon your own experience, write the comparison of high school and college teachers begun above. Remember your audience is high school students who are apprehensive about facing college teachers.

Analogy

Earlier in this chapter we saw that often two things can be compared that don't appear very much alike at first glance. A comparison of one thing to another thing quite different from it is called an *analogy.* The main purpose of analogies is to clarify a concept; but since analogies are surprising, they are memorable too. If you say people using the telephone are like two insects touching antennae, you emphasize the closeness of the contact in a memorable way (reminiscent of Bell Telephone's slogan, "Reach out and touch someone.").

Elements of an analogy must have at least one similar quality. Often, however, writers will write an *extended analogy,* showing all of the surprising ways two unlike things are similar. In the following passage, Loren Eiseley draws an analogy between our position in the cosmos and the position of a single white blood cell in our bodies. Notice that Eiseley describes the position of the white blood cell in detail and lets his readers infer the points of similarity with our position in the cosmos.

> So relative is the cosmos we inhabit that, as we gaze upon the outer galaxies available to the reach of our telescopes, we are placed in about the position that a single white blood cell in our bodies would occupy, if it were intelligently capable of seeking to understand the nature of its own universe, the body it inhabits. The cell would encounter rivers ramifying into miles of distance seemingly leading nowhere. It would pass through gigantic structures whose meaning it could never grasp—the brain, for example. It could never know there was an outside, a vast being on a scale it could not conceive of and of which it formed an infinitesimal part. It would know only the pouring tumult of the creation it inhabited, but of the nature of that great beast, or even indeed that it was a beast, it could have no conception whatever. It might examine the liquid in which it floated and decide, as in the case of the fall of Lucretius's atoms, that the pouring of obscure torrents had created its world.—*The Invisible Pyramid*

Analogies help us understand new concepts by linking them to concepts we are familiar with. But analogies can be misleading too. We must remember that the two things compared are alike only in one way or from one perspective. A *false analogy* is the use of an analogy to draw invalid conclusions. For example, if I am arguing against gun control, I might say that proper use of a gun is like proper use of an automobile. Used correctly, both are safe. But the analogy obscures an important difference—guns are designed to kill; automobiles are designed to be driven.

Exercise

Write some brief paragraphs creating analogies for the following subjects or similar subjects of your choice. Your audience consists of people who have never had these experiences.

— failing an exam
— whitewater canoeing
— an automobile accident
— interviewing for a job

Summary

Making comparisons is one of the most commonly used and useful patterns of thinking. In writing, comparisons can show your audience the ways in which your subject is similar to or different from something they are familiar with. Comparisons enable the audience to understand your subject more quickly.

In writing comparisons, either tell about one of the things being compared and then the other, or choose certain qualities as the basis for comparison, and describe each thing being compared in relation to those qualities. The first pattern gives your audience a whole picture of each thing; the second emphasizes points of comparison and is often easier to follow.

Comparing two unlike things is called *analogy*. Analogies can contribute clarity and memorability to your writing.

You Can't Just Pick Up the Key

You received a letter the other day from the daughter of a friend of your mother. She will be attending State University next year, and, since you have been at State two years, your mother gave her friend your address and said she was sure you'd be glad to give the daughter any information she needed. Mothers are so helpful!

Here's the letter:

Dear _____ ,

I know you don't know me, but my mother is a friend of your mother. Your mother said that since you go to State University, it would be all right if I contacted you about a problem I have. I hope you don't mind.

I have a problem that I can't make up my mind about. Some of my friends who are at college live in dormitories, and they say it's the only way to go. They say if you don't live in the dorm, you won't meet anybody, and your social life will be almost non-existent. On the other hand, I have two other friends who say that living off campus in an apartment is the only way to do it. They say you avoid the hassles of curfews, and the food is better because you fix it yourself. They also say it's easier to study because there aren't so many people around all the time. And they say it's just as easy to meet people because you see them in class and in the Student Center.

Since I don't know anyone who has attended State, I thought perhaps you wouldn't mind giving me some advice about whether it's better to live in a dorm or an apartment there. I would really appreciate it because I have to make up my mind soon so I can put down a dorm deposit if that's what I decide. My parents aren't crazy about the idea of my living in an apartment, but they have said that if that's what I decide to do, they'll go along with it. Deep down, I think that's what I really want to do.

I'm looking forward to hearing from you and to coming to State. I hope I get a chance to meet you in person during the time I'm there.

Thanks a lot.

The reason that your response is so hard to write is that you believe that each person has to decide what's best depending upon his or her personality, and since you don't know this person at all, you don't see how you can advise her on the problem. However, you can understand her dilemma, and you want to try to answer her in some useful way. One fear that you have is that since she seems so dependent on her friends' opinions, she might be the kind of person that would be swayed in whatever direction you support. You surely don't want the blame if that direction doesn't work out. However, she *has* asked your opinion. You turn to some of your friends for help—one who lives in an apartment and another who lives in the dorm. Here are your notes on what they said.

The friend who lives in the apartment:
— you're on your own
— can have guests over anytime

— can eat when and what you want to
— divide chores with roommate
— neighbor had stereo stolen last month
— privacy to study for exams
— better grades since living in apartment

The friend who lives in the dorm:
— almost forced into friendships, which is good if you're shy
— lots of people dropping by, asking for class notes
— don't have to cook or clean
— more time to study, be with friends, watch TV
— can't drink in room
— noisy neighbors a problem
— always someone to listen to problems

Assignment 1
Write to the high school student comparing dorm life to apartment living. Use as much or as little of the material above as you wish. Add any information you have collected from friends and class discussion of the case.

For class discussion
1. What other advantages are there to dorm or to apartment living that the two friends failed to mention?
2. What kind of person prefers living in a dorm? What kind prefers living in an apartment? How could you incorporate this information into your letter?
3. Should you offer the student any direct advice?

Assignment 2
After mailing your letter, you remember a later conversation you had with your friend who lives in an apartment. You discussed the fact that a person who decides to live in an apartment needs to be aware of all the financial obligations involved in living off-campus. You decide, since you've already done so much work on this problem, to write an open letter for your school paper on dorm versus apartment life, including the relative costs.

Your apartment friend gives you this list of costs:

1. Rents—Efficiency, $125-$250
   One bedroom, $150-$320
   Two bedroom, $200-$350
   Three bedroom, really scarce, $300 and up
2. Gas and electric—$20-$30 (varies a lot with apartments)
3. Telephone—$5.25 a month plus long distance charges
4. Deposits—$50-$250. Landlord must return it within 30 days after you move out. Normal wear and tear OK. Deduct damages from deposit. Have heard story of landlord who charged $5 for every nail hole.
5. Cooking and cleaning supplies—$50-$200. Get unbreakable stuff.
6. Food prices. Take these for granted when living with parents. Inflation is outrageous. With common sense, from $15-$50 a week.

You live in the dorm, and you draw up this list of costs:

1. Room and board—$_____ per semester
2. Telephone—free local service, but pay phone for long distance
3. Snacks and eating out when miss cafeteria hours—$5 a week.

(You may add the dorm cost for your school and revise any figures if they differ considerably from the area in which you live.)

Making Decisions

Just before you left for college, your parents called you in and had the typical "going away to college" talk. They told you that they would no longer be as much a part of your life and that you would now have to be making decisions on your own. You took all of this quite seriously, and in your first month at college, you feel that you have been handling things well. While some students have been partying all night and getting poor grades, you have managed to be level-headed enough to be able to have a good time while remembering all of the reasons you are at college.

You were really surprised, therefore, when you paid your first visit home the weekend before last, and your father gave you a hard time about your coming in at three on Sunday morning after a night out with the gang. You are gradually realizing that the "going away to college" talk may have meant one thing to you and quite a different thing to your parents.

Chris called this week on Monday night. You have been going together for two years. Although you were quite serious in high school, you both agreed that your dating would be much more casual in the future since you decided to go out of state to college. Chris called to invite you to drive up this weekend for the homecoming game at the university and the party afterward. Excited about seeing Chris again and about the idea of a campus weekend, you immediately said yes.

At first you decided not to call your parents at all. This trip was going to be another example of your ability to make good decisions on your own. By Tuesday, however, you decided to give them a call about your plans because you might stop by to see them on Sunday afternoon on the way back to college and have some of your mom's famous roast beef and chocolate pie. To your surprise, however, when you explained your plans to them, they both became angry. Your father said that you were making too many trips back and forth and that he just didn't have that kind of money to spend on gasoline. Your mother tried to avoid asking the question she really wanted to ask—where you would be staying—and asked instead what Chris' parents would think about your coming up for the weekend. Finally, they said that they could not stop you from going, but that you would disappoint them enormously if you decided to go anyway.

You suspect that the real reason for their anger is that they don't want to face your spending the weekend with Chris. Your father did make a valid point, though—he is paying for the gas. Although you had a job last summer, you spent all of your wages on buying your car. Your parents are supporting you fully this year as a way of helping you get adjusted to college life without the hassle of a job.

All the rest of Tuesday you were upset by the whole incident. You talked to several people, and each person had different advice. However, most of your best friends said that you should go because parents just don't understand these kinds of things.

You still weren't sure, however, so you decided to go to the only older person on campus that you know well enough to discuss the matter with—your dorm advisor. You explain the situation and ask for advice. The advice you get is that you should make your decision based upon who will be hurt the most in the situation. The dorm advisor points out that your parents will be immediately hurt by the situation if you go. Since they made their wishes known to you, they will see your going as deliberate disobedience. The advisor also points out, though, that your parents might be hurt worse in the future if you have to go against their wishes in some larger and more serious matter. It might be easier to begin to lay the ground-work for increased responsibility now. Chris will be hurt by your not going because plans have been made. Chris also might see this as a first step toward breaking off your relationship. Chris could be appeased by an invitation to your upcoming homecoming weekend and might not stay hurt as long as your parents would. You will probably be a little hurt either way.

For class discussion

1. What is the problem in this case?
2. How do you make decisions now—peer advice, past parental guidance, your own best judgment?
3. What possible sources of advice would be available to you in a similar situation?
4. If you were in the situation just described, would you go or not? Why? Would you tell your parents if you decided to go?

Assignment 1

To help you think through the problem clearly, make some notes comparing the results of each of your possible decisions. Use these notes to make your decision whether or not to go, and write a letter to Chris if you decide not to go or to your parents if you do go. Use the comparison that you have made to persuade your audience of the correctness of your decision.

For class discussion
1. If you decide not to go, what reasons will you give Chris?
2. If you decide to go, what attitude should your letter to your parents express?

Assignment 2
Now that the weekend is over, you realize that the situation has just begun. You see that you are going to have to make your parents understand your need for independence. Write a letter to them explaining how the person you are now compares with the person you were in high school. Try to persuade them of your need for more trust.

For class discussion
1. What can you know about the parents in this situation?
2. What kind of tone can you predict that they will respond best to if you use it in your letter?
3. What points of comparison between you in high school and you in college are most likely to be convincing to your parents?

Pink or Blue or Long Green?

You and your fiancé have been having a long-standing argument for the past year. Although you are compatible in almost all of your opinions, when the subject of having babies comes up, you can never agree. Both of you like children. Your fiancé grew up as an only child, but has always enjoyed cousins' and neighbors' children. You have two brothers and adore their children.

The problem is that you are both very serious about your careers. Your fiancé is a first-year law student, and you are in your last year of working on a degree in accounting. Both of you fully intend to pursue your careers for the rest of your lives and like the idea of the financial security two incomes will bring you. *You* see no problem with double careers and having children. With so many day care centers available and with industry moving more and more toward the idea of shared responsibility for parenting and release time for both husbands and wives, you feel that it is possible for you and your fiancé to have careers and children both.

Your fiancé feels quite differently, and often says, "Statistics show that many women successful in careers are divorced. This situation is hard on children." Also, your fiancé believes that one parent or the other should stay home with the children full time for the first two years. Since neither of you is willing to give up your careers completely for any period of time, your fiancé is strongly against the two of you having children after you are married. Lately, almost every time you are together you have had an argument over this problem.

This semester you are taking a sociology course called "Current Social Problems." Your professor has asked you to write an essay analyzing a social problem that affects your life. You will turn in the essay two weeks from now. Because of your recent discussions with your fiancé, you decide to write on the problem of careers and children. You decide to approach the problem as openly as possible. Perhaps this will be a chance to get things clearer in your own mind.

Sitting at your desk, you make a list of reasons why people have babies. You divide your list into what you consider good reasons and bad reasons:

Good	Bad
1. To add depth to an already good relationship.	1. Never thought about not having kids.
2. For a feeling of security and a close relationship after own parents die.	2. To save a marriage.
3. For the challenge of having something meaningful to do.	3. For someone to take care of you when you're old.
	4. For a son to carry on the family name.
	5. For something to do.

To determine if there are other reasons to have a baby or not, you decide to do some research on your own. Since you have two weeks for the project, you will have time to ask some people you know about why they decided to have a baby or not and whether careers and children mix.

Assignment 1

Begin with a telephone call to your parents. Explain to them the reason for your question, and ask them why they decided to have children. As they talk, take careful notes on what they say. After you hang up, write up your notes in a more complete form for later use.

Assignment 2

Another idea occurs to you. By now you have several friends who are married, and some of the older ones already have children. Invite two couples—one with children and one without—to lunch. Explain the project to them, and tape the conversation that follows. Afterwards review the tape and list all the pros and cons of having children that are mentioned.

Assignment 3

Now that you have mulled the issue over in your mind and have done some surveying, you feel ready to write the essay your sociology professor asked for. Write an essay in which you compare the benefits of a two-career couple having children or remaining childless.

Assignment 4

Working through the idea of whether or not to have a baby has made the issue clearer for you. You decide to send a copy of your essay to your fiancé, hoping it will help clarify the issue that has been the source of tension between you. Compose a letter to your fiancé to send with the essay using a tone that will encourage openmindedness. In your letter, anticipate and deal with some of your fiancé's possible objections to what you say in the essay.

CHAPTER 6

DEFINITION AS A WAY OF THINKING AND WRITING

After reading this chapter, you should be able to:

define terms and ideas as a way of discovering what you want to say;

recognize when it is necessary to define terms for your audience;

define terms in such a way that your audience understands those terms in the precise way you intend.

Curiously, when you ask people to define a word, they often go directly to the dictionary. Dictionary definitions tell us how the general public uses words at the time the dictionary was published. But words are always changing in meaning, and sometimes it is more important for you to figure out and tell your audience what you mean when *you* use a particular word. A *definition* limits what you mean by a word, a phrase, or an idea. It places a term into a class of similar terms, then shows how the term differs from all other members of that class. If I write, for example, that *"dancercise* is a strenuous physical activity combining the motions of modern dance and exercise designed by insidious young physical education instructors to make young people feel supple and beautiful and middle-aged people feel clumsier and creakier," you immediately recognize that the definition has a definite personal edge. I have placed *dancercise* into a class—strenuous physical activity. This class also includes many other activities like swimming, football, and tennis. To differentiate *dancercise* from those other activities, I say that *dancercise* combines the motions of modern dance and exercise. But note that the last part of my definition, "designed by insidious young physical education instructors . . .," is hardly universally accepted. It is, instead, what *I* mean by dancercise as I sit here, barely able to move with my body sore from my last dancercise class. At the moment, it is more important to me that you recognize what I mean by the term than what the rest of the world means.

Parts of a Definition

Let's examine for a moment a formal definition from a dictionary.

> **flatbed press** A printing press in which the type, locked into a chase, is supported by a flat platen (in older models) or by a cylinder against which the bed moves.— *The American Heritage Dictionary*

First, *flatbed press* is placed into a class of things—*printing presses*. Next, it is distinguished from all other printing presses: "the type, locked into a chase, is supported by a flat platen (in older models) or by a cylinder against which the bed moves." Formal definition, then, is composed of two steps:

1. Place the term into a class of things that it is like.

Examples: *Hate* is an *emotion*.
Mimosa is a *kind of tree*.
Writing is a *physical and mental activity*.

2. Explain how the term is different from other members of that class.

Examples: *Hate* is an emotion in which *intense dislike is felt for another person or thing*.

A *mimosa* is a kind of tree *having clusters of pink flowers and complex, lacey leaves*.

> *Writing* is a physical and mental activity in which *thoughts are placed on paper in such a way as to persuade, inform, entertain, or engage a reader.*

Exercise

1. Identify the two parts of a definition in each of the following:

a. Justice is the insurance which we have on our lives and property; to which may be added, and obedience is the premium which we pay for it.—William Penn

b. A Conservative is a man with two perfectly good legs who, however, has never learned to walk.—Franklin D. Roosevelt

c. buyers' market.   A market condition characterized by prices at or near cost, occurring when the supply of commodities exceeds market demands.—*The American Heritage Dictionary*

2. Give your own personal definition of each of the following terms or of other terms you have a personal interest in.

a. Adidas
b. boredom
c. work
d. homesickness
e. success

When to Define Your Terms

You will remember that when we discussed writing as the process of solving problems or answering questions in Chapter 3, we said that defining the problem or question was the first step. Just as defining how you feel about a problem helps you begin writing about it, so defining terms and ideas you want to use in your writing helps you discover what you want to say. For example, perhaps you've defined a problem you want to write about as a fear of success—you freeze when you're taking exams because you fear that success will put more pressure on you to do even better next time. If you go on to define what *success* means to you, you may discover more ideas that help explain your problem. Whether or not definitions appear in your finished product, defining is an essential mode of thought in a great deal of the writing you do.

The most obvious time you will want definitions in your writing is when you are using terms that are connected with a special subject and thus not likely to be understood by your audience. Almost all special fields of study use terms that are unique to that field. Most artists and art historians, for example, will readily understand what is meant by the terms *funk, patina, pointilist,* and *plasticity,* whereas many non-artists might not recognize these words at all. The scientist might understand *olfactory epithelia, spirochetes,* and *symbionts,* but the rest of us probably need some explanation.

Writing to the general readers of *Time* magazine, the author of "Those Baffling Black Holes" begins with a definition:

> If Einstein's theory is correct, black holes are the natural consequences of the death of giant stars. In what astronomers call catastrophic gravitational collapse, most of the matter contained in such a dying star begins falling in toward the stellar center. If the conditions are right, the matter crushes together with such enormous force that it literally compresses itself out of existence. The star becomes what mathematicians call a "singularity." Its matter is squeezed into an infinitesimally small volume, and it simultaneously becomes infinitely dense and has an infinitely high gravitational force. At the point of singularity, time and space no longer exist. "Imagine," says Harvard Astrophysicist Jonathan Grindlay, "you take an enormous mass and shrink it down to nothing. A very disturbing idea."

Exercise

Look back over the assignments you've written in this course so far. Are there any specialized terms you used that you could have defined for your audience? Select an instance where a definition is most needed and revise your writing, including a definition in the new version.

Another good time to define a term is when you use that term in an unusual or not widely accepted way, as was true of my definition of *dancercise.* If, for example, you want to write about being poor, but for you being poor had less to do with financial situation and more to do with a state of mind, then you need to tell your audience what sense of *poor* you are using:

> Curiously enough, I've never felt poor. Many people define "being poor" as not having very much money. There have certainly been plenty of those times for me. Once I can remember having three dollars to last for food for five days. It was an unpleasant shock the first evening when the grocer charged me 50¢ for one orange. I guess most people would call that poor. I never felt that way, though. Always around me were the books and objects that I liked best. And I always knew that I would be smart enough to figure out a way to survive if I had to. No, "being poor," for me, is not an absence of money. "Being poor" is the feeling of being a victim in a world over which you have no control.

You should also define a term when you want your audience to understand that you are using a limited meaning for a term that usually has a much broader meaning. In the following paragraph, G. K. Chesterton uses *sentimental* in a very limited sense. Knowing that the word is likely to remind the audience of a kind of sweet, almost maudlin feeling, Chesterton begins his essay by separating what he means by *sentimental* from its usual connotations:

> We shall never attain to a serious and complete school of criticism so long as the word "sentimental" is regarded as a term of depreciation. That "passionate" should be a complimentary form and "sentimental" a hostile one is as utterly unmeaning and ridiculous as it would be if "blue" were complimentary and "green" hostile. The difference between passion and sentiment is not, as is so often assumed, a difference in sincerity or wholesomeness or reality of feeling. It is a difference between two ways of looking at the same unquestionable facts of life. True sentiment consists in taking the central emotions of life not as passion takes them, personally, but impersonally, with a certain light and open confession of them as things common to us all. Passion is always a secret; it cannot be confessed; it is always a discovery; it cannot be shared. But sentiment stands for that frame of mind in which all men admit, with a half-humorous and half-magnanimous weakness, that they all possess the same secret, and have all made the

same discovery. *Romeo and Juliet,* for example, is passionate. *Love's Labour's Lost* is sentimental. No man, perhaps, was more sentimental than Thackeray; a certain kind of cynicism is akin to sentiment in that it treats the emotions openly and lightly. To the man of passion, love and the world are new; to the man of sentiment they are infinitely old.—"Sentimental Literature"

Extended Definition

Sometimes an entire piece of writing will be what is called an *extended definition*—a definition that is expanded by more information and qualifications of the meaning. It often uses many of the other modes of development (description, examples, comparisons, analogies) as well. Extended definitions have many uses. A writer may wish to evaluate a particular instance of something on the basis of what it really should be. For example, a writer might define the concept of *United States senator* in order to evaluate how well a particular candidate lives up to the idea. Or a writer may wish to persuade the audience to decontrol oil prices by defining capitalism. Or a writer may simply wish to explore and understand a concept in some depth.

When writing an extended definition, begin with the definition of the term you are concerned with. Then, go on to explore each of the parts of that definition in more detail, expanding the audience's understanding of the definition.

The following essay by Lance Morrow represents extended definition that is used to make an argument. You might not recognize that the essay is definition at first because it defines something we are familiar with—the necktie.

narrative

During the fuel shortage four years ago, the federal energy boss, John Sawhill, tried to persuade men to take off their neckties: it would cool them down a degree or two and save on power for air conditioners. The Sawhill movement, intelligent for reasons besides conservation, vanished faster than a Nehru suit. The men's neckwear lobby protested, and Sawhill backed down. Well, fellas, he said, just *loosen* your ties. But the look he proposed was wrong anyhow. When a businessman in full regalia removes only his tie (retaining the dark shoes, the suit, the shirt buttoned at the wrists), then he looks like a sharecropper—or an executive being held by terrorists. Something is missing.

class

Still, Sawhill was thinking in the right direction. The necktie—that vestigial bib, that morning noose—is a strange and sinister article of clothing. When a man feels ill, the first thing to do is loosen his tie; it is, after all, pressing against the carotid arteries, impeding the flow of blood to the brain. Practically, the necktie is as supererogatory as those little belts and buckles that used to adorn the backs of men's

comparison

trousers. The tie has no function except to clean eyeglasses, and even that it does badly. It makes as much sense as the grenade loops on a trench coat, or perhaps even less, since the man in the trench coat can at least carry grenades if he wishes.

beginning
of
differentiation

But it would be wrong to say that the tie is useless or pointless. Dress is language. The tie has many meanings, many symbolic and psychological uses. It is an inverted exclamation mark hanging from the throat. It subtly directs attention away from the wearer's physicality. Worn with full business suit, it can be a form of armoring, a defense and an assertion of power. It can also be a gesture of compliance. White House Aide Hamilton Jordan, tieless and amiably scruffy for years, has started dressing (almost contritely) in suit and tie in the wake of stories about his drinking and raffishness. Often, the tie is a uniform signaling solidarity among certain kinds of men, a semaphore announcing that

example

"we all speak the language." It gives men a feeling of security, a certain formality, a necessary distance. Although the tie may be physically uncomfortable, they take psychic comfort from it.

differentiation

Ties differentiate social classes, kinds of jobs. They can be flags of social ordering. The difference between blue collar and white collar has almost always meant the difference between no tie and tie on the job. While some men in, say, the professorial classes go tieless, wearing blue work shirts under their tweed jackets, plenty of factory workers aspire

examples

to jobs that involve ties. In William Inge's *Picnic*, Hal Carter speaks wistfully of a job "in a nice office where I can wear a tie and have a sweet little secretary." When dressing up, blue collar workers often like a loud yell of garish color, while upper middle class men tend toward more discretion.

continued differentiation Looping around the neck like a reiterated threat of the garrote, a necktie can serve to restrain and discipline. That, at least, is the theory behind having little boys in private schools wear them; it doesn't always work. Neckties also represent a gesture of respect. A lawyer always advises his client to appear in court wearing a coat and tie. It shows that you have the deference to make yourself uncomfort-

examples able. Several years ago, a Florida judge cited a lawyer for contempt of court when the lawyer showed up wearing a gold medallion around his neck instead of a tie.

Dress codes in clubs, restaurants and schools are a form of social discipline resting on the premise that certain kinds of dress will preclude certain kinds of behavior and, of course, certain kinds of people. Reluctantly, some of the nation's fancier restaurants have started admitting the tieless. But not La Cara-velle in New York City. Says Co-Owner Fred Decré: "If you give in on ties, then people will start showing up without jackets. Next you will have shirts with short sleeves, or unbuttoned to the navel, with hairy chests and gold chains all over the place. That would be intolerable."

It is possible that neckties accomplish a certain amount of symbolic good. A suit and tie make a rather democratic outfit; the richest men wear them, and so do the poorer when dressing up, even if they do not spend $600 to cover their nakedness. Class and regional distinctions are usually evident in choices, however. Consider the outfit, prevalent in

example Ohio, known as the "Full Cleveland": a bright blazer (red or green), plaid trousers, white shoes, white belt and white tie.

There are symbolic, if not practical, uses for the necktie. But can it be defended simply on the grounds of adornment, of what looks good, regard-less of function? Sometimes. The neckwear industry promotes ties as discretionary plumage, the one item with which a man can express a bit of flamboy-ance. That argument may hold for men in properly neutral suits, but what do you say to the man in the

Full Cleveland? *Everything* he is wearing is as loud as the roof on a Howard Johnson's.

analogy

Neckties are a little like wasp-waist corsets for women: even if one admires the look, he must wonder why they need to be uncomfortable. To be neat, the tie requires a shirt buttoned snugly at the Adam's apple. So, especially of course in summer, the body notices that it is airlessly bound at waist, wrists and neck. Food for the stomach and air for the lungs must pass down this strait constricted to appease teachers, bosses and headwaiters.

narrative

It is possible to defend dress codes while still finding it ridiculous that this oddly shaped rag, knotted at the throat, has come to define respectable dress in a man. The necktie did not arrive with any compelling mandate from nature. Its origins were whimsical enough. After the Croatians defeated the Turks in a battle during the 17th century, the victorious regiment was given a welcome in Paris; admiring Frenchmen copied the soldiers' flowing scarves—*cravates.* Over the centuries, the tie has gone through thousands of fitful and pointless variations: stocks, string ties and once during the 19th century, a crescent-shaped bowtie worn with a choker collar so high and stiff that the wearer could neither see to the side nor turn his head. This year, fashion designers have ordained that, along with lapels, the thing must shrink again to '50s proportions (about three inches at the widest place).

examples

Are there alternatives? If the tie is one of a man's few opportunities to peacock a bit, then presumably a substitute must involve some color too—a brocade vest, a plumed hat. For summer at least, the newly revived turn-of-the-century collarless shirt, without the celluloid attachable collar, has possibilities. It is neat and extraordinarily comfortable. If only the collarless shirt did not reek so disagreeably of a sort of Bloomingdale's chic, which has the effect of somehow trivializing the wearer. For years Filipino men have managed to be both elegant and comfortable in the *barong tagalog,* the embroidered shirt that is a kind of national costume. The caftan might not pass as suitable business attire, and the clergyman's Roman collar can bite the neck. But among the tunics, togas, jerkins, buff coats, cassocks, sweat-shirts, turtlenecks and other garments that humans have experimented with down the long centuries, there must be some arrangement that will get a man past the maître d'. A necktie cannot be the final answer. A man's clothes should not throttle him.—"The Odd Practice of Neck Binding"

The point here is that, though a tie is a useful social symbol, as an article of clothing it is a "strange and sinister" device. The author begins by recounting an incident involving a tie, then, in the second paragraph, he places *tie* in the class of clothing and notes its deficiencies as a member of this class. In the third paragraph, he places *tie* in another class—like all clothing ties are symbols. Then he differentiates ties from other symbols by explaining what they symbolize. He concludes by suggesting that men find a less uncomfortable garment to symbolize their social status. Note how he uses other modes of thought throughout his extended definition.

Exercise

Choose a familiar item (tennis shoes, pocket calculator, foreign car) and define it in terms of its social function. Examine how well its physical characteristics serve its function and make any recommendations for change you think are needed.

Summary

Definition allows you to explore and set limits on what you mean by an idea, a concept, or an object. Brief definitions make communication with your audience surer. We live in a time of constant complaints about the proliferation of jargon in almost every field of study. If those in a particular field of study can't keep up with the vocabulary of that field, then certainly none of us can hope to have knowledge of all of the words that a writer might use. This makes definition an even more important way of writing than ever. By giving adequate definitions for terms that might be misunderstood, you help your audience understand what you mean and also help insure that they follow your thoughts.

Always define terms that your audience might be unfamiliar with and terms that you are defining in a special way.

A definition usually consists of two basic parts. The first part places the term into a class of which it is part. It classifies the term with other like terms. The second part tells how the term differs from other members of that class. An *extended definition* explores the concept in more detail, often using other modes of development.

Outward Bound and Downward Bound

You have just been hired as director for an Outward Bound program sponsored by the YMCA. The program is designed to put a group of fifteen twelve-year-olds from inner-city schools through a rigorous physical training program in order to create a sense of pride about their physical well-being.

You were a bit surprised when you received the call from the Westside YMCA saying that you have been hired. You are in your third year of college, and your only experience with kids was as a lifeguard at the pool during the summer between your junior and senior years in high school. Your only other qualifications are that you love sports and are in fair physical condition yourself. You play racketball regularly and run three miles every day. But the program director for the Y said that the main requirements for the job are enthusiasm and the ability to work with people, and that the letter of recommendation from the manager of the fast food restaurant you worked for during the past three years convinced her that you were the person for the job.

As you start the job, you first read through the schedule of activities to see what preparations you will have to make. You notice that one of the rigorous activities the kids will engage in is rappelling. You have been allotted $200 to hire an expert for a week of instruction.

All you know about rappelling is that it has something to do with rock climbing, so you take a look at the dictionary definition:

rappel (ra pel′)—the act or method of descending from a mountainside or cliff by means of a double rope passed under one thigh and over the opposite shoulder.

That doesn't help much, so you go to the library to find an article on rappelling. You find only general articles on climbing, and you decide that you'll have to rely on your expert for your information.

At the pay you're offering, you are not likely to entice someone with a full-time job to come in for a week. You decide to place an ad on the campus bulletin board and hope that you can find a summer school student with climbing experience who would like to earn some extra money.

Assignment 1
Compose the "Employment Available" ad for the campus bulletin board, requesting letters of application to be sent directly to you at the Westside YMCA, 1000 W. Slade.

Assignment 2
In answer to your ad, you receive the following three letters:

Dear Director:

I hope that you will accept this letter as an application for the position that you advertised of teaching rappelling to Outward Bound students. I am a sophomore here at the college with a physical education major, and climbing is my special hobby and has been for three years.

For the last two summers I have had extensive experience in the Sierras and in the Rocky Mountains. I have also had some experience working with younger children in my high school's program of summer gymnastics for the elementary schools.

I would appreciate any consideration that you can give me. I am available for an interview at your convenience. For references, please contact:
    Joe Boynton
    Physical Education Instructor
    Green High School
    Green, Idaho 79911

Rudy Moose, Instructor of Physical Education
Department of Physical Education
This Campus

Sincerely yours,
Ralph Swanson

Dear Director:

I took up climbing last summer and like it a lot. Me and a couple of buddies went mountain climbing at Mt. Spindle every weekend. I really need a summer job, and I hope you will consider me your man and give me a call at 694-5826.

Sincerely,
Bob Benton

Dear Director:

I was excited to see your ad for someone to teach rappelling. It is an activity that I have enjoyed since my father introduced me to mountain climbing five years ago.

Last summer I worked as a counselor at Camp Wahoo, and part of my duties were to instruct nine and ten-year-olds in rappelling. I am happy to report that there were no injuries in my class throughout the summer.

I am here this summer taking some extra courses toward my business major, and I would welcome the opportunity to earn some extra money.

You may contact me at the above address. I would be happy to provide you with the name of some references and to come for an interview.

Sincerely yours,
Becky Sarnes

For class discussion
From your initial reactions to the letters, who seems the most qualified for the job?

On the basis of the letters alone, you decide not to interview Bob Benton. You do interview the other two candidates, and in your interviews, you take the following notes:

Ralph Swanson

Age 24. Real jock. Talks sports constantly. Knows his stuff about rappelling. Observable strengths—confident manner and commanding voice. Could probably keep kids in line. Says he likes kids. Thoroughly enjoyed working with them in his high school program. Admits to having very few skills in organization. Might need some help here. But, sure could handle the active end of the program.

Becky Sarnes

Age 20, alert, athletic build. Bubbly and friendly. Genuinely seems to like kids. Says she likes the responsibility of organizing day-to-day activities. *Very* knowledgeable about rappelling. Drawback—heavy school schedule, six semester hours. Would she have time for program? She seems confident she would.

Decide which candidate to hire for the job based on the letters of application and your notes from the interviews. Write a letter expressing regret to the candidate that you do not hire.

Assignment 3
You have hired your instructor, and it is the week before the rappelling classes take place. To prepare the kids for the program, you are holding a meeting to build their enthusiasm for rappelling, an activity most never have heard of. You plan to show a short film and then talk to the kids about what's involved. You asked the person you hired to give you an extended definition of rappelling. Using this definition and your knowledge of the instructor, write your presentation. Define rappelling in a simplified way and acquaint the kids with their new instructor. Here is the definition sent to you.

> Rappelling is the act of descending a cliff by support of a rope passed through a carabiner. A carabiner is a steel oval with a spring-loaded gate. The rope is around your waist.
> In rappelling you hold the rope in the right hand behind the back and levy control. A glove is worn on the hand. When you want to speed up, bring the hand from behind the back and let the rope pass through the gloved hand. If you want to slow down or stop, put your hand behind your back again and clamp onto the rope.

Beyond the basics of rappelling, there are many styles that can be developed. You can take long smooth leaps from ledge to ledge. The leaps can consist of as much as fifty feet. As yo do these leaps, you are almost horizontal to the vertical wall. Another technique that can be used is pushing out from the cliff and lowering yourself about twenty-five feet. After you land, you push off again in another direction. In a third style, you push off as far from the wall as you can and let the rope slide through your hand. You travel about fifty feet from the cliff and drop about sixty feet.

Rappelling is difficult and very strenuous, but a good combination of skill and creativity can make it a very graceful activity.

For class discussion
1. What can you assume these kids know about this subject, and how are they likely to feel about it?
2. What words in the extended definition will you have to modify for your audience?
3. What material seems unnecessary for your audience to know at the beginning of their program?
4. What material might you add to build enthusiasm?
5. What will you tell the kids about their instructor?

The Mental Health Bill

Since you've been working for Congressman Rusk you have learned a lot about politics and even more about how little freshman members of the State House sometimes know. The House serves as a training ground for novices in public office, and your congressman certainly is in the beginning stages of his education! You trust him, though, and you know he is genuinely concerned about those he represents; therefore, as his aide, you are willing to overlook his shortcomings and help him out.

Recently he passed a letter along to you with a memo saying "Get on this right away!"

Dear Congressman Rusk:

I was in the audience last month when you spoke at the State Public Health Officials Convention. I was frankly shocked at how little knowledge you have about our state mental health programs. Surely you are familiar with the Mental Health Code, yet you stumbled when someone asked if the Code didn't need revision.

I want to urge you to vote for at least $35 million for the community mental-health centers program. Last year's slash set our programs back ten years. Your comments at the Convention that we need cutbacks in state spending are valid. But we have to set priorities.

Sincerely,
Alice Longworthy, Community Mental Health Center, Pleasantview

Congressman Rusk obviously doesn't want to send his form letter: "I appreciate your view on the issue, and I will keep it in mind when the vote comes up." As he often has done in the past, he asks you to give him the information he needs to write an informed reply.

Assignment 1
First, you'll have to find out about the Mental Health Code. Using these notes that you gathered in your research, write an explanation for your congressman.

Mental Health Code—1948
Hospitalization procedures:
voluntary commitment (submit self, 10 days; remain then until release or 96 hours after request for discharge)
emergency involuntary (peace officer submits; can be held 96 hours)
temporary commitment (county judge decides on basis of medical testimony; commitment up to 90 days. Open hearing, counsel, jury trial)
indefinite commitment (judge also, safeguards including jury)

Assignment 2
Next, research the mental health programs in your state. Write your notes in a form you can pass on to Congressman Rusk.

Assignment 3
After you send your reports, you receive this memo from the congressman:

> You're the expert. Write Ms. Longworthy. I'll sign. Make sure she knows I'm better informed. I'll support the bill, but make no commitment about the funding.

Write a letter to Ms. Longworthy in which you define the mental health program in such a way that it is clear that Congressman Rusk supports it. You may wish to do more research on the mental health program in your state in order to write a more convincing letter.

For class discussion
1. What classes of terms could the state's mental health program be considered a member of? Which classification might be most useful for achieving your purpose in the letter?
2. How does the state's mental health program differ from other governmental programs? How does it differ from the mental health programs in other states?

The Responsible Parent

For several months you couldn't get an advertisement you had seen in the paper out of your mind. You clipped it out and put it on your bulletin board. Every time you were sitting at your desk and your eye caught the ad, you reminded yourself that some day soon you were going to do something about it.

The ad said:

NEEDED IMMEDIATELY!

Responsible volunteers are needed desperately at the Parenting Center. You do not have to be a parent to qualify. We are seeking persons with a strong desire to help others and in the process reward themselves.

You are needed to serve as a parent partner to counsel disturbed parents referred to the center. Training classes meet

once a week for six weeks in the evenings, and your volunteering can be scheduled according to your preferences.

Won't you please help? We promise you won't regret it.

Parenting Center
1900 North Indiana

You have been increasingly interested in giving some of your time to help others. You have plenty of free time, you are secure in your job, and your salary is more than adequate for your needs. Your own two children are much more independent now. One is in the last year of middle school, and the other is in the sixth grade. This volunteer job interests you more than others. Your experience raising your own two children has been fairly typical—some good times, some bad times, but all worthwhile times.

You can easily understand, however, how a parent can have problems raising a child. During the times when money wasn't so readily available or when pressures at work were at their greatest, you've been less than a good parent. And other times when your children have been passing through particularly difficult stages of their development, you have understood how easy it would be to develop a terrible relationship with your children. Somehow, though, you have managed to weather the bad times.

Child abuse interests you too. Before you became a parent, child abuse was one crime you could have no sympathy for. After you were a parent for a while, you saw how easy it was to lose your temper with your children, and you realized the struggle it took to maintain an even relationship with them. Now, though you still abhor child abuse, you feel great pity for those involved, and you want to share some of your understandings with them.

Finally, you called the Center and asked if they were still in need of help. The next evening you found yourself beginning the first two-hour session of your six-week training course in being a Parent Partner.

In the first session, you were given a history of the Center and were shown a film of a psychologist working with a parent who is a child abuser. You learned that this is the major problem the Center deals with.

Then the leader explained what you would be doing. A

Parent Partner serves as a responsible, guiding person the disturbed parent can confide in. The Parent Partner listens, responds as rationally as possible, and makes suggestions. But, in order to be most effective, he or she maintains an objective, neutral relationship with the parent. You are not to become a close friend and under no circumstances do you take the responsibility for solving problems for the abusing parent. You were somewhat relieved at the last statement.

The leader then discussed some of the behavior the Center tries to encourage in a parent. You took some notes during this part:

1. Democratic society—children have rights. Ideal situation— mutual respect between parent and child.
2. All misbehavior has a purpose—an effective parent learns to look for that purpose.
3. Good listening a key to understanding. Includes reflective listening, listening for keys to meaning beyond what other person is actually saying.
4. Parents must decide if problem is their problem or child's problem. Example: messy room—whose problem?

Your leader concluded the session by giving an assignment. The leader asked each of you to write an extended essay defining what you each think it means to be a *responsible parent*. He suggested that you consider how a responsible parent meets the physical, emotional, economic, social, and sexual needs of a child. He asked you to be as precise as possible in your definition, perhaps even giving examples of what you mean.

Assignment 1
Write the extended definition of a *responsible parent* that the leader asked for. You will want to consider all of the needs he suggested, but you may emphasize some more than others. Remember that giving examples and making comparisons are two ways to communicate your meaning more precisely.

Assignment 2
In the next session, the leader explains that your first step in any Parent Partner case will be to set reasonable goals for

what you hope to accomplish. Those goals will include such things as advising the parent how to search for a job, supplying information on hygiene and nutrition, counseling the parent on how to obtain legal aid if a divorce seems to be the answer, and offering reasonable guidance through trying situations.

The leader gives you a copy of a sample case that you might be assigned to as a Parent Partner. He asks you to describe the goals you would consider most important in working with that case and explain how you might accomplish them.

Read the following case and write the description the leader called for.

SAMPLE CASE: Alice Montgomery

Alice Montgomery has been referred to the Center by the Department of Human Resources. Two of her three children were picked up by a police officer after he spotted them wandering aimlessly down one of the busiest thoroughfares in their neighborhood. All three of Alice's children are age four and under.

Alice Montgomery is nineteen years old. While living at home with her parents, she was sexually abused by her father from the age of eleven to the age of fourteen. Her mother was aware of this abuse but did nothing to stop it.

Alice married at the age of fifteen to escape from her unhealthy home life. Her husband is five years older than Alice and works as a machine operator in a broom factory. He makes just enough to pay the rent on their tiny apartment and to feed inadequately the five of them. He is completely unsupportive of Alice's complaints about her life. He says that she has a soft life—staying home all day watching television. He occasionally beats her for small things like not having dinner ready when he gets home.

Alice does not have a phone (her husband says they can't afford one), and she does not drive. She is completely isolated from her neighbors who will have nothing to do with her because of the unsanitary way the family lives. Her husband discourages any friendships she does initiate, saying she doesn't have time and should be at home with the kids.

Except for shopping for necessities, Alice stays at home alone all day with the three children and the two dogs that live with them in the apartment.

When the case worker first entered the apartment, she was overcome by the stench of the place. The children were filthy and half-clothed. The oldest child had bruises on his legs. Alice quickly explained that he had fallen, but the child privately told the case worker that his mother had beaten him because he had taken candy from his little sister. Dog excrement was in plain sight in the kitchen. Unwashed dishes were piled in the sink, and most of the chairs were filled with dirty clothing. Alice was in her nightgown in the living room watching television.

The case worker learned after working with Alice for a while that she was extremely depressed about her situation and wanted to change it, but just didn't know how. At the current time, Alice has been helped to the extent that she now gets dressed every day and is keeping the house a little neater.

For class discussion
1. In what ways does Alice Montgomery not fit the definition of a responsible parent you formulated in the last assignment?
2. Look at Alice's life from her point of view. What are her problems and what caused them?
3. Look at the case history from the children's point of view. What are their problems and what caused them?
4. What solutions are possible for these problems? What consequences do the solutions have?

Assignment 3
You are nearing the end of the training sessions, and it is almost time for you to be assigned as a Parent Partner. As a final assignment, the leader of your training sessions asks you to describe a situation from your own childhood in which there was a problem between you and your parents. You are to explain and evaluate how your parents handled the situation and suggest alternative measures your parents might have taken. These essays will be discussed in the final training session next week. Remembering your audience and what you have learned, write the essay.

CHAPTER 7

CLASSIFYING THE WORLD AROUND YOU

After reading this chapter, you should be able to:

see how classification helps you understand new information and use what you know;

devise classes that suit your purposes in writing;

devise classes according to the needs of your audience.

Imagine walking into a grocery store where the owners have made no attempt at classification. The toothpaste is on the shelf next to the canned peaches, the toilet paper is beside the dog food, and the beer is next to the cantaloupes. Since it would be difficult both to find what you need and to remember where everything is once you've found it, chances are you wouldn't return to that store. Our minds cannot handle large numbers of things without creating some classes or categories to place them in.

As a baby, you may have called all men "Daddy," often embarrassing your mother. The problem was not that you couldn't recognize your father. Rather, you knew that there was a group of human beings that fit roughly into the same class as that human being you knew as "Daddy." So you chose a collective term to refer to all humans in that class—"Daddy." Unfortunately it was the wrong term. Later, you learned the proper term for that class—*men.* Very rapidly, you learned to classify men into subclasses in a variety of ways depending upon your needs at the time. Men might have become (1) Daddy, (2) uncles, (3) grandfathers, and (4) friends. Or, they might have been (1) men that gave you candy and (2) men that didn't. Or, they might have been (1) familiar men and (2) strange men. You began to understand classification.

Classification

Classification is a natural way of thinking about the world. When you encounter something for the first time, you understand it by placing it into a class or classes with other things that seem to be similar to it. As we noted in Chapter 6, one step in defining something is to classify it. Evidence of classification systems is all around us. For example, if you go into a record store to buy an album, you will find the albums grouped according to type of music—jazz, classical, country and western, rock, and many others. Your school bookstore classifies books according to academic discipline—anthropology, English, history, government, chemistry—or subject matter—poetry, cooking, biography, reference, self-help. When you fill out income tax forms, you are classified according to marital status and income. *Classification is the systematic grouping of ideas or items into categories based upon shared characteristics.*

But a large group of ideas or items can be classified in any number of ways, depending on which characteristics you choose to look at as a basis for classification. Your purpose in classifying and your audience determine the characteristics you choose. For example, if you were compiling a course guide for fellow students, you might classify professors on the basis of their teaching ability. You would pay no attention to their ages, appearances, or ranks, and group them into classes that revealed how well they perform in the classroom. You then have to consider what characteristics make for a good teacher. You might decide on the following classes:

excellent (engaging and knowledgeable);
good (boring, but knowledgeable);
fair (engaging, but stupid);
poor (boring and stupid).

In contrast, if you're talking to a friend about professors' personalities, you might classify them on the basis of clothing style. In this case, you would pay no attention to their teaching abilities, ages, or ranks, and would group them into classes that revealed how they express themselves through their clothes. Again, you would have to carefully define the classes you use:

high fashion (stepped out of the pages of *Vogue* or *GQ);*
outdoorsy (stepped out of the pages of the L. L. Bean, or EMS or R.E.I. catalog);
low-price (shops at Salvation Army);
classic (conservative and tailored);
eclectic (mixes styles—for example, a three-piece linen suit with hiking boots).

Choosing bases for classification requires you to think carefully about what characteristics are important for your purpose and your audience. And, most importantly, the characteristics you choose must clearly separate the ideas or items into unified classes.

Exercise

1. Colleges classify courses by academic discipline because of the organization of professors into departments. You may wish to classify courses for other purposes. Devise alternate systems of classification for college courses, and state the purpose of each.
2. Devise some classifications for automobiles and state the purpose and audience for each.

Since you use classification in your writing to help your audience see a subject in the same way you do, one of the first questions to ask when you decide what classes to use is, What do my readers already know about my subject?

If you were writing about the economic structure of small towns for a general audience, you might classify them on the basis of major source of employment: factory towns, college towns, farm towns, mining towns, resort towns. If you were writing with the same purpose to a more specific audience—

for example, residents of Minnesota—you might label the classes with the names of familiar towns, and describe each class in terms of that town: Red Wing (factory), Northfield (college), Owatonna (farm), Hibbing (mining), Ely (resort). Finally, if you were writing a paper for a sociology class, you might classify towns at a higher level of generality: industrial (including factory and mining), agricultural (farm and packing), white-collar (education and small business), recreation (resorts and park entrances).

The classes you chose not only fit your purpose—to examine the various sources of economic support for small towns—but also fit your audience by explaining the classes in terms they are familiar with. It may seem that nature readily falls into classes, but keep in mind that our names for those classes (birds, mammals, reptiles) were created by humans. Classification is a dynamic, changing process. You can make your classes fit your purposes and the needs of your audience.

In the examples so far, we divided items into one set of classes, but often you want to make further subdivisions. *Subclasses,* smaller categories into which classes are divided, can be created in two ways. One way is to classify on several bases at once. If you're trying to decide what restaurant to go to tonight you might start by classifying restaurants on the basis of type of food—do you want Italian, Mexican, or Chinese? Once you've decided it's Chinese, you classify the Chinese restaurants on the basis of quality. Then, having narrowed your choices to the two good Chinese restaurants in town, you make your final decision on the basis of price—Fung-wa's is the less expensive of the two. Because quality and price are characteristics equally applicable to the other types of restaurants, the classification you have used divides restaurants on the basis of three characteristics at once. Here are the classes and subclasses that result:

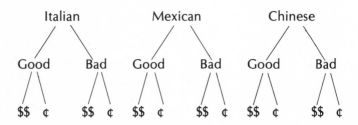

The other way to create subclasses is to divide each class further on the basis of characteristics unique to each class. For example, the first small town classes we mentioned above could be subdivided in this way:

— Factory (on the basis of product): glass, automobiles, canneries, optical equipment;
— College (on the basis of source of funding): state, private;
— Farm (on the basis of crop): cotton, potatoes, wheat, dairy;
— Mining (on the basis of resource found): iron, copper, taconite, salt;
— Resort (on the basis of activities offered): fishing, golf, gambling.

A general question to ask yourself in setting up classes and subclasses is: Are my classes inclusive and mutually exclusive? If many of the items you are sorting don't fit any of your classes or fit into more than one class, your classification won't be very useful. For example, if you were dividing games into adult games and children's games, you would soon discover many games that fit in both categories: monopoly, checkers, backgammon. You would then reconsider your classification and create an additional class: games for all ages. And if your town has many restaurants serving types of food other than Italian, Mexican, and Chinese, the classification suggested above would have to be expanded. Of course, there will always be exceptions to any classification—one thing that fits none of your classes or fits two at once. A Chinese-Italian restaurant would fit two of the restaurant classes, while a Salvation Army free lunch wouldn't fit at all. The final test in devising a classification is whether it works for your purpose and audience.

How Classification Helps You Write

When you write, classification serves you in two ways. First, it provides you and your reader with a way of clarifying and exploring your subject. As you create classifications that fit your purposes, you discover many characteristics and similarities among individual items that you didn't think of at first.

Classification also serves you in a second way. As you place your subject into a class and then divide that class into subclasses, you find a natural means of organizing your writing. Of course, you still have several options. You may describe each subclass fully before going on to the next one. You may compare and contrast subclasses on each characteristic. Or you may eliminate some subclasses as unimportant and discuss only the important ones.

The authors of the following passage are helping the readers of a camping handbook understand the choice of lanterns for outdoor use. Lanterns are classified into types, and each type is described.

Lanterns

The camper has a wide choice of lanterns manufactured for outdoor use.

Gasoline lanterns. The familiar old gasoline pressure lantern, now redesigned into a more compact shape, is still widely used. It uses white gasoline, which can be purchased in sealed cans in some sporting goods stores. (If you have your own can, you can often buy white gas at supply points near recreational areas, although it is difficult to find elsewhere.) The lantern gives off a brilliant white light. Gasoline lanterns have built-in pumps to pressurize the fuel.

LP-gas lanterns. A similar lantern burns LP-gas, using replaceable tanks. These are convenient to use—they don't have to be pumped up periodically—but you must carry additional storage tanks. A new model has a refillable LP-gas container with hoses which can be connected to both a stove and lantern; its only drawback is limited portability.

Both the gasoline and LP-gas lanterns use mantles; carry a supply of extra mantles in case you damage those in the lamp.

Electric lanterns. There are dozens of electric lanterns on the market, powered by 6-volt batteries. These appeal to campers who dislike carrying extra fuel. Many of them are all-purpose, but some are concentrated spotlight-only models.

There are good portable units handy to use inside a tent—one you can use for a reading lamp, another is fluorescent and can also be plugged into 110-volt lines.

The 6-volt battery is advertised as good for 100 hours of intermittent use, but if accidentally left on, it will use up the battery in a day. You probably should carry an extra battery or two.—"Assembling Your Equipment," *The Sunset Camping Book*

The authors take the class "lanterns" and divide it into three subclasses—gasoline, LP-gas, and electric. Because the authors expect the readers to know very little about lanterns, they then describe each of the three types of lanterns and the properties of each. If the intended audience had been seasoned campers, the three subclasses chosen might have remained the same, but chances are the descriptions of each of the classes might have changed drastically.

Creating subclasses for a subject that is normally not classified can often be a useful and enlightening activity. In the following passage, Aldous Huxley divides the class "snobberies" into several subclasses, and in so doing, provides us with some interesting insights into the people of his time.

Disease-snobbery is only one out of a great multitude of snobberies, of which now some, now others take pride of place in general esteem. For snobberies ebb and flow; their empire rises, declines, and falls in the most approved historical manner. What were good snobberies a hundred years ago are now out of fashion. Thus, the snobbery of family is everywhere on the decline. The snobbery of culture, still strong, has now to wrestle with an organized and active low-browism, with a snobbery of ignorance and stupidity unique, so far as I know, in the whole of history. Hardly less characteristic of our age is that repulsive booze-snobbery, born of American Prohibition. The malefic influences of this snobbery are rapidly spreading all over the world. Even in France, where the existence of so many varieties of delicious wine has hitherto imposed a judicious connoisseurship and has led to the branding of mere drinking as a brutish solecism, even in France the American booze-snobbery, with its odious accompaniments—a taste for hard drinks in general and for cocktails in particular—is making headway among the rich. Booze-snobbery has now made it socially permissible, and in some circles even rather creditable, for well-brought-up men and (this is the novelty) well-brought-up women of all ages, from fifteen to seventy, to be seen drunk, if not in public, at least in the very much tempered privacy of a party.—"Selected Snobberies"

Exercise

What subclasses of snobberies would Huxley find in our present world?

As a final example, Marshall McLuhan in this paragraph shows that sometimes two subclasses are enough to explore a subject thoroughly:

> There is a basic principle that distinguishes a hot medium like radio from a cool one like the telephone, or a hot medium like the movie from a cool one like TV. A hot medium is one that extends one single sense in "high definition." High definition is the state of being well filled with data. A photograph is, visually, "high definition." A cartoon is "low definition," simply because very little visual information is provided. Telephone is a cool medium, or one of low definition, because the ear is given a meager amount of information. And speech is a cool medium of low definition, because so little is given and so much has to be filled in by the listener. On the other hand, hot media do not leave so much to be filled in or completed by the audience. Hot media are, therefore, low in participation, and cool media are high in participation or completion by the audience. Naturally, therefore, a hot medium like radio has very different effects on the user from a cool medium like the telephone—*Understanding Media*

McLuhan uses two subclasses to classify all media—hot and cool. Hot media give the receivers most of the information that they need. Cool media leave much of the information to be filled in by the audience.

Exercise

Take one of the subjects that you classified in the first exercise in this chapter and expand your classifications by creating subclasses. Give examples of your subclasses.

Summary

Classification is a useful and dynamic process—the systematic grouping of ideas or things into categories based on shared characteristics. These groupings make it possible for us to cope with large numbers of items. Placing ideas or objects into classes helps a writer explore a subject and helps the audience see the subject the same way the writer does. Major considerations for devising a system of classification are the purpose of the classification and the type of audience the classification is intended for.

Subclasses are the smaller classes into which larger classes may be divided. The subclasses that you choose should be inclusive and mutually exclusive.

One last word of caution about classification. When we are placing people, objects, or ideas into classes, it is easy to forget that those classes are composed of *individuals*. No two individuals are *exactly* alike, as shown in the following passage by Lewis Thomas:

> Minnows and catfish can recognize each member of their own species by his particular, person-specific odor. It is hard to imagine a solitary, independent, existentialist minnow, recognizable for himself alone; minnows in a school behave like interchangeable, identical parts of an organism. But there it is.
> —*The Lives of a Cell*

For some purposes, considering individuals only as members of a class is justified. But forgetting that classes are composed of individuals also makes it possible to treat the members of classes as if they were alike in all characteristics rather than just in one or two—all jocks are stupid, all frat rats are snobs, all Republicans are rich. Taken to the extreme, these *hasty generalizations* can cause us to draw conclusions about individuals that are not true. A hasty generalization is the fallacy of drawing conclusions based on too little evidence. When we place people or things into classes, we must still be able to recognize their individual identities.

The Alarming Drop-Out Rate

Alvin Collins, Vice-President for Student Affairs, put down the phone. He had a troubled look on his face. He had just talked to the dean of the College of Arts and Sciences, and things were just as bad as he was afraid they would be. The drop-out rate of freshmen at the end of the spring semester was way up over last year's rate. For the last five years, the drop-out rate of freshmen at the end of their first year has been steadily increasing. Freshmen always have feelings of frustration and often experience problems adjusting to college life, but to Alvin the problems seemed to be increasing. Over the five-year period the percentage of freshmen who dropped out at the end of the first year rose from 20 percent to 33 percent. This figure included those who quit school completely and those who transferred to another school. Although the national average rate for freshman drop-out is 30 percent, Alvin still felt alarmed. At that moment he decided to form a committee to determine some of the reasons for the increase. The committee would study academic problems, as well as social and emotional problems. Collins appointed to the committee Dr. Robert Wilkes, English; Dr. Fred Martin, sociology; Dr. Alice Wilkins, psychology; Dr. Mildred Miller, education; Dr. Jane Wynander, Dean of Arts and Sciences; and Mary Plan, student representative.

As the fall semester began, the committee met and formed their plan of action. The first tool used by the committee would be statistical information gathered from the various divisions regarding enrollment and drop-out ratios. As the reports began to come in, the committee found that, not surprisingly, the school reporting the greatest number of drop-outs was Arts and Sciences because freshmen are placed in that school until they declare a major. Out of 475 freshmen enrolled in Arts and Sciences in the fall semester of last year, 150 left school after the spring semester (45 transfers, 105 drop-outs). The average grade point of those 150 was 1.85.

The second highest drop-out ratio was in the School of Business. There, out of 390 freshmen enrolled in the fall semester, 99 left at the end of the spring. Their average grade point was 1.63.

The lowest ratio was reported from the School of Education. Out of 198 freshmen declaring education as a major in the fall semester, only 25 left after the spring semester. Their average grade point was 2.32.

The second tool to be used by the committee would be a number of essays to be written in freshman English classes concerning factors that affect whether or not a freshman stays in school. Teachers were asked to discuss in class probable factors such as intimidation by the whole college experience, accessibility of faculty members, dorm life, lack of knowledge about procedures for registering and adding and dropping courses, academic appeals, and a lack of knowledge about the availability of counseling, academic, and tutorial facilities. The committee will use these essays as a spring board to make recommendations regarding any needs that arise, such as more adequate counseling, more urging of professors to keep regular office hours, and better orientation sessions.

For class discussion
1. What other factors are probable causes of freshman attrition on campus?
2. What do the statistics on the drop-out rates in the various divisions imply?
3. What characteristics would be best to use as bases of classification?
4. Of the factors named, which is probably most important?

Assignment 1
You are Mary Plan, representing the students on the committee. As a freshman, you are interested in the problem because a number of your friends have dropped out. You didn't start school until the spring semester last year, and of the friends that you met, two of your closest friends as well as several other acquaintances did not come back this fall. You decide, when you are assigned the essay in class, that you will do some research that will help you write a more well-informed essay. Two of the most obvious categories of freshmen problems seem to be grade problems and homesickness problems. Together with your class, make a list of all the problems freshmen encounter. Next, decide on bases for classification, and group the problems into classes. Then rank the classes in order of importance, from those that are most likely to cause a student to drop out to those that are least likely.

Assignment 2
Write an essay classifying and describing the most important factors for determining whether or not a freshman stays in school. Use the categories that you developed in Assignment 1. Make any recommendations that you can to the committee for improvement. Keep in mind that the committee will report

to the Vice President for Student Affairs, and your suggestions could result in the formation of new programs and facilities for students, as well as changes in existing ones.

The Twin Oaks Apartments

This fall, you and two friends moved into an apartment both as an adventure and as a way of saving money. The Twin Oaks Apartments had a number of advantages—rent was low, the apartments were only two blocks from campus, and you'd be near your fiancé's apartment building. Unfortunately, the Twin Oaks hasn't turned out to be a very good deal.

Early in November, just when the weather began to get cold, the heat switch on your window unit went out. You reported the problem to the manager, and although you sent numerous reminders, it is now the third week of November and nothing has been done. When you called the manager and asked why the unit hadn't been repaired, he made some excuse about waiting for an OK from the owners in New York. Angry and cold (you and your roommates have to rely on your oven for heat), you began to ask other tenants if they had had any problems recently getting things done. It was then that you learned that almost everyone around you had some complaint. The older man in the apartment next to yours complained of a backed-up toilet that he had reported two days ago. He has been using the toilet in the laundry room. The young couple in the apartment above you said that they had a leak in their bedroom roof that had been there since March. Although they had reminded the manager countless times, nothing had been done.

Seeking advice about your rights, you call the Housing Office on campus. The woman who answers tells you that you have several options. You can leave the apartment and sue the landlord for moving expenses. You can organize a tenants' association and collectively withhold your rent until the problems have been dealt with. Or, if there is a health problem involved, you can hire a lawyer and present the case before a judge who can order that the problems be taken care of.

Because you don't want to move, you decide that collective

action is the most reasonable alternative. And the idea of being a junior union organizer appeals to you. You write an open letter to the tenants of your apartment building urging them to come to the first meeting Friday night of the Twin Oaks Apartments Tenants' Association.

Assignment 1
The turn-out for the first tenants' association meeting was gratifying. Everyone was there except two tenants who had to be out of town. All of you were amazed at how numerous the complaints were. Everyone had at least one complaint—some as many as three or four. You asked everyone to list their complaints and give the lists to you. After that was done, the group decided that the first action should be to advise the manager that the tenants were organized and to give him one last chance to make repairs. As organizer, you were chosen to write the letter to the manager. Looking at the list of complaints before you, you decide that your letter will be more effective if you classify the types of complaints and give some examples of each to make your point about how numerous and varied the complaints are. To your letter you will append the list of specific complaints. Write the letter to the manager.

Complaints List

Apt. 16—Leaking roof over closet.
　　　Hazardous light socket in bathroom (sparks fly from it).
Apt. 1—Toilet backed up.
Apt. 2, 3, 8, 10—Heater broken.
Apt. 6—Kitchen oven doesn't work.
　　　No screen on back window.
　　　Dripping faucet in bathtub.
Apt. 9—Refrigerator light doesn't work.
　　　Fan broken on stove vent.
　　　Garbage disposal doesn't work.
Apt. 14—Leg broken off dining table.
　　　No dead-bolt lock.
　　　No cover for front porch light.
Apt. 15—Safety latch pulled off front door.
　　　Caulking almost gone from around tub.

Bathroom sink leaks.

Window won't open in living room.

Apt. 12—Dripping faucets.

Apt. 13—Electrical wiring messed up (have to turn on kitchen light to make hall light come on).

Apt. 5—Neighbors play stereo too loudly.

Apt. 4—Key broken off in mailbox so it won't lock.

All Apartments: Two clothes dryers won't work.

One washer has no hot water.

Pool filthy.

Bushes grown up in front of windows.

Safety lights out near laundry room.

Bannister broken off stair at left entrance.

Not enough garbage cans so they overflow by pick-up day.

For class discussion

1. What classes will best suit your purpose in writing?
2. What classes will help the manager see the problem in your way?
3. What tone should you use in the letter to the manager?

Assignment 2

The manager replied that he was doing all that he could, but that the owners in New York were not sending enough money to make the necessary repairs. You held a second meeting of the tenants' association where it was decided that the next step would be to collectively withhold the December rent. You figure this action may get the manager to put some pressure on the owners. Write a letter to the manager telling him what the association has decided to do.

For class discussion

1. What tone should this letter have?
2. How should you refer to the complaints?

Assignment 3

Still nothing has been done, and it is the end of the first week of December. The association meets again and decides to go to court. After the meeting, you and two other members contact a lawyer. The lawyer asks you to come to his office and bring a list of the complaints that can be classified as health problems. Make the list for the lawyer.

Assignment 4
You won your case in court! The judge has ordered that the manager fix the health problems within two weeks. You are elated. The campus newspaper hears of your apartment's organized efforts and asks you to write a brief summary of no more than 500 words explaining how you accomplished what you did. Write the summary.

Open Air Learning Center

You are a junior member of a new and growing architectural firm, and you are excited by a recent project of yours. The Parent Teacher Association of the Hubbard Elementary School asked you to design an open air learning center for a portion of the school grounds. The school system approved the project, and the PTA raised about $80,000. They hope to raise $100,000 in all.

The PTA asks only that the following facilities be included —an amphitheatre to seat 50, a garden and greenhouse, a picnic area, moving water, and a small zoological garden. Other possibilities and details will be left up to you. The school has had two acres of land donated to it; therefore, the facilities can be varied.

Assignment 1
You are to meet with representatives of the PTA next week to present your preliminary ideas before you show them actual plans and drawings. That meeting will give them a chance to rule out anything that seems immediately undesirable or infeasible. Brainstorming is important here. All of the details and dimensions will be worked out later. Write out your preliminary description of the Learning Center, classifying the kinds of facilities that you envision by the educational goal they are intended to achieve. Be as imaginative as you like; these suggestions are intended as exciting possibilities.

For class discussion

1. What additional areas, other than those suggested by the PTA, would make other kinds of learning possible at the Center?

2. What materials, new and old, would work best in this environment?

3. What particular kinds of knowledge and skills could a Center of this kind encourage?

4. How could these particular kinds of knowledge and skills be grouped into classes that emphasize more general educational goals?

5. How can you characterize these educational goals in a way that will help the PTA see them the same way you do?

CHAPTER 8

NARRATION AND OTHER PROCESSES

After reading this chapter, you should be able to:

see how chronological sequence helps you analyze and understand your experiences;

recount in your writing an experience or an incident or follow a sequence of events in such a way that the audience understands the progression;

use details and information in the recounting of the events in a way appropriate to your purpose—to inform, to explore, to entertain, to persuade;

explain in your writing a series of steps or actions in such a way that the audience follows those steps and understands a process.

"It's all in the telling" is a familiar cliché. And like most clichés, it's true. Recently a friend remarked that he wished he had had a tape recorder to record the stories that his older relatives told him when he was a child because how they told them was as important as the stories themselves. And everyone has had the experience of retelling a funny joke and having no one laugh. Both these examples illustrate the truth of the cliché. When you tell a story, when you describe actual or fictional events, you are narrating.

But *narration,* arranging the events in a story in chronological order, is also a way of thinking about those events. Your memory of the time the bear visited your campsite at dawn may consist of a set of vivid images—beady eyes reflecting the light of your flashlight, the bear calmly scratching its rump on a tree as you yelled at it to go away, the heap of camping gear piled up in your canoe as you beat a hasty retreat. But as you begin to recount the experience, either to yourself or to others, you begin to think about everything that happened more carefully. Which events were most important? Many things happened that didn't affect what the bear did or your reaction to its presence—a loon called on the lake, your air mattress sprung a leak and was flat, the mouse who woke you up disappeared in the brush. One of the first things you do while thinking in a narrative way is to separate out important events.

As you figure out which events happened when, you think about the relationships among the events. The bear's circling around the campsite, away from the tree with the food pack suspended in it, made you hope it might be getting discouraged, so you yelled and banged a cooking pot on the aluminum canoe. The bear's persistence in coming back for seconds after having finally reached the food pack and carried off some food made your friend so angry that she advanced on the bear brandishing a canoe paddle, an action that startled the bear into running off into the bushes. Selecting details of what happened and arranging them in a chronological sequence helps you understand the experience more completely.

A narrative can be part of a larger piece of writing, or it can be the whole piece of writing in itself. And when you're writing, you will find that a narrative can serve a variety of purposes. If you are trying to persuade your local city council that a traffic light is needed at the end of your block, you might recount a near-miss two neighborhood children and a car had at that corner. Or, in writing a letter to a friend, you might tell him or her a funny story about something that happened to you. The story would be the entire reason for writing; your purpose might be to amuse or to entertain. Or, you might write in your journal about something that happened to you just to give yourself a record of that event for the future.

Sometimes, as in diaries and journals, you are the only

intended reader of your narration. But in other kinds of narrative someone else will read what you write, and you are consciously aware of that reader. In those instances, "it's all in the telling" has a real meaning. Your ability to select important facts, to arrange events in logical progression, and to give enough detail is essential to all narrations. It helps you and your audience understand the incident. Your ability to use vivid detail and describe your thoughts and feelings affects how your audience responds to you. The extent to which they can see and feel the incident in the same way you did will determine whether they finish reading your narrative.

Exercise

Think of an important incident that happened to you in the past year. Write down everything you can remember about the incident. Now, think about who you might want to tell about this incident and why you would want to tell them. When you have decided on an audience and a purpose, look over your notes, select the important facts, and arrange them in a logical sequence.

Chronological Order

Narration is concerned with time. Often when you write narrative you follow a chronological progression; that is, you place one event after another in the order in which they occurred. Occasionally events that happened long before the events you are narrating may be important to understanding your narrative. In that instance, you might use a technique called the *flashback*. In a flashback you interrupt the chronological order to tell a significant event that happened earlier. The purpose of the flashback is usually to help the audience see how two events, while unrelated in time, are related in significant other ways.

Narratives whose purpose is mainly to inform often contain large passages in which events are arranged strictly in chronological order, as in the following excerpt by Carl Bernstein and Bob Woodward.

Woodward had waited in the hallway for about 20 minutes when the Mitchells' security guard, a large black man, left the suite and took the elevator down. Woodward went down to a telephone booth in the lobby and called Room 710. Martha Mitchell answered. She sounded jovial and happy for the chance to chat. They talked about Washington, politics, the upcoming election, Manhattan . . . The operator broke in, saying it would take another five cents to keep talking.

"I wouldn't want Katie Graham to spend another nickel on me," Mrs. Mitchell said.

Woodward popped a quarter into the pay phone. But she was starting to sound anxious, and said she had to run. Woodward took the elevator back to the seventh floor.—*All the President's Men*

The authors don't mention everything that happened. Woodward must have put a coin in the phone and dialed the number in the course of calling Room 710. And he surely hung up the receiver before he "took the elevator back to the seventh floor." But every event that is recounted is placed in the order it occurred with relation to every other event.

Order of Importance

In newspaper stories, in contrast, events are reported in the order of their importance. The chronological sequence must be inferred by the audience based on their knowledge of how things normally occur and on words in the story that signal time-relationships among events. For example, here is the beginning of a story from the *New York Times*.

20,000 Flee a Volcanic Eruption on Indonesian Island of Ternate

JAKARTA, Indonesia, Sept. 6 (Reuters)—Thousands of people have fled a volcanic eruption on the tiny island of Ternate, in the North Moluccas, officials said today, but there were no reports of casualties.

They said 20,000 people had sought sanctuary on the southern tip of the island or fled to neighboring islands after the 5,625 foot Gamalama volcano erupted three times in 24 hours. They said the Government would ship rice and tents to the refugees.

Residents of the island's capital, also called Ternate, said that black ash at least four inches deep covered buildings and roads.

If the events were told in chronological order, we would hear first about the eruption (reported at the end of the first sentence in the second paragraph), then about the ash covering buildings and roads (reported in the third paragraph), then about the flight of the island's residents (reported first), and then about the government's promise to ship rice and tents (reported at the end of the second paragraph). But because most of us are more interested in people's lives than geologic events, we hear about the effect of the eruption on people first. We infer the order of events from our knowledge that ash covering buildings and roads is a result of, and thus follows, a volcanic eruption. We also know that ash falls quickly and that evacuations take time, so that four inches of ash probably was on the ground before everyone got to safety. And we know that the people fled after the volcanic eruption rather than before because the story uses the word *after* to establish this time sequence.

Exercise

Take a news story and rearrange the events into chronological order. Mark the words in the story that help you figure out the sequence of events, and explain why the writer of the story arranged events as they were.

Order of Narrator's Perspective

We have seen that narratives can be arranged chronologically and in the order of the importance of events. Many narratives follow an additional order. The events are told in a way that shows how the narrator views the events and the relationships between them. Typically, a sequence of events is seen as causing some effect on the narrator and on the surrounding world. In short stories and in novels, we call this the *plot*. It is useful to consider plot for a moment because plot patterns generate some questions that may be of help in constructing your own narratives. The following plot pattern was developed by William Labov.

1. Abstract
2. Orientation
3. Complication
4. Evaluation
5. Resolution
6. Coda

The *abstract* (not found in all narratives) tells why the story is being told. At the beginning of *Paradise Lost*, John Milton says he's telling the story of Adam and Eve in order to "justify the ways of God to men." Similarly, you may begin telling a story to a friend by saying, "Something awful happened to me yesterday." The *orientation* introduces the time, scene, and characters. The *complication* relates a series of events. The *evaluation*, which reveals the narrator's or the characters' attitude toward the events, is the climax of the story. The *resolution* explains how the story ended, what final effect the events had. And the *coda*, which, like the abstract is optional, brings the audience back to the present day: "And so they lived happily ever after."

These elements of plot suggest a series of questions that might be useful to you as you write your narratives:

1. Why am I telling this story?
2. What orientation information will my audience need to understand this story?
3. How are the events I am going to narrate related causally?
4. How did the people involved in the events react?
5. Does the resolution clearly follow from the events I am telling?
6. What happened after the events I am narrating?

Most stories that you tell, most events that you narrate, will follow this pattern rather naturally.

Exercise

Use the series of questions suggested above to help you write a narrative account of the incident you analyzed in the first exercise in this chapter.

Narrative Words

Whether or not you report events in chronological sequence, in narration you want to help your audience understand the order in which events occurred. Consequently, certain kinds of words are characteristic of the narrative. Words such as *first, second, third* help readers keep sequences straight. *"First,* we cleaned our bikes and checked the air in the tires. *Second,* we attached our prepared picnic to our bikes using elastic straps. *Finally,* we pulled into the street, one by one, off on what was to be one of our most enjoyable bike excursions." Other words that are useful in narrative are adverbs and adverbials and prepositional phrases that refer to when something was done: *before, then, after, finally, later, now, at that time, often, previously, at night, the next day.*

Read the following example by Maya Angelou noticing how often she uses words that signal time relationships.

> The school band struck up a march and all classes filed in as had been rehearsed. We stood in front of our seats, as assigned, and *on a signal from the choir director,* we sat. *No sooner* had this been accomplished *than* the band started to play the national anthem. We rose *again* and sang the song, *after which* we recited the pledge of allegiance. We remained standing *for a brief minute before* the choir director and the principal signaled to us, rather desperately I thought, to take our seats. The command was so unusual that our carefully rehearsed and smooth-running machine was thrown off. *For a full minute* we fumbled for our chairs and bumped into each other awkwardly. Habits change or solidify under pressure, so in our state of nervous tension we had been ready to follow our usual assembly pattern: the American national anthem, *then* the pledge of allegiance, *then* the song every Black person I knew called the negro National Anthem.—*I Know Why the Caged Bird Sings*

Since narratives emphasize action, the verbs you use in narrative are important. Verbs can be used to describe actions precisely, as in this passage by Robert M. Pirsig.

The coals die lower and lower. We smoke our last cigarettes. Chris is off somewhere in the darkness but I'm not going to shag after him. John is carefully silent and Sylvia is silent and suddenly we are all separate, all alone in our private universes, and there is no communication among us. We douse the fire and go back to the sleeping bags in the pines.

I discover that this one tiny refuge of scrub pines where I have put the sleeping bags is also the refuge from the wind of millions of mosquitoes up from the reservoir. The mosquito repellent doesn't stop them at all. I crawl deep into the sleeping bag and make one little hole for breathing. I am almost asleep when Chris finally shows up.—*Zen and the Art of Motorcycle Maintenance*

Verbs like *die, smoke, shag, douse, go back, discover, doesn't stop, crawl, make,* and *shows* help describe actions as they recount them. Notice how much less you would see of the scene if Pirsig had written the first two sentences as follows: "The fire goes out. We finish our cigarettes."

Exercise

1. Look over the narration you wrote in the previous exercise, and underline the words you used to help your audience see how the events are related sequentially. You might find that you want to add a few more words and phrases where the sequence isn't as clearly indicated as you want it to be.
2. Now underline all the verbs you used in your narration. Do the verbs help your audience see the scene as well as understand the story? Make any changes you think would make your narration more descriptive.

Describing Processes

Another way of thinking that is concerned with the chronological sequence of events is process analysis. In narration we were concerned with *what happened,* but in process we are concerned with *how* a result is achieved. A *process* is a series of actions, steps, operations, or functions that brings about an end or a result. In describing a process, you are figuring out how that end result is accomplished.

A process analysis tells the logical pattern of steps that lead to the final conclusion. In process writing the order of the steps is as important to understanding the process as are the steps themselves. When you write about a process, you teach someone else how to do something, you explain how something works, or you describe a natural change. Process is the kind of writing that makes it possible to put together a child's bike on Christmas Eve or to bake a delicious fudge cake. But process can be used for more exalted endeavors as well. Process is the kind of writing that teaches us about the creation of the universe or the evolution of man. When you write about *how* to do something, you are writing about a *scientific* process. When you write about how something actually *was done*, you are writing about a *historical* process.

As you write about a process, first divide your subject into stages, steps, or operations. Make sure you present the steps in the order they must occur to lead most efficiently and smoothly to the result. You will once again want to signal the time relationships using the vocabulary that helped you write narratives: *first, second, third, fourth, then, next, before, after.*

Three examples of writers using process writing follow. You will notice that as with narration, a process description can serve many purposes. The first example is an advertisement in which the manufacturers of a bourbon are informing the audience about the process used to make the bourbon, hoping to impress the audience with the quality of the bourbon and the care taken to produce it. In the second example, Robert Jastrow describes how a star is born, intending to inform his audience. In the final example, Robert Greene instructs his audience about how to buy stereo speakers. As you read all three, pick out the logical progression that the writers are using and look for the words that signal that progression to the audience.

ANY BOURBON THAT CLAIMS TO BE THE WORLD'S BEST, BETTER HAVE THE PROOF.

Old Weller does. 107 proof, to be exact. Aged seven long years with the most loving care dedicated bourbon lovers could give it. We start with meticulously selected ingredients, including the Weller family secret "whisper of wheat." We seal it in barrels of handpicked white oak, charred on the inside to enhance the mellowing. We store it near a long row of windows at the top of the distillery, opening and closing the windows every morning and evening so the whiskey can breathe during the day without getting chilled at night. After seven years, it has become our pride and joy. This careful aging coupled with bottling at 107 proof produces a unique bourbon whiskey with a more sophisticated taste for the true bourbon connoisseur. High in proof, but incredibly smooth and mellow. As we like to say, "a great spirit, tamed but unbroken."

And since we consider what goes into a bottle of Weller 107 as good as gold, we actually spin a veil of 22-carat gold over the entire surface of each and every bottle.

Seek some Weller 107 out soon. It may be a bit hard to find, but then, the best things usually are.—Ad for *Old Weller Bourbon*

The stars seem immutable, but they are not. They are born, evolve and die like living organisms. The life story of a star begins with the simplest and most abundant element in nature, which is hydrogen. The universe is filled with thin clouds of hydrogen, which surge and eddy in the space between the stars. In the swirling motions of these tenuous clouds, atoms sometimes come together by accident to form small pockets of gas. These pockets are temporary condensations in an otherwise highly rarefied medium. Normally the atoms fly apart again in a short time as a consequence of their random motions, and the pocket of gas quickly disperses to space. However, each atom exerts a small gravitational attraction on its neighbor, which counters the tendency of the atoms to fly apart. If the number of atoms in the pocket of gas is large enough, the accumulation of all these separate forces will hold it together indefinitely. It is then an independent cloud of gas, preserved by the attraction of each atom in the cloud to its neighbor.

With the passage of time, the continuing influence of gravity, pulling all the atoms closer together, causes the cloud to contract. The individual atoms "fall" toward the center of the cloud under the force of gravity; as they fall, they pick up speed and their energy increases. The increase in energy heats the gas and raises its temperature. This shrinking, continuously self-heating ball of gas is an embryonic star.

As the gas cloud contracts under the pressure of its own weight, the temperature at the center mounts steadily. When it reaches 100,000 degrees Fahrenheit, the hydrogen atoms in the gas collide with sufficient violence to dislodge all electrons from their orbits around the protons. The original gas of hydrogen atoms, each consisting of an electron circling around a proton, becomes a mixture of two gases, one composed of electrons and the other of protons.

At this stage the globe of gas has contracted from its original size, which was 10 trillion miles in diameter, to a diameter of 100 million miles. To understand the extent of the contraction, imagine the Hindenburg dirigible shrinking to the size of a grain of sand.

The huge ball of gas—now composed of separate protons and electrons—continues to contract under the force of its own weight, and the temperature at the center rises further. After 10 million years the temperature has risen to the critical value of 20 million degrees Fahrenheit. At this time, the diameter of the ball has shrunk to one million miles, which is the size of our sun and other typical stars.

Why is 20 million degrees a critical temperature? The explanation is connected with the forces between the protons in the contracting cloud. When two protons are separated by large distances, they repel one another electrically because each proton carries a positive electric charge. But if the protons approach within a very close distance of each other, the electrical repulsion gives way to the even stronger force of nuclear attraction. The protons must be closer together than one 10-trillionth of an inch for the nuclear force to be effective. Under ordinary circumstances, the electrical repulsion serves as a barrier to prevent as close an approach as this. In a collision of exceptional violence, however, the protons may pierce the barrier which separates them, and come within the range of their nuclear attraction. Collisions of the required degree of violence first began to occur when the temperature of the gas reaches 20 million degrees.

Once the barrier between two protons is pierced in a collision, they pick up speed as a result of their nuclear attraction and rush rapidly toward each other. In the final moment of the collision the force of nuclear attraction is so strong that it fuses the protons together into a single nucleus. At the same time the energy of their collision is released in the form of heat and light. This release of energy marks the birth of the star.

The energy passes to the surface and is radiated away in the form of light, by which we see the star in the sky. The energy release, which is one million times greater per pound than that produced in a TNT explosion, halts the further contraction of the star, which lives out the rest of its life in a balance between the outward pressures generated by the release of nuclear energy at its center and the inward pressures created by the force of gravity.

The fusion of two protons into a single nucleus is only the first step in a series of reactions by which nuclear energy is released during the life of the star. In subsequent collisions, two additional protons are joined to the first two to form a nucleus containing four particles. Two of the protons shed their positive charges to become neutrons in the course of the process. The result is a nucleus with two protons and two neutrons. This is the nucleus of the helium atom. Thus, the sequence of reactions transforms protons, or hydrogen nuclei, into helium nuclei.

The fusion of hydrogen to form helium is the first and longest stage in the history of a star, occupying about 99 percent of its lifetime. In the second stage, which takes up most of the remaining 1 percent of the star's life, three nuclei of helium combine to form the nucleus of the carbon atom. Afterwards, the nuclei of oxygen and other still heavier elements are fabricated, at an increasingly rapid pace, until all elemen:.s have been built up. In this way the elements of the universe are manufactured out of hydrogen nuclei at the center of the star during the course of its life.—*Red Giants and White Dwarfs*

Of all the parts of a stereo system, loudspeakers are not only the most difficult to choose but also the most likely to make the difference between good, so-so, and downright rotten sound. How, then, do you go about making the right decision? To make the process just a little less ominous, understand right off that there is no one "right" decision. Unless your situation is most extraordinary, you would probably find a number of speakers quite satisfying.

Before you go out shopping, however, get into the game forearmed; read up on speakers, particularly reviews in the hi-fi magazines. If all the technical jargon is beyond you, don't worry, just read the nontechnical portions where the reviewers give a general statement of how they feel about the unit in question. This preparation will at least give you an idea of what to expect from systems of various levels of complexity and price. (Note, however, that *not* finding a review of any given speaker doesn't necessarily indicate that it's not worth considering. It's impossible for more than a small percentage of the available models to be covered.)

In addition to reviews, scan the advertisements in this and other national magazines (not local retail ads) to become familiar with brand names. This is not to say that everything made by national advertisers is equally good or equally suited for you, but such companies have reputations to protect and you can reasonably expect help from them in the unlikely event of trouble with any of their products. Be wary of speakers with an unknown brand name or those sold by only one store; these may be so-called "house-brand" or "private-label" speakers. You might happen on some that are just dandy, but it's not unheard of for a dealer to have such speakers made up inexpensively to be sold at a huge "discount" or to lower the cost of a "package" that includes other, name-brand components.

Don't let yourself be impressed just because one system has more drivers in it than another. A four-way system will not *automatically* produce better sound than a three- or even a two-way system. All of the components in the cabinet may be there for sound engineering reasons, but one or two of the drivers might have been included merely to make the system seem more "technically" attractive—or to permit charging a higher price. Given any two speaker systems, the simpler or less expensive one *might* be more accurate than its higher-price competitor. "Accurate" is the operative word here; "better" and "worse" are subjective matters, but accuracy—meaning correspondence of the speaker's acoustic output with the electrical audio signal from the amplifier is not. Of course, not everyone will *prefer* a more accurate speaker, but *experienced* listeners will always go for an accurate speaker over one designed for boom and sizzle.

Since your listening room effectively becomes an acoustic part of any speaker system played in it, and because speakers interact differently with different rooms, the ideal way to select a speaker is to audition the possible choices in your home before you buy. Failing this, try listening to how your friends' systems sound in their homes. This will at least give you some experience in critical listening.

At some point you'll have to visit a dealer. But before you do, measure your listening room's dimensions (including height) and determine its acoustic character—"live" and bright (lots of hard surfaces) or "dead" (lots of soft furniture, heavy carpets, drapes, etc.). Stand in the middle and clap your hands a few times. In a live room the sounds will "ring" or reverberate back at you; in a dead one they will, naturally, die out immediately. Also try to determine where you would put the speakers: on the floor or up on shelves and near or far from adjacent walls.

All this information will help a dealer to assist you in choosing a speaker from among those he stocks. It will also help him figure out how powerful an amplifier or receiver you'll need to drive the speakers you decide you want in the room where you'll be listening to them. It's at this point that the question of speaker efficiency comes up. *Efficiency* is often confused with *quality*, but it is only an indication of how much power is needed to drive the speaker to a given volume (or sound-pressure) level. All else being equal, a relatively efficient speaker (none is *very* efficient) will require less power from the amplifier. Your listening habits enter into this too, since a chamber-music aficionado isn't likely to require the same power levels as a rock or disco fan.

Once you're actually at the point of selecting speakers in a store, there are some precautions you should bear in mind. *Don't* try to compare more than two sets of speakers at one time; you'll only confuse yourself. Some people even suggest auditioning single speakers—with the amplifier's controls set to mono—rather than stereo pairs. (This also gives you the option of later switching to the opposite member of a stereo pair to judge how much the room position might be influencing your evaluations.)

Listen to several *male* announcers on different FM stations. One or two may sound boomy because of drawbacks in the stations' facilities, but if *all* of them do then the speaker you're auditioning is probably putting out too much volume at around 100 Hz. This may make for a nice heavy bass in pop or rock music, but it's at the cost of clarity in the upper bass—and probably a lack of really *low* bass too. Another indication of good low-end performance is if the speaker lets you hear the differences between similar-sounding bass instruments.

The midrange frequencies (brass instruments, etc.) should not be shot out into your lap or recede too far into the background; the former indicates a boost in that area and the latter an attenuation. A boosted midrange will also tend to make female voices sound nasal or "honky," while too subdued a midrange will make them sound distant or withdrawn.

For the high frequencies, listen to recordings that include cymbals and triangles. These instruments should appear to "shimmer" and sound bright and airy. Also, normal tape hiss and record-surface noise should be audible but not exaggerated. (A speaker that shows up *no* flaws in ordinary program material is probably obscuring desirable sonic details.)

Except for the announcer test mentioned earlier, *don't* use FM radio as a program source for auditioning speakers; you have no way of knowing the quality of the broadcast material or the transmission at any given time, and both can vary widely. To introduce at least one constant into a situation otherwise made up entirely of variables, carry your own test records with you. Try not to use anything too flashy, as this might be deceptive.

Finally, keep in mind that a speaker system should not intrude itself on your listening; the best thing that could be said of a loudspeaker is that, once it's installed, you simply forget that it's there and listen to the music.—"Selecting a Speaker"

Exercise

Take a process that you are expert at, such as making pizza, convincing your parents to send you more money, or getting from your bed to your first class in less than ten minutes, and break it into steps. Write out those steps in such a way that your audience can be as successful in performing this task as you are.

Summary

Narration and process are two patterns of thought that are concerned with time. The difference between the two is that narration concerns "what happened," and process concerns "how" a result was achieved. Narrative order can be chronological, but it is often arranged according to the importance of events or by the narrator's perspective. In process writing there is a logical ordering of the steps to achieve the result.

In both narration and in process writing you must be concerned with your audience. An audience should be able to understand the narrative through the order in which you place the events. And in process writing, an audience should be able to understand how each step follows logically to achieve the desired result.

Some people are better storytellers than others, but in writing we can all learn to narrate a series of events or describe a process in a clear and orderly way so that we can be understood.

Your Writing Process

This time you are yourself, nearing the end of the major chapters in your case rhetoric text. A friend has been taking a different kind of composition course this semester, a course concentrating on grammar. From the beginning of the semester, your friend was curious about the case method, asking you all sorts of questions about what a case is and how you go about approaching a case.

Last week when you and your friend were having lunch, he took up the subject again. He said he had learned all the grammar rules, but he still had a hard time thinking of anything to say and getting something down on paper. While he feels his composition course this semester helped him master grammar and its use, he still doesn't know *how* to write a paper. He explained that every time he is assigned something to write, he agonizes over it for a long time finally coming up with something to say at the eleventh hour. He hates to write because he is afraid that he will draw a blank at the last minute.

He said that you seem to write your papers for your composition course almost effortlessly. You had to laugh at that. You! The same person who sweats blood at the type-writer every week! Nonetheless, he asked if you would help him out by writing a description of the process you use in writing your assignments. He wants information about where you write, how you get your ideas, how you revise, how many drafts you make, and any special tricks you know. He said that although he had seen articles about how famous writers go about writing, he had never read anything that showed him how people who aren't experts write. Since he is majoring in history, which requires a lot of writing, he is feeling desperate.

You protest that he's probably asking the wrong person. But he seems so sincere, you just can't turn him down. Besides, you think you may learn something useful yourself by thinking about how you write.

Assignment 1
Describe exactly how you wrote your last paper for your friend. Be as honest and complete as you can.

For class discussion
In what way has the case approach changed your process of writing? Has it made some things easier? Has it made some things harder?

Assignment 2
Write an essay for your friend giving realistic advice about how to write an adequate paper.

Activity for the Blind

As the new physical education director at the Center for the Blind, Andrea Phillips is appalled at how little physical activity the adults are encouraged to participate in. When Andrea observed the activities in progress at the center, she was excited by the work being done with children and teens. The children were being taught tag games and were participating in some exercises and learning skills needed later in team sports. The teens were being taught the rudiments of team sports.

But when Andrea arrived at the area where the adults were having physical education, she observed only minimal activity. Some of the adults were being led in simple exercises like knee bends. Others were running in place. Still others were engaged in simple body responses to music. Andrea went back to her office determined to change all that. Convinced that given proper instructions, the blind adults could be taught many activities, Andrea would first have to show her staff how to teach those activities. She decided to write a manual for her staff describing how physical activities could be taught to blind adults.

Assignment 1
You are Andrea. Write the instructions to your staff for teaching one physical activity. Choose an activity that blind persons could conceivably do. It can be a dance step, an exercise, a sport, or a game. Give your staff the exact words to use in teaching the activity.

For class discussion
1. What special considerations will have to be made in instructing the blind adults?
2. What attitude toward the blind adults do you want to encourage in your staff teachers?

Assignment 2
You now must write the introduction to the manual. You want to emphasize the importance of more physical activity for blind adults, but you don't want to offend those who have

been trying to do a good job. In your files you found a letter from one of your most dependable staff members to the former director in which she complained that the director had "failed to treat the staff like professionals and seemed to have made the assumption that the staff was trying to avoid doing a good job." Write the introduction to the manual.

For class discussion
1. What does your audience value? How can you appeal to those values in order to get your message across?
2. What does your audience know about physical activities for the blind? What might they not know that might help them understand your new proposals?

Rock Star

For ten years now you have been playing guitar. Occasionally, you jam with a group, Angel Flight, at Fat Man's on Saturday nights. But it has long been your dream to form your own band. For a couple of years you've been talking about when *you* get your band together, and most people thought you were just kidding. Now, though, you have decided that it's time to do something about your dream. You've managed to interest several other musicians in the idea, but frankly none of you knows anything about getting started. You all have enthusiasm and talent, but that's about it.

One idea occurs to you. If you can find out how other bands got to the top, you can compare those processes and determine the quickest way for your group to get there. You're determined not to be part of just another hometown group playing only locally. You're going to make it big!

Assignment 1
Pick out a few bands that play the kind of music you would like to play. Do some research on how they got to the top. Write out a summary of the process that each group followed.

For class discussion
What are some possible sources for this kind of information?

Assignment 2
Interview any local bands that you can to find out what they think is the best and quickest way to get to the top. Take notes on your interviews and write them up in usable form.

Assignment 3
Making use of the information that you have gained, write a scenario that will serve as a guide for your group's future activities in getting to the top the quickest way.

Assignment 4
Deciding on a name for your group may be the hardest part. You and the other members decide to place all of your suggestions anonymously in a box and then to choose from among the suggestions. That way personalities won't get involved. Each of you is to make a list of your suggestions with an explanation of why each would be a good name. Make your list.

For class discussion
1. What image do you want the name to convey?
2. What words have connotations that would support this image?

CHAPTER 9

EXPLORING CAUSE AND EFFECT RELATIONSHIPS AND SYLLOGISTIC REASONING

After reading this chapter, you should be able to:

explore your subject for its possible causes and effects, both major and minor;

use the causes and effects of your subject to help you inform or persuade your audience;

make use of syllogisms to help you analyze your subject and argue effectively.

When a group of tribesmen prepare for the hunt, they carefully apply poison to the end of their darts. In addition, they engage in a series of rituals and incantations. They are convinced that these rituals have as much to do with their success in the hunt as does the poison. A scientist would say that it is the poison on the darts that kills the animals. It may be, however, that the rituals and incantations are, at least indirectly, also a cause of the kill. If the hunters believe strongly in the effectiveness of the rituals, then those rituals may in fact *be* a real cause of success. The hunters may be braver after performing the rituals. Certainly their group morale is higher.

Often effects may be the results of many causes, some of them hidden. As you look for causes and effects, you will want to search out as many as possible.

A *cause* is that which produces a result or a consequence, and an *effect* is that result. An effect is logically dependent on a cause; a cause is responsible for an effect. For example, smoking has been proven to be a *cause* of lung cancer. There are other identifiable causes, but smoking is at least one.

It is important to realize that because one thing precedes another in time, it is not necessarily a cause. This kind of reasoning is the fallacy of *post hoc, ergo propter hoc,* or "after this, therefore because of this." One thing may succeed another and yet the two things may have no relationship to each other. Advertising is often filled with this kind of fallacious cause and effect reasoning. A cigarette ad pictures a rugged merchant seaman enjoying his favorite brand aboard ship. The copy reads: "Brand X. Nobody does it better. This is your world. This is your Brand. Taste it all." The advertisement implies that smoking Brand X enables you to taste everything, to enjoy your life, and perhaps that smoking Brand X will make you into a he-man like the sailor in the photo. But, in fact, smoking impairs your sense of taste, nor is smoking likely to make you more attractive or manly. In Charles Dickens' *Great Expectations,* the young hero detects the same kind of fallacious reasoning in a friend's explanation that he finds working in a counting-house (accounting firm) rewarding because it enables him to keep an eye out for opportunities:

> "But the thing is," said Herbert Pocket, "that you look about you. *That's* the grand thing. You are in a counting-house, you know, and you look about you."
>
> It struck me as a singular implication that you couldn't be out of a counting-house, you know, and look about you . . ."

Exercise

Explain the *post hoc, ergo propter hoc* fallacy in each of the following advertisements:

a. Does your family's safety mean anything to you? Can you afford to risk their lives by not investing in Quick Signal Smoke Alarms?

b. Use Spinaker After-Shave. The girls will follow you everywhere.

c. The federal government has forbidden mining in national reserves and prohibits the burning of high-sulfur coal. That's the reason we have an energy shortage, and the reason everyone should support the National Coal Company.

Causes

In the following passage, Barbara Tuchman explores both the actual and imagined causes of the fourteenth-century plague:

Ignorance of the cause augmented the sense of horror. Of the real carriers, rats and fleas, the 14th century had no suspicion, perhaps because they were so familiar. Fleas, though a common household nuisance, are not once mentioned in contemporary plague writings, and rats only incidentally, although folklore commonly associated them with pestilence. The legend of the Pied Piper arose from an outbreak of 1284. The actual plague bacillus, *Pasturella pestis,* remained undiscovered for another 500 years. Living alternately in the stomach of the flea and the bloodstream of the rat who was the flea's host, the bacillus in its bubonic form was transferred to humans and animals by the bite of either rat or flea. It traveled by virtue of *Rattus rattus,* the small medieval black rat that lived on ships, as well as by the heavier brown or sewer rat. What precipitated the turn of the bacillus from innocuous to virulent form is unknown, but the occurrence is now believed to have taken place not in China but somewhere in central Asia and to have spread along the caravan routes. Chinese origin was a mistaken notion of the 14th century based on real but belated reports of huge death tolls in China from drought, famine, and pestilence which have since been traced to the 1330s, too soon to be responsible for the plague that appeared in India in 1346. . . .

The earthquake was blamed for releasing sulfurous and foul fumes from the earth's interior, or as evidence of a titanic struggle of plants and oceans causing waters to rise and vaporize until fish died in masses and corrupted the air. All these explanations had in common a factor of poisoned air, of miasmas and thick, stinking mists traced to every kind of natural or imagined agency from stagnant lakes to malign conjunction of the planets, from the hand of the Evil One to the wrath of God. Medical thinking, trapped in the theory of astral influences, stressed air as the communicator of disease, ignoring sanitation or visible carriers. The existence of two carriers confused the trail, the more so because the flea could live and travel independently of the rat for as long as a month and, if infected by the particularly virulent septicemic form of the bacillus, could infect humans without reinfecting itself from the rat. The simultaneous presence of the pneumonic form of the disease, which was indeed communicated through the air, blurred the problem further.—*A Distant Mirror*

Tuchman first explores the *real* cause of the plague—the bacillus in its bubonic form was transferred to humans by the bite of either a rat or a flea. She then goes on to list the imagined causes of the plague—earthquakes, a struggle of plants and oceans, stinking mists from stagnant lakes, a malign conjunction of the planets, the devil, God's wrath, and so on. Through Tuchman's words, we see the people of the medieval period looking everywhere for the causes of the plague except in their own houses.

In an article from *Time* magazine, a writer traces the causes of apathy and cynicism among symphonic musicians in our country.

What has gone wrong? Schuller, former president of the New England Conservatory of Music, parcels out the blame in three directions. The musicians' union, or at least the union mentality of the players, has fostered a grudging, clock-watching approach to rehearsing and performing, he says; jet-age music directors have left their orchestras in an artistic lurch while pursuing second and third careers elsewhere; managements and boards of trustees have run the show with the box office uppermost in their minds. "Out of sheer ignorance or arrogance, many boards have time and again made lamentable decisions," argues Schuller. "We should have obligatory training courses for prospective trustees." —"Symphony of Dissonance"

The causes of musicians' apathy, according to this report, are the union mentality of the players, the scattered interests of the music directors, and the decisions by money-hungry boards of trustees.

Looking at what caused something you're writing about can be a way of exploring what to say about it or of arriving at a solution to a problem. Suppose, for example, that you were interested in country and western music and you wondered about its surge in popularity. You might at first think one cause was the popularity and wide recognition of some of its stars. But what did people find attractive about the stars and their music? After all, most of those celebrities had been around for over a decade. One question you might ask is whether the interest in this down-home style of music might be connected with other events on the entertainment scene. Perhaps the C & W soundtracks for popular movies and TV shows had an influence. Or maybe many people were tired of and repulsed by other forms of music.

Searching deeper, you might ask if changes in American society might provide other reasons for people to turn to country music. You might conclude that this type of music has always thrived on a longing for simplicity, naiveté, and down-home, self-reliant feelings Americans were hungry for after the disillusionment of Vietnam, Watergate, and the energy crisis. You might also look at the way the music was promoted. Stars took their music, in a slick form, to the clubs of the big cities where it was appropriated by city dwellers who found it "quaint." Or, you might just say that it's good music. To do a good job in exploring the subject, you would want to investigate as many causes as possible.

The causes that you choose to emphasize will depend upon your purpose in writing. If you are writing to inform your audience, you will probably want to include all of the causes that you can and help them see how the various causes interact. If you are writing to persuade your audience that certain causes are the predominant ones, you may place special emphasis on those causes. Nonetheless, you will want to mention other causes to reassure your audience that you are not blind to the fact that other causes exist.

Exercise

Determine as many causes as you can of the decline in the American automobile industry. You may wish to look up articles on this situation in magazines like *Time* and *Newsweek* and in newspapers like the *Wall Street Journal,* the *New York Times,* the *Los Angeles Times,* and the *Detroit Free Press* in order to decide which factors actually caused the decline. Bring your list of causes to class and compare them with the lists drawn up by your classmates.

For class discussion
1. Which of the causes were the most important?
2. Which of the causes would you emphasize if you were writing a letter to your representative urging him or her to support restrictions on foreign car imports?
3. Which causes would you emphasize if you were analyzing the structure of American corporations in a paper for your class on introduction to business administration?

Effects

Sometimes as you write, you want to look forward rather than backward, and you want to explore the *effects* of a particular action or situation. Considering effects is especially important when you are proposing a change or a solution. You might be writing to the City Council about the adverse effects on your neighborhood of the absence of a traffic light at a busy corner. Or, you might be writing a letter to the editor citing the positive effects a procedural change in student body elections would have.

Here John Holt writes of the effects that pressure in school can have on a child.

> Under pressure that they want to resist but don't dare to resist openly, some children may quite deliberately *go stupid;* I have seen it and felt it. Most of them, however, are probably not this aware of what they are doing. They deny their intelligence to their jailers, the teachers, not so much to frustrate them but because they have other and more important uses for it. Freedom to live and to think about life for its own sake is important and even essential to a child. He will only give so much time and thought to what others want him to do; the rest he demands and takes for his own interests, plans, worries, dreams. The result is that he is not all there during most of his hours in school. Whether he is afraid to be there, or just does not want to be there, the result is the same. Fear,

boredom, resistance—they all go to make what we call stupid children.—*How Children Fail*

In this paragraph Holt describes the effects of the pressure of school on certain children as (1) fear, (2) boredom, (3) resistance, and (4) the labeling of a child as "stupid."

The effects Holt describes follow soon after their cause; we call such effects short-term effects. But some effects take much longer to develop. In this article, Steven H. Wodka explains the long-term effects on farm workers of organophosphates:

> Besides the obvious hazards of DDT and the herbicides, the farm worker faces an additional problem from the organophosphates. Organophosphates are a class of chemicals originally developed by the Germans during World War II in their search for what is commonly called nerve gases. The organophosphates are among the most deadly chemicals known to man. Over 75,860,000 pounds of organophosphates were produced in the United States during 1968. They go by names like parathion, methyl parathion, TEPP (tetraethyl pyrophosphate), azodrin, and malathion. Malathion is the allegedly safe organophosphate only because the mammalian liver renders it relatively harmless. Otherwise the organophosphates destroy a protective body enzyme called cholinesterase. Under normal body conditions, an impulse passes from nerve to nerve with the aid of a chemical called acetylcholine. The acetylcholine is in turn destroyed by the cholinesterase. If the cholinesterase is absent, the impulses continue to flash from nerve to nerve. The movements of the whole body become uncoordinated: tremors, muscular spasms, convulsions, and death quickly result. Repeated exposures may lower the cholinesterase level in the blood until an individual reaches the brink of acute poisoning at which he may be pushed over by a very small additional exposure. But up to that point his symptoms are, unfortunately, usually taken for the flu.—"Pesticides Since *Silent Spring*"

The short-term effects of malathion on people are flu-like symptoms; the long-term effects can be death. When you consider the effects of a situation or action, you will want to think not only of immediate effects but also of those effects which may develop later.

Suppose that instead of the causes of the boom in country and western music, you are now interested in its effects. You think about changes in society that may have been caused by this revolution in taste. Certainly it's not so easy to spot a real cowboy because many people wear jeans and western shirts, cowboy hats, boots, and silver-buckled belts. You note also that many radio stations have changed their formats to country and western. You remember reading that pickup trucks are in greater numbers on the nation's highways. These are short-term effects. What long-term effects might the country and western craze have had? Will this style of music continue to affect other types of music or other forms of art? Did teenagers who listened to country music choose different occupations from those of the acid-rock era? Did more people decide to move to the western parts of the country?

You might want to concentrate on effects in just one area of life—fashion, for example, or on the entertainment industry. But mention as many effects as possible in order to convince your audience that the rise in popularity of this music was an important cultural phenomenon.

When you identify the causes or effects of a situation, you must be careful that they indeed are causes or effects, that the causes actually preceded the effects and that there is a real link between them. Were movies with country and western themes causes or effects of the popularity of that type of music? You'll need to determine exactly when the upsurge in popularity occurred and check the dates of the release of the films. Was the increased popularity of pickup trucks really the effect of the increased popularity of country music, or were both the effect of some more general social change? Or is it, perhaps, just a coincidence? You'll have to look into who began buying pickups and what reasons they gave for their choice.

Barbara Tuchman pointed out the problems caused in the Middle Ages by the identification of the wrong causes of the plague. That is just one instance where false assumptions about the causes or effects of a particular problem or situation have caused unnecessary grief, trouble, or horror. Sometimes wrong assumptions affected large groups of people. In some incidents in our own early history, Native Americans who were unjustly thought to be causing trouble were killed. Doubtless some Germans believed that the Jews, the Poles, the Greeks, and others who were killed during the time of Hitler were a cause of many of the problems of the world. Such mistakes must be constantly guarded against.

Exercise

List the short- and long-term effects of imposing restrictions on the number of foreign cars that could be imported into the United States. Bring your list to class to compare with the lists of your classmates.

For class discussion
1. What areas of life might be affected by these restrictions?
2. What effects would favor imposing these restrictions?
3. What effects would lead you to oppose these restrictions?

Syllogistic Reasoning

Whether we know it or not, syllogistic reasoning underlies most of the conclusions we come to and most of the arguments we make. If you argue to your employer that you should not have to work on Martin Luther King, Jr.'s birthday, you are using the following syllogistic pattern of thought:

1. Employees are excused from work on birthdays of nationally important figures.
2. Martin Luther King, Jr., is a nationally important figure.
3. Employees should be excused from work on Martin Luther King, Jr.'s birthday.

A syllogism is a conclusion drawn from two related assumptions, called *premises.* The first assumption is called the *major premise,* and it should be an assumption that is generally agreed on. In the preceding example, everyone agrees that employees don't work on President's Day (a joint celebration of Washington's and Lincoln's birthdays). The second assumption is called the *minor premise,* and it is related to the major premise in that it offers a particular example of something mentioned in the major premise. In the example, Martin Luther King, Jr., is offered as a particular example of a nationally important figure. The *conclusion* follows from the two premises by relating the particular example offered in the minor premise (Martin Luther King, Jr.) to what the major premise says should be done (employees should be excused from work) about what was mentioned in the major premise (nationally important figures). We can diagram how a syllogism works:

A stands for a general person, place, thing, or idea.
B stands for a particular example of **A.**
C stands for what is said about both **A** and **B.**

MAJOR PREMISE	A ——————▶ B
MINOR PREMISE	B = A
CONCLUSION	B ——————▶ C

When thinking about a subject, look at your assumptions about that subject and try to figure out how your assumptions are related. By arranging your ideas in a syllogistic pattern, you are able to draw a conclusion. As you think of writing about a subject, you repeat this process over and over, abandoning old assumptions, making new assumptions, and rearranging assumptions into different patterns. Syllogistic reasoning helps you figure out what you think about a subject.

Syllogistic reasoning also helps you think about your audience. When you argue for or against a point, you worry whether your audience will agree with the assumptions expressed in your premises. Using syllogistic reasoning correctly does not guarantee that your conclusions will be true. It simply ensures that the relationships among the parts of the argument are logical. If the syllogism is correctly constructed, whether or not the conclusion is true depends on whether or not the premises are true. But in the syllogisms we use in arguments, as opposed to the logical syllogisms constructed by philosophers, we are more concerned with probability than with truth. We don't argue over whether or not Greeks are mortal (a conclusion of a classic logical syllogism); we can verify the premises (all people are mortal; Greeks are people) by appealing to fact. We *do* argue over such things as whether or not pollution regulations should be abolished.

A ⟶ C
MAJOR PREMISE Anything that is not cost effective / should be abolished.

B = A
MINOR PREMISE Pollution regulations / are / not cost effective.

B ⟶ C
CONCLUSION Pollution regulations / should be abolished.

We cannot just look at facts to establish whether or not all things that are not cost effective should be abolished and whether or not pollution restrictions are cost effective. People disagree on these questions, though they may use facts to help support the answer they find most in line with their values and beliefs. So we use syllogistic reasoning to make our arguments logical, and in constructing syllogisms, we rely on premises our audience will agree with in order to make our arguments as convincing as possible.

In his autobiography, Benjamin Franklin gives an example of the convenience of being a creature who is able to reason.

> I believe I have omitted mentioning that, in my first voyage from Boston, being becalmed off Block Island, our people set about catching cod, and hauled up a great many. Hitherto I had stuck to my resolution of not eating animal food; and on this occasion I considered, with my master Tryon, the taking every fish as a kind of unprovoked murder, since none of them had or ever could do us any injury that might justify the slaughter. All this seemed very reasonable. But I had formerly been a great lover of fish, and, when this came hot out of the frying-pan, it smelled admirably well. I balanced some time between principle and inclination: till I recollected that, when the fish were opened, I saw smaller fish taken out of their stomachs: Then thought I, if you eat one another, I don't see why we mayn't eat you. So I dined upon cod very heartily, and continued to eat with other people, returning only now and then occasionally to a vegetable diet. So convenient a thing it is to be a *reasonable creature,* since it enables one to find or make a reason for everything one has a mind to do.—
> *Autobiography*

You probably noticed that the reasoning that allowed Franklin to eat fish is not entirely convincing. If we look at the syllogism that underlies his reasoning we can see why:

$$A \longrightarrow C$$

MAJOR PREMISE Anything fish do / is something I can do.

$$B \quad = \quad A$$

MINOR PREMISE Eating fish / is / something fish do.

$$B \longrightarrow C$$

CONCLUSION   Eating fish / is something I can do.

This syllogism is correctly constructed. The major premise presents a general idea (anything fish do) and says something about it (is something I can do). The minor premise offers a particular example of the general idea in the major premise. And the conclusion says the same thing about the particular example that the major premise says about the general idea. The problem with Franklin's argument is that few people would agree with his major premise. There are many things fish do that people can't do and often wouldn't want to do. Relying on premises that are not generally agreed on is one of the major causes of unconvincing arguments.

You'll also notice that Franklin doesn't state the major premise of his argument anywhere. This is not a fault. Major premises are commonly left unstated in written arguments. When the audience completely agrees with the major premise, stating it might seem insulting or a waste of time. Why tell your audience something they already know? When the major premise is left unstated and only the minor premise and conclusion of a syllogism are presented, the argument is called an *enthymeme*. Franklin's statement, "if you [fish] eat one another, I don't see why we mayn't eat you" is an enthymeme. Enthymemes sometimes have the form Franklin uses here:

IF (minor premise), THEN (conclusion).

But they just as often have this form:

(Conclusion) BECAUSE (minor premise).

Here's an example of an enthymeme that uses the second form. I couldn't attend class yesterday BECAUSE I was ill. The unstated major premise, which we would all agree with, is that ill people can't attend classes.

Exercise

State the major premise (assumption) that stands behind each of these enthymemes. Who would agree with these premises? Who wouldn't?

a. We should protect endangered species of animals because the animals cannot protect themselves.

b. If learning to deal with alcoholic beverages is an educational experience, then alcoholic beverages should be allowed on college campuses.

c. Nuclear warfare is more desirable in the long run than conventional warfare because nuclear wars are of short duration.

d. The Equal Rights Amendment is unnecessary because the rights for women that it ensures are already accepted by most people.

e. The excess burros in Death Valley should be shot because they are upsetting the ecologic balance of the area.

Relying on assumptions that your audience doesn't agree with is not the only thing that can make your argument unconvincing. Your syllogism or enthymeme must be correctly constructed. Many arguments fail because the minor premise simply redefines the conclusion rather than presenting an example of the general person, place, thing, or idea mentioned in the major premise. Arguments on the topic of abortion, whether for or against, usually fail for this reason:

Conclusion

Women who want abortions should have the right to obtain

minor premise

abortions BECAUSE women should have the right to control their own bodies.

Conclusion

Women who want abortions should not have the right to

minor premise

obtain abortions BECAUSE women should not have the right to kill another human being.

As suggested by the form of the enthymeme, the minor premise should provide reasons or evidence for the conclusion. But simply redefining abortion as either "controlling one's own body" or "killing another human being" gives no reason for the conclusion that abortion should or should not be allowed. Neither of these arguments can be made convincing using just these assumptions, because when the syllogisms are made logically correct, we see that the minor premises present assumptions that many people do not agree with and that are impossible to support with evidence.

A ⟶ C

MAJOR PREMISE Control of their own bodies / is a right women should have.

B = A

MINOR PREMISE Abortion / is / a method of controlling one's body.

B ⟶ C

CONCLUSION Obtaining abortions / is a right women should have.

A ⟶ C

MAJOR PREMISE Killing other human beings / is a right women should not have.

B = A

MINOR PREMISE Abortion / is / killing another human being.

B ⟶ C

CONCLUSION Abortion / is a right women should not have.

To construct a convincing argument, you must find a minor premise that presents a reason for your conclusion and can be supported with evidence.

Exercise

Explain what's wrong with these incorrectly constructed enthymemes. How could the arguments they suggest be made convincing?

a. The government should provide free life insurance for all government employees because government agencies should offer employee benefits to employees.
b. Children should be raised in an extended family setting because it's important for children to deal with aunts and uncles and grandparents as well as with their mother and father.
c. If infant mortality rates were reduced, then more babies would live.

Though syllogistic reasoning underlies most arguments, syllogisms, or even enthymemes, are rarely presented in written arguments in any simple, straightforward fashion. Writers instead develop the relationships among their premises and conclusions in various ways, weigh alternatives, present evidence for their premises, and even present subordinate arguments to support parts of their premises and conclusions. In presenting a complicated argument on a controversial subject, writers often add three more elements to the syllogistic thinking pattern—a *qualification* of the conclusion, a *reservation* about the general applicability of the major premise, and *backing* for the major premise. A *qualification* shows your audience that you realize that your conclusion cannot be completely proven, although you think it is the most probable conclusion. In the following enthymeme, the first clause, introduced by *even though,* expresses a qualification of the conclusion.

> *Even though we must respect students' own dialects,* we have an obligation to teach them the "standard" dialect because they need facility in this dialect in order to achieve financial success.

A *reservation* shows your audience that you realize that your major premise may not hold in all situations, although you believe it is generally true. If you were arguing from the premise that an unstable balance of political power leads to war, you would probably want to acknowledge that nuclear weapons may deter war even when power imbalances exist. Providing *backing* for your major premise gives your audience reasons to agree with the assumption on which your argument rests. Say you wanted to make this argument:

$$A \longrightarrow C$$

MAJOR PREMISE A soothing environment / encourages plants to flower.

$$B \qquad = \qquad A$$

MINOR PREMISE Classical music / provides / a soothing environment.

$$B \longrightarrow C$$

CONCLUSION Classical music / encourages plants to flower.

You would want to discuss the results of scientific studies that show that plants grown in a quiet, conflict-free environment flower more profusely (though the difficulty of finding such studies might cause you to abandon this argument).

In the following essay, Lance Morrow argues a very controversial subject. As you read his discussion of the problem of what to do about handguns, try to figure out the syllogism that underlies his argument, and notice how he develops his assumptions, qualifies his conclusion, and suggests reservations about and backing for his major premise.

IT'S TIME TO BAN HANDGUNS

By a curiosity of evolution, every human skull harbors a prehistoric vestige: a reptilian brain. This atavism, like a hand grenade cushioned in the more civilized surrounding cortex, is the dark hive where many of mankind's primitive impulses orginate. To go partners with that throwback, Americans have carried out of their own history another curiosity that evolution forgot to discard as the country changed from a sparsely populated, underpoliced agrarian society to a modern industrial civilization. That vestige is the gun—most notoriously the handgun, an anachronistic tool still much in use. Since 1963 guns have finished off more Americans (400,000) than World War II did.

After one more handgun made it into American history last week (another nastily poignant little "Saturday night" .22 that lay like an orphan in a Dallas pawnship until another of those clammy losers took it back to his rented room to dream on), a lot of Americans said to themselves, "Well, maybe *this* will finally persuade them to do something about those damned guns." Nobody would lay a dime on it. The National Rifle Association battened down its hatches for a siege of rough editorial weather, but calculated that the antigun indignation would presently subside, just as it always does. After Kennedy. After King. After Kennedy. After Wallace. After Lennon. After Reagan. After . . . the nation will be left twitching and flinching as before to the pops of its 55 million pistols and the highest rate of murder by guns in the world.

The rest of the planet is both appalled and puzzled by the spectacle of a superpower so politically stable and internally violent. Countries like Britain and Japan, which have low murder rates and virtual prohibitions on handguns, are astonished by the over-the-counter ease with which Americans can buy firearms.

Americans themselves are profoundly discouraged by the

handguns that seem to breed uncontrollably among them like roaches. For years the majority of them have favored restrictions on handguns. In 1938 a Gallup poll discovered that 84% wanted gun controls. The latest Gallup finds that 62% want stricter laws governing handgun sales. Yet Americans go on buying handguns at the rate of one every 13 seconds. The murder rate keeps rising. It is both a cause and an effect of gun sales. And every few years— or months—some charismatic public character takes a slug from an itinerant mental case caressing a bizarre fantasy in his brain and the sick, secret weight of a pistol in his pocket.

Why do the bloody years keep rolling by without guns becoming subject to the kind of regulation we calmly apply to drugs, cars, boat trailers, CB radios and dogs? The answer is only partly that the National Rifle Association is, by some Senators' estimate, the most effective lobbying organization in Washington and the deadliest at targeting its congressional enemies at election time. The nation now has laws, all right—a patchwork of some 25,000 gun regulations, federal, state and local, that are so scattered and inconsistent as to be preposterously ineffectual.

Firearms have achieved in the U.S. a strange sort of inevitability —the nation's gun-ridden frontier heritage getting smokily mingled now with a terror of accelerating criminal violence and a sense that as the social contract tatters, the good guys must have their guns to defend themselves against the rising tribes of bad guys. It is very hard to persuade the good guys that all those guns in their hands wind up doing more lethal harm to their own kind than to the animals they fear; that good guys sometimes get drunk and shoot other good guys in a rage, or blow their own heads off (by design or accident) or hit their own children by mistake. Most murders are done on impulse, and handguns are perfectly responsive to the purpose: a blind red rage flashes in the brain and fires a signal through the nerves to the trigger finger—BLAM! Guns do not require much work. You do not have to get your hands bloody, as you would with a knife, or make the strenuous and intimately dangerous effort required to kill with bare hands. The space between gun and victim somehow purifies the relationship —at least for the person at the trigger—and makes it so much easier to perform the deed. The bullet goes invisibly across space to flesh. An essential disconnection, almost an abstraction, is maintained. That's why it is so easy—convenient, really—to kill with one of the things.

The post-assassination sermon, an earnest lamentation about the "sickness of American society," has become a notably fatuous genre that blames everyone and then, after 15 minutes of earnestly empty regret, absolves everyone. It is true that there is a good deal of evil in the American air; television and the sheer repetitiousness of violence have made a lot of the country morally weary and dull and difficult to shock. Much of the violence, however, results not from the sickness of the society but the stupidity and inadequacy of its laws. The nation needs new laws to put at least some guns out of business. Mandatory additional punishments for anyone using a gun in a crime—the approach that Ronald Reagan favors—would help. But a great deal more is necessary. Because of the mobility of guns, only federal laws can have any effect upon them. Rifles and shotguns—long guns—are not the problem; they make the best weapons for defending the house anyway, and they are hard for criminals to conceal. Most handguns are made to fire at people, not at targets or game. Such guns should be banned. The freedoms of an American individualism bristling with small arms must yield to the larger communal claim to sanity and safety—the "pursuit of happiness."

That would, of course, still leave millions of handguns illegally in circulation, the penalties for possessing such weapons, and especially for using them in crime, would have to be severe. Even at that, it would take years to start cleansing the nation of handguns. Whatever its content, no substantive program for controlling guns probably stands any chance of getting through Congress unless Ronald Reagan supports it. He ought to do so, not because he has been shot in the chest but because it should be done.

The indiscriminate mass consumption of guns has finally come to disgrace Americans abroad and depress them at home. It has been almost 90 years since the historian Frederick Jackson Turner propounded his famous thesis about the end of the American frontier. But the worst part of the frontier never did vanish. Its violence, once tolerable in the vast spaces, has simply backed up into modern America, where it goes on blazing away.

The syllogism underlying Morrow's argument is this:

$$A \longrightarrow C$$

MAJOR PREMISE Dangerous vestiges of the past / should be controlled.

$$B \quad = \quad A$$

MINOR PREMISE Guns / are / dangerous vestiges of the past.

$$B \longrightarrow C$$

CONCLUSION Guns / should be controlled.

Nowhere in the essay does Morrow directly state the premises of his argument, but he states the conclusion in his title and near the end of the seventh paragraph. The essay begins with some backing for the major premise. Our primitive impulses, he says, originate in the vestige of our evolutionary past, the reptilian brain. Morrow emphasizes the dangerousness of the reptilian brain by comparing it to a hand grenade, and everyone would agree that it is important to control primitive impulses in civilized societies. He then suggests that guns are a similar vestige of our past.

Morrow offers a wealth of evidence for his minor premise. He points out that since 1963 guns have been responsible for 400,000 deaths in America, more Americans than died in World War II. He refers to the shootings of John Kennedy, Martin Luther King, Jr., Robert Kennedy, George Wallace, John Lennon, and Ronald Reagan. He notes that in Britain and Japan, where handguns are not readily available, murder rates are low. He says that "most handguns are made to fire at people." He also constructs a subordinate syllogism to support his minor premise:

$$A \longrightarrow C$$

MAJOR PREMISE Impulse / triggers murders.

$$B \qquad = \qquad A$$

MINOR PREMISE Guns / are responsive to / impulse.

$$B \longrightarrow C$$

CONCLUSION Guns / trigger murder.

In this case he states both of his premises and his conclusion:

MAJOR PREMISE "Most murders are done on impulse"

MINOR PREMISE "and handguns are perfectly responsive to the purpose"

CONCLUSION "That's why it is so easy—convenient, really —to kill with one of the things."

In acknowledging that "it is very hard to persuade the good guys that all those guns in their hands wind up doing more lethal harm to their own kind than to the animals they fear" Morrow shows that he realizes that not everyone will agree with the premises of his main argument. And he offers a reservation to his major premise when he notes that controlling people's actions restricts their freedom. But he argues that this reservation is a minor consideration: "The freedoms of an

American individualism bristling with small arms must yield to the larger communal claim to sanity and safety."

Morrow qualifies his conclusion in three ways. First, he restricts the prohibition on guns to handguns, excluding rifles and shotguns. Second, he acknowledges that the ban he proposes will not immediately rid the nation of handguns. Third, he points out that even though a majority of Americans favor restrictions on handguns, "no substantive program for controlling guns probably stands any chance of getting through Congress unless Ronald Reagan supports it."

Morrow has made his argument as strong as he can. It is logical, for the syllogism on which it is based is correctly constructed. He has given his audience reasons to believe his major premise (backing) and offered evidence for his minor premise. His minor premise offers a reason for his conclusion. He acknowledges a reservation many people have about his major premise, and he qualifies his conclusion. Still, whether any particular reader will be convinced depends on whether or not he or she agrees with the premises. All that writers can do is make sure their arguments are logical and well-supported with evidence. Asking yourself these questions will help you make your arguments as strong as you can:

1. Who will agree with my major premise?
2. Who will not agree with my major premise?
3. What backing could I offer for my major premise?
4. Are there any reservations I should make about my major premise?
5. What evidence can I supply for my major premise?
6. Does my minor premise offer a reason for my conclusion?
7. Should I qualify my conclusion in any way?

Exercise

Construct a syllogism arguing a point you feel strongly about. Then ask yourself the questions listed above.

Summary

Exploring causes and effects can be a useful pattern of thought in helping you discover what you want to say. Citing the causes of an event, a problem, or an idea can help you and your audience understand your subject more completely. Looking for the effects of an event, a problem, or an idea can sometimes help you and your audience understand why something is true or what can be done to change an undesirable condition.

Causes produce consequences, and *effects* are those consequences. As you write, you should identify as many causes and effects related to your subject as you can. You may only want to focus upon certain of those causes or certain of those effects in your writing. Being aware of all of the possible causes and effects, however, will increase the chance that the causes and effects you are concentrating on are the right ones.

Like exploring cause and effect relationships, syllogistic reasoning focuses on relationships between events or ideas. The syllogism reasons from two assumptions, or premises, to a conclusion. The major premise should be an assumption that your audience will agree with. The minor premise should offer a reason for your conclusion and should be an assumption you can support with evidence. In arguing on complex subjects, you may also want to qualify your conclusion, offer reservations about the general applicability of your major premise, and present backing for your major premise.

Marijuana in the Schools

This year you are chairman of your fraternity's social services project. You must come up with a worthwhile service project for the fall semester. You had an idea several weeks ago on a visit home when your twelve-year-old brother confided in you that he had been "smoking dope." Though shocked that he would be trying it at such an early age, you certainly weren't going to rat on him to your parents. You did try to tell him, however, some of the things that you thought were harmful about marijuana for such a young kid. Because he thought he was so "cool," your remarks seemed to have little effect on him.

During the trip back to campus, your idea for a service

project began to take shape. The members of your fraternity could offer to speak about marijuana use to the various junior highs in the area. Since you are "college guys" and since most of you have tried marijuana and would be willing to admit it, the kids might be more attentive to what you have to say about its use than they would to their teachers. As you thought about it, the project seemed more and more worthy of your time. In a way, you felt that the project would not only be helping kids *like* your kid brother, but might also help *him* indirectly, too. If you knew more of the facts, you might be able to help him better understand the consequences of marijuana use and abuse.

One problem is that while none of your fraternity brothers abuse marijuana, some use it occasionally and a number are regular cigarette smokers. They might feel hypocritical warning kids not to smoke. You're going to have to make it clear that the purpose of the project is to give the kids information, not to preach at them. The kids that they talk to will be making their decisions about whether or not to smoke marijuana, and the job of the fraternity members will be to make those decisions informed ones. They will be concentrating on giving the kids the necessary facts that they need to make a choice.

Assignment 1
Write a presentation about the project to be read at your next fraternity meeting. Do all that you can to eliminate any feelings of hypocrisy that your brothers might have about the project.

Assignment 2
Your brothers agreed to the project, although some were reluctant. Maybe that will insure that you won't have to be chairman again next year! Anyway, as chairman, you have naturally been asked to prepare the talks for the other members.

You first go to the library and locate a technical article that seems to be a competent rehearsal of the most recent data regarding marijuana use. That done, you have to decide how to think about and present the facts. Your article talks mostly about effects of smoking marijuana, but you feel that concentrating on these will turn your talk into a warning. You decide to also consider the various causes of marijuana use.

Using the following technical article about marijuana use, prepare a talk for your fraternity brothers to give at the junior highs.

As with any widely used drug, concern exists regarding possible harmful health effects of marijuana use. Such concern extends to potential acute toxicity, as well as deleterious effects from long-term use. And because marijuana is an illicit drug in our society, the basic nature and quality of the substance being used cannot be assured. Therefore, research on the pure drug cannot be generalized to all forms of the substance found "on the street."

Nevertheless, marijuana is rapidly becoming one of our most researched drugs. Since synthesis of its psychoactive ingredient [Δ-9-Tetrahydrocannabinol (THC)] in the mid-60s, extensive and systematic investigation has been done. To date, however, more questions about the health effects of marijuana have been raised than answered.

Various studies conducted throughout the world have found differing results from marijuana use. The major areas of concern include: potential birth defects from chromosome breakage; brain damage; amotivational syndrome; psychosis; impaired sexual function from lowered testosterone levels in males; reduced immune response; and basic heart and lung impairment. None of these alleged effects has been demonstrated adequately enough to draw a definitive conclusion. More and better controlled experiments, along with the passage of time, are necessary before a final judgment can be made.

For each of the aforementioned health concerns, conflicting studies exist. Interestingly, in many instances, the more carefully designed follow-up investigations failed to corroborate the initial adverse findings. Further, preliminary investigations conducted during the first decade after the synthesis of THC were often not designed to control for use of other drugs and correlated factors. Therefore, some of the early deleterious findings ascribed to marijuana use could have been caused by other drugs, including alcohol and tobacco.

Nevertheless, because of the tragedy of cigarette smoking in our society, special concern exists regarding the long-term consequences of marijuana smoking. Like tobacco cigarettes, marijuana reefers contain hundreds of substances, many known to be carcinogenic. Although the average tobacco user smokes many more cigarettes per day than even the heavy marijuana smoker, the fact that the joint is unfiltered, plus the way in which it is smoked, both increase the relative insult to the respiratory system. Moreover, the strength of marijuana on the street has increased in recent years. Further, many marijuana smokers also smoke tobacco cigarettes, thereby possibly compounding health risks. . . .

One study, by Leuchtenberger and associates, tested the effects of tobacco and marijuana smoke on human lung explants. Over 1300 cultures of normal lung tissue, removed during surgery, were exposed in a Filtron CSM 12 smoking machine. The authors concluded that fresh smoke from cigarettes made of marijuana had essentially the same impact on lung tissue as did smoke from tobacco. Similar abnormalities in DNA metabolism, mitosis, and growth in fibroblastic cells were found from both types of exposure.

Huber and his colleagues investigated the effect of marijuana smoke on the bacteriocidal effectiveness of pulmonary alveolar macrophages. In this study, graded amounts of fresh marijuana smoke were added to tissue flasks containing alveolar macrophages from rats. (THC content of the smoke was 2.2 percent.) The macrophage cultures were then incubated *in vitro* with staphylococcus bacteria. After three hours, control macrophages (not exposed to marijuana smoke) had inactivated 78 percent of the staphylococcal challenge. However, the bacteriocidal activity of those macrophages exposed to marijuana smoke was lessened, and the depression was dose dependent. While the authors note that *in vitro* studies on macrophages from rats cannot be totally extrapolated to humans, they also point out the significant role of pulmonary alveolar macrophage in phagocytosis and normal lung physiology.

Tashkin *et al.* studied 28 healthy young males who were experienced marijuana smokers. Thorough pulmonary function tests were done on each subject. After 57 to 59 days of smoking 5.2 joints per day with 2.2 percent THC, another set of readings was taken. The posttest findings showed slight but highly significant changes in lung function, notably in large airways. Follow-up studies in six of the original 28 subjects showed only partial reversal after a week of marijuana smoking cessation. The authors concluded:

. . . *[C]ustomary social use of marijuana may not result in detectable, functional respiratory impairment in healthy young men; whereas, heavy marijuana smoking for 6 to 8 weeks causes mild but statistically significant airway obstruction.* . . .

Listed among the possible adverse health effects of marijuana

is something called "amotivational syndrome," which refers to personality changes among marijuana users, including lessened energy and concentration, depression, stress reduction, and memory loss. Though formal research in this area has been inadequate to date, parents have been advised to be alert to symptoms that their children may be "hooked" on marijuana. These symptoms include: decreasing school performance, impaired short-term memory, cough, chest pains, depression, lessened intensity of involvement, and dramatic mood changes.
—"Marijuana: Assessing the Cost," *The Science Teacher*

For class discussion
1. What do junior high students know about marijuana use? What might they not know?
2. How much technical information should be given to the junior high students?
3. What values do junior high students have that you could appeal to in your talk?
4. What are some techniques that the fraternity brothers can use at the beginning of their talks to catch the attention of their audience?
5. What clichés about marijuana use should you avoid in your talk?

Assignment 3
Your next job is to contact the schools. Compose a letter to be sent to the principals of the local junior highs explaining your project and asking if they are interested. Since the principals might be skeptical, you will have to convince them of the usefulness of your project.

For class discussion
1. What objections might principals have to your project?
2. What arguments can you use to convince them to participate?

Assignment 4
Congratulations! The project was successful, and your fraternity was commended by all the principals involved. Something is still bothering you though. Your kid brother needs this information too. Write him a letter about marijuana use.

Teacher Activist

Fran Kahn, a history teacher at your son's high school, was involved last year in a blockade of the Green Trees Nuclear Power Plant, located about twenty miles from your city. Arrested, tried, and fined for her part in the blockade, Ms. Kahn is continuing her campaign against nuclear energy this fall. On weekends she participates in rallies against nuclear energy and in marches on the power plant. Because the demonstrators have curtailed some of their more aggressive activities, there have been no new arrests. Some of Fran Kahn's students are participating in the marches and rallies, too, and *that's* the problem.

Fred Glower, as representative of the parents of participating students, called Leo Giammalva, the school principal, to protest Ms. Kahn's open campaign against nuclear energy. Mr. Glower charged that Ms. Kahn was using her classroom to encourage the students to "hit the streets" (his words) in protest against nuclear energy. Declaring that Kahn had no right to use the classroom in this way, Glower, on behalf of the angry parents, demanded that Mr. Giammalva make a full investigation.

After questioning over twenty-five students enrolled in Ms. Kahn's history classes, carefully examining ten different sets of students' class notes, talking with Fran Kahn, and checking her lesson plans, Giammalva was fully satisfied that both sides of the issue of nuclear energy had been presented to the students. In fact, Ms. Kahn had invited an electric power company official to speak to the class on the value of nuclear energy. Giammalva could find no evidence that Fran Kahn had advocated protest on the part of the students.

Hoping to calm the angered parents, Mr. Giammalva sent the following letter home to the parents of all students in Ms. Kahn's classes:

Dear Parents,

Some of you have protested what you consider to be Frances Kahn's advocacy of protest against nuclear energy. I have made as complete and thorough an investigation of the matter as possible.

That investigation revealed that, while Ms. Kahn did express her personal opinion against nuclear energy and present a case for eliminating its use, she also invited an electric power company spokesperson to present the case for nuclear energy.

As long as both sides of the issue of nuclear energy were presented, I believe that Ms. Kahn is within her rights. Those rights are defined for us by the United States Court of Appeals in Tinker versus Des Moines School District, 1969. The ruling is that teachers' rights go with them into school. Teachers can express personal views, challenge established beliefs, and deal with controversial issues if they are relevant to the subject that they are teaching and if both sides are presented.

Apparently the letter did nothing to calm the parents because two days later your son Rich brought this letter home from Mr. Giammalva:

Dear Parents,

At the request of several parents, I have agreed to an open discussion session concerning Ms. Kahn's right to speak out against nuclear energy in her classroom. The parents believe that the subject of nuclear energy is inappropriate in the course Ms. Kahn is teaching—American History since World War II.

I have, therefore, called a meeting for Thursday, December 6, at 7:30 in the main auditorium. To save time, please bring prepared statements lasting no more than four minutes. That way we will have adequate time for a question-and-answer period at the end of the meeting.

You are interested now because you believe you know what will happen at the meeting. Parents will get so caught up in arguing about whether or not nuclear energy is relevant to the history class that they will lose sight of the central issue—the rights of teachers to free speech and to determine the content of their classes. You decide to read a prepared statement at the meeting, addressing those effects.

Assignment 1
First, state the syllogisms that underlie the parents' two arguments—that Ms. Kahn should not speak against nuclear energy and that a discussion of nuclear energy has no place in

an American History class. Do you agree with the premises of the arguments?

Now you are ready to prepare your statement. Discuss the effects of a teacher's taking a side in an issue, or discuss the effects of preventing a teacher from taking a stand, or discuss the effects of allowing parents to determine class content. Construct a syllogism that presents your argument, then write your statement.

For class discussion
1. What effects could this situation cause?
2. What reasons could you offer for the various possible conclusions?
3. What tone should your statement take to be most effective in this situation?

Assignment 2
Describe an incident from your own experience in which a teacher expressed a personal opinion in class. What effect did that opinion have on you? On your classmates? Did you agree or disagree with the opinion? Did the teacher have the right to make the statement based upon the criteria defined in the Tinker versus Des Moines School District case?

The Stress Test

You have been suffering from severe depression for over a week now. Your problems are probably not atypical of the problems of a number of people you know, but you don't seem to be able to handle them. You are nineteen, a sophomore, and from a small town in a neighboring state—about a four-hour drive away. You were a member of the honor society in high school, ran track, and were chosen Senior Favorite. Your ambition is to become a dentist, and high grades up to now have insured the fulfillment of that goal. You are in college on an academic scholarship, and you have maintained a 3.8 grade-point average.

Even before coming to college, you made the decision that almost all of your time would have to be given to studying in order to earn the grades that would guarantee admission to dental school. By the end of the first year, you were spending almost every hour outside of class studying. This intensive study program came at the sacrifice of friendships, socializing, and running track. Your austere way of life bothers you if you think about it much, but most of the time you are too busy to worry.

This last week you received a D on a biology midterm, and you immediately felt like giving up. Spending more and more time alone and deeply depressed, you believe that all hope is lost for getting into dental school and that nobody really cares but you. You have only confided in one person, your room-mate Pat. Your mother thinks that you can do no wrong, and would be no help at all. Your father has placed such heavy responsibility on you to do well in college that you could never talk to him honestly.

Last night your roommate tried to talk you into going to see the campus psychologist. Only a couple of months ago you both read an article in the campus paper that quoted him as saying that as many as 75 percent of the students on campus suffer from depression and stress every school year. In many of the cases the problem is great enough to seek professional help. Campus suicides are 50 percent more frequent than suicides among those who do not go to college. The psychologist invited students to visit his office. He said counseling was available free to all registered students. He also mentioned a stress test that he could give to students to determine the severity of their problems.

At first you were angry with your roommate for suggesting it. You *aren't* a nut! But after three hours of almost unbearable silence, you finally broke down, "I just feel like killing myself. I guess I better go before I do something drastic."

Assignment 1
After a few moments of getting acquainted, the psychologist asks you to take the following stress test. Respond as honestly as you can.

QUESTIONNAIRE
Pick the statement that best describes how you have been feeling over the past week. Use that statement as the opening statement

of a paragraph in which you expand your answer. Tell what you think the causes of that feeling are.

1. I feel really excited when I think about the future.
   The future scares me.
   I have no hope for the future.
2. I am more successful than I have been for a long time.
   I am a failure too much of the time.
   I am a failure all of the time.
3. I am basically a happy person.
   I am sad much of the time.
   I am so sad sometimes that I don't think I can go on.
4. I can't remember the last time I cried.
   I cry sometimes, but usually for a good reason.
   I cry almost all the time, and I can't stop myself.
5. I sleep well.
   I have trouble sleeping.
   I haven't been sleeping much lately.
6. My studies are going well.
   I have to push myself to get my work done.
   I haven't been doing any studying lately.

Assignment 2

The psychologist has suggested that you drop one of your courses (you're carrying six instead of the normal five, and introduction to sociology, a distribution requirement, is offered every term), go out for track, or at least find someone to run with regularly, and force yourself to spend at least half an hour every day talking to other students in the dorm about something other than classwork. When you protest that you couldn't possibly do any of these things, the psychologist tells you to respond to what he's suggested in the journal he's asked you to keep. He tells you to write down your fears about how taking the time to do these things would affect your future, to examine the validity of your fears, and to explore the other effects these activities could have on your life.

CHAPTER 10

PERSONA

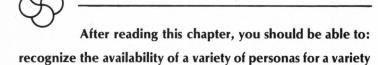

After reading this chapter, you should be able to:

recognize the availability of a variety of personas for a variety of purposes;

create a persona appropriate for the writing situations you are involved in.

Every time you write, the readers of your writing hear an imagined voice. The kind of voice they hear determines their willingness to listen, believe, and act on what they hear. This voice is the result of the particular words you choose and the way you combine these words to form phrases and sentences. From your word choice and sentence arrangement, readers draw inferences about who is talking and about your attitude toward your subject and your audience. Mark Twain consciously creates a voice in *Huckleberry Finn*:

> "Well, three or four months run along, and it was well into the winter, now. I had been to school most all the time, and could spell, and read, and write just a little, and could say the multiplication table up to six times seven is thirty-five, and I don't reckon I could ever get any further than that if I was to live forever. I don't take no stock in mathematics, anyway."

We know it's a young person talking because of what's being discussed, and we know that the speaker's attitude towards schooling is not positive from what he says in the last sentence. He doesn't apologize for this attitude or try to disguise it, so we assume he is being honest with us. And we know he is not highly educated because of his use of nonstandard forms such as *run,* and *don't* take *no* stock.

You aren't helpless in creating a voice; that is, you don't have to be content with just one voice every time you write. Just as during the course of the day you adjust your behavior to the situation you are in, so in writing you have many alternative voices available for the writing situation you are in. Your changing behaviors are not artificial; they are a real part of you. You behave one way with your friends, another way with your professors, another way with your family—but you're not being phony in any of those instances. The same is true in your writing. You have many ways of writing to your audience—and none of them need be phony or artificial.

We use the word *persona* to refer to the created voice, the character who speaks to the audience. The Latin word *persona* means *mask.* When you write, the voice that the audience hears may or may not be exactly the same as the real you, but the persona, the created image, is all that an audience can know about you. In other words, the persona is all the audience has to determine if your voice is worth hearing. You won't be there to show what a fascinating, insightful, vivacious person you are. Your writing has to stand on its own. You can't rely on gestures, smiles, frowns, and raised eyebrows in your writing. You have to create a voice that the audience will trust, listen to, or feel sympathetic toward.

You may have read a piece of writing in which the writer sounded artificial or phony. The problem may have been the writer chose the wrong persona for the writing situation. For example, in the following passage the writer probably was expressing very real sentiments. Unfortunately, she has chosen a mixture of personas. Sometimes she sounds like a real person talking; sometimes she sounds as if she is writing to impress her English teacher.

> As I perused my new textbooks, I got really scared. How was I ever going to accomplish the goals I had set for myself? How would I ever attain my cherished degree in business? But then, I took hold of myself. One must do these things a step at a time. Developing enough maturity to know that one can accomplish any job he or she sets out to do, if one can just stick to it, isn't easy. But I'm

bound and determined to keep reminding myself that one's goals and aspirations are within reach with enough determination.

Let's use that paragraph to illustrate how it is possible for you to control the persona the audience hears. First, using roughly the same ideas, that passage can be made to sound like someone talking.

I got back to the dorm and looked over my textbooks, and I got really scared. I just didn't see how I was ever going to graduate from college. How would I ever get a degree in business? Then I got hold of myself. I said, "Just go a step at a time." I have a hard time remembering that you can get almost anything done if you just stick to it. But I'm going to keep telling myself that every day until I graduate.

The addition of some contractions, the use of some colloquial expressions like "a hard time" and "got hold of," the elimination of subordinate clauses and words like *perused* and *cherished,* and the substitution of *you* for *one* have created a persona that sounds like someone talking.

That passage also can be made to sound more general and formal.

As I perused my textbooks, a fear crept over me. How was I ever to accomplish the goals I had established for myself during the next four years? How would I ever attain that desirable degree in business? At that point, I mastered my emotions. The key to accomplishing one's goals is to complete one task at a time. It is sometimes difficult to remember that one's success depends on strong resolve. Yet I shall continue to remind myself that my goals and aspirations are within reach with enough determination.

The formal persona in this passage was achieved by replacing particular details with general statements (for example, "to graduate from college" becomes "to accomplish the goals I had established," and "you can get almost anything done" becomes "one's success"), adding subordinate clauses, using less colloquial verbs and nouns ("attain" instead of "get," "mastered" instead of "got hold of"), replacing "you" with "one," and substituting "shall" for "will."

Neither the colloquial nor the formal passage is better than the other, but in some situations one may be more appropriate than the other. The formal version would seem odd as an entry in a personal journal; the colloquial version would not be effective as part of a valedictorian's speech at graduation.

Exercise

Write about a significant experience you had using a persona appropriate for a journal entry. Then rewrite the passage substituting a persona appropriate for an autobiography of a famous and highly respected person.

Another way in which personas can vary is in the amount of confidence about themselves and their opinions they demonstrate. The voice in this passage sounds uncertain:

> I seem to remember that my first blind date was kind of awful. He was rather good-looking and appeared to be knowledgeable and intelligent. But he seemed to talk a lot about liberal politics and his experiences campaigning for Kennedy. When I mentioned that I thought liberal economic policies were a bit out of date, he didn't even comment on what I said. Instead he went on doing most of the talking during dinner, dancing, and the bus ride back to my apartment. I said goodnight and I guess I slammed the door in his face. I don't really mind discussing politics on a date, but I think if I had wanted to hear a speech, I could have gone to a rally.

Does she remember the date clearly or does she only seem to remember it was awful? Are liberal economic policies out of date or not? Did she slam the door in his face or not? Sometimes we aren't certain about things we want to say, and we should admit it. But this writer is not uncertain about what happened. Rather she is afraid to directly say what she knows and believes, either because she doesn't want to be impolite or because she's afraid you won't be very interested. This passage can easily be rewritten in a voice that sounds confident and engaging:

> My first blind date was awful. He was good-looking—tall, well-built, blue eyes—knowledgeable, and intelligent. But he talked non-stop about liberal politics and his experiences campaigning for Kennedy. When I said that liberal economic policies were out

of date, he didn't even comment on what I said, but continued his monologue through dinner, dancing, and the bus ride back to my apartment. I said goodnight and slammed the door in his face. I don't mind discussing politics on a date, but if I want a speech I'll go to a rally.

Now the writer's purpose is clearer; she wants to convince us she had a bad experience and to express her opinions on the kind of behavior she expects from someone she goes out with. The difference in persona comes from leaving out qualifying words like *seem, kind of, rather, appeared, thought, a bit, guess, most, really,* and *think.*

You will notice that what's wrong with the first passage is not just that the persona sounds uncertain, but that this uncertainty is inappropriate to the writer's purpose. Had her purpose been to demonstrate how she, like most of us, forgets details of bad experiences, she would have created a persona who sounded even more uncertain:

I remember that my first blind date was awful in some way. Such a feeling of revulsion comes over me when I think of it that I've forgotten most of the details. I think he might have been good-looking and intelligent—but I may be wrong about that. I do seem to remember him talking a lot about politics or some such topic, and I remember feeling as if he didn't know I was there. When he took me home I think I might have slammed the door in his face. For years afterward I absolutely forbade anyone to arrange dates for me.

For some purposes you may want to sound uncertain; for other purposes sounding uncertain will work against what you want to achieve. The thing to remember is that the persona you choose must not only be appropriate to the situation you're writing in, it must also be appropriate to your purpose.

Exercise

Describe the persona in each of the following selections:

a. Getting through the night is becoming harder and harder. Last evening, I had the uneasy feeling that some men were trying to break into my room to shampoo me. But why? I kept imagining I saw shadowy forms, and at 3 A.M. the underwear I had draped over a chair resembled the Kaiser on roller skates. When I finally did fall asleep, I had that same hideous nightmare in which a woodchuck is trying to claim my prize at a raffle. Despair.

—Woody Allen, *Without Feathers*

b. I have often wondered, and it is not a pleasant wonder, just what white Americans talk about with one another. I wonder this because they do not, after all, seem to find very much to say to *me,* and I concluded long ago that they found the color of my skin inhibitory. This color seems to operate as a most disagreeable mirror, and a great deal of one's energy is expended in reassuring white Americans that they do not see what *they* see. This is utterly futile, of course, since *they do* see what *they* see.—James Baldwin, *Unnameable Objects, Unspeakable Crimes*

c. Suppose I were to violate decorum by telling a joke at this solemn moment, and suppose further—oh fond fantasy!— that it is as uproariously successful as the best joke you've heard in the last year. And then suppose a critic were to tell you that you do not know whether I was joking or not, that for all you really can prove, I was intending to communicate my tragic sense of life. What we know, in his view, is what we can prove, in his notion of proof. I submit that we would have every right to call him unreasonable, dogmatic, and in fact a bit foolish, because our communally shared knowledge of joke telling, its purposes, its conventions, its effects, is very secure stuff indeed. My joke would of course reveal other intentions than merely to make you laugh: you would know, at this stage of my third lecture, that I intended the joke and the laughter as illustrative. If the critic tried to convince you that I intended anything else by it than to make you laugh in order to illustrate our communal understanding, you would have every right to call him unreasonable, or even—if you wanted to be playfully contentious—unscientific.—Wayne Booth, *Modern Dogma and the Rhetoric of Assent*

Persona and Purpose

In Chapter 1 we talked about the purposes that writing can

have—expressive, informative, and persuasive. Here let's look at the kind of personas that are appropriate to these different purposes.

If your writing has an expressive purpose, you choose a persona that matches your mood and what you're trying to express. Since the emphasis is on exploring your own emotions, ideas, and attitudes, you are free to explore the voices that also speak those attitudes, emotions, and ideas.

Contrast, for example, the two very different personas in the following expressive passages. Pay attention not only to *what* they're expressing, but *how* they do it—what words and sentence patterns they choose.

August 17—

Ah! if I could so live that there should be no desultory moment in all my life! that in the trivial season, when small fruits are ripe, my fruits might be ripe also! that I could match nature always with my moods! that in each season when some part of nature especially flourishes, then a corresponding part of me may not fail to flourish! Ah! I would walk, I would sit and sleep, with natural piety! What if I could pray aloud or to myself as I went along by the brooksides a cheerful prayer like the birds! For joy I could embrace the earth; I shall delight to be buried in it. And then to think of those I love among men, who will know that I love them though I tell them not! I sometimes feel as if I were rewarded merely for expecting better hours. I did not despair of worthier moods, and now I have occasion to be grateful for the flood of life that is flowing over me. I am not so poor: I can smell the ripening apples; the very rills are deep; the autumnal flowers, the *Trichostema dichotomum*,—not only its bright blue flower above the sand, but its strong wormwood scent which belongs to the season,—feed my spirit, endear the earth to me, make me value myself and rejoice; the quivering of pigeons' wings reminds me of the tough fibre of the air which they rend. I thank you, God. I do not deserve anything, I am unworthy of the least regard; and yet I am made to rejoice.—Henry David Thoreau, *The Journal*

The word was my agony. The word that for others was so effortless and neutral, so unburdened, so simple, so exact, I had first to meditate in advance, to see if I could make it, like a plumber fitting together odd lengths and shapes of pipe. I was always preparing words I could speak, storing them away, choosing between them. And often, when the word did come from my mouth in its great and terrible birth, quailing and bleeding as if forced through a thornbush, I would not be able to look the others in the face, and would walk out in the silence, the infinitely echoing silence behind my back, to say it all cleanly back to myself as I walked in the streets. Only when I was alone in the open air, pacing the roof with pebbles in my mouth, as I had read Demosthenes had done to cure himself of stammering; or in the street, where all words seemed to flow from the length of my stride and the color of the houses as I remembered the perfect tranquility of a phrase in *Beethoven's Romance in F* I could sing back to myself as I walked—only then was it possible for me to speak without the infinite premeditations and strangled silences I toiled through whenever I got up at school to respond with the expected, the exact answer.—Alfred Kazin, *A Walker in the City*

The images you remember from Thoreau's journal entry are the blue flowers above the sand, smelling of wormwood, and pigeons' wings quivering in the air. The images Kazin leaves you with are a plumber fitting together pipes, and a word, somehow like a tender object, being forced quailing and bleeding through a thornbush. Thoreau speaks about what he wishes for himself and what is true of him in the present, using words like *cloud, should, might, may, would,* and the present tense—I love, I feel, I can smell, the flowers feed, endear, make me value myself. Kazin speaks of the past—I had to meditate, I was always preparing, only then was it possible, I toiled. Thoreau's sentences are much shorter, and they contain fewer of the descriptive phrases and clauses that make Kazin's sentences so much longer and more tortuous to read. Look, for example, at Kazin's last sentence, which begins, "only when," and which contains so much description of "when" that he has to repeat "only when" halfway through the sentence so his readers won't get lost. Kazin's sentences are as laborious as the efforts of the young man he describes to speak.

If your writing has an informative purpose, your persona will be more self-effacing. You will not want to draw attention to your voice because in informative writing the emphasis is on the message. You will avoid getting in the way of the transmission of that information. But even in informative writing, there is still a voice we are asked to listen to. That voice may be almost unidentifiable, but it is there.

In the following news story, we can know little about the persona other than that he or she is in command of the facts and wants to present them in the clearest and most unbiased way possible.

Louisiana Town Sets Curfew After Three Are Wounded

OAKDALE, La., April 14 (AP)—Riot-equipped state police were on duty in this south Louisiana town today after a white policeman and two black men were wounded by shotgun pellets in a confrontation in a predominantly black section.

Mayor George Mowad imposed an indefinite curfew, ordering the 8,000 residents off the streets between 8 P.M. and 6 A.M. The town's high school and junior high school were closed today.

Sheriff Claiborne Durio of Allen Parish said he believed that the confrontation late last night was linked to noontime racial fighting at Oakdale High School.

And the school fight may have been touched off, in turn, by a Saturday night incident in which several white teenagers went to a black section of town, Sheriff Durio said. There was some name-calling and a gun was fired, he said, but no one was injured.

In the following piece of informative writing, the persona is more human, someone who might forget or might want to revolt. Notice how at the end of the passage E. M. W. Tillyard relates his subject to himself and his readers by using the words *we, ourselves, you,* and *yourself.*

The conception of world order was for the Elizabethans a principal matter; the other set of ideas that ranked with it was the theological scheme of sin and salvation. However widely biblical history was presented in medieval drama and sermon, even though many Protestants may have had the Gospels by heart, the part of Christianity that was paramount was not the life of Christ but the orthodox scheme of the revolt of the bad angels, the creation, the temptations and fall of man, the incarnation, the atonement, and regeneration through Christ. And this is as true of the Middle Ages as of the Age of Elizabeth. Here was another pattern as powerful in its imaginative appeal as the divine order of the universe, standing out clean and distinct from all other theological lore. It had been the pattern St. Paul imposed on the

Christian material and it persisted in spite of all disputes and eruptions as a great formative force in men's lives, until with the scientific revolution of the seventeenth century it slowly receded into this and that citadel. We should never let ourselves forget that the orthodox scheme of salvation was pervasive in the Elizabethan age. You could revolt against it but you could not ignore it. Atheism not agnosticism was the rule. It was far easier to be very wicked and think yourself so than to be a little wicked without a sense of sin.—*The Elizabethan World Picture*

In informative writing, whether or not you choose to involve yourself and your audience in the discussion, the goal is to present your subject as clearly and objectively as possible.

Exercise

Describe some event you observed—a concert, a game, or a rally—first in order to express how you reacted to it and then to inform someone else about what happened. What differences in the two versions help establish your different personas?

Finally, if your writing has a persuasive purpose, you are interested in changing your audience's thinking or behavior. And if you expect your audience to believe you, you cannot give them reason to doubt you. There are no rules to follow that will always result in your audience believing what you say. There are, however, three general ways of going about persuading people—*logical* means, *emotional* means, and *ethical* means. They are a fit conclusion for these ten chapters because they illustrate how a writer decides what kind of relationship to have with both the subject and the audience.

Logical Means

Logos, or logical argument in writing, calls on facts and reasoning. If you choose to persuade through logical means, your first concern will be to present your subject to your audience clearly, honestly and with as much appeal to authority, reason, and facts as possible. Your attitude toward your subject will be so if you explore your subject fully and well. If you present your subject in as much detail as seems necessary, the subject itself will persuade your audience. Express confidence that you have mastered your subject well and that you have looked at it with a critical eye. Address your audience as logical, reasonable, and intelligent people who will understand your subject in the same way you do.

The following paragraph by Norman Luxenburg persuades us by statistics of the rapid increase of automobile ownership in Europe after World War II:

> Thus, by 1967, the United Kingdom alone, with more than ten million autos, had more cars than all of Europe together had had only thirteen years earlier, and both France and West Germany had more cars than did the United Kingdom. While it was undoubtedly true that a large number of persons had more than one car, an increase from two million to ten million cars in France, and an increase from 1.1 million to ten million in West Germany in the period from 1953-66 meant that there were now more than twenty million cars, the overwhelming majority of very recent vintage, for a population of only about 105 million. Millions of persons in 1966 could obviously afford cars who could never have done so in the pre-1953 Europe.—*Europe Since World War II*

Emotional Means

Pathos, or emotional appeal, calls on your audience's emotions. Few thoughtful people are persuaded by a purely emotional appeal; there has to be more. The writer has to give evidence of an understanding and exploration of the subject, of a fairness toward the issues, of a reason to be believed. But emotions are an important part of writing. To be angry or indignant about your subject, to be impassioned, to be sympathetic or compassionate, and to let these or other emotions appear to your audience is, on occasion, persuasive. Your attitude toward your audience is that they are humane, caring, and thoughtful, and that they too will be indignant or impassioned about your subject.

In the following brief example, we see the writer Susan B. Anthony, letting her strong devotion for her cause show through her writing. Her anger at the condition of women is evident in her strong language: *degradation, in chains, debasing.*

> So while I do not pray for anybody or any party to commit outrages, still I do pray, and that earnestly and constantly, for some terrific shock to startle the women of this nation into a self-respect which will compel them to see the abject degradation of their present position; which will force them to break their yoke of bondage, and give them faith in themselves; which will make them proclaim their allegiance to woman first; which will enable them to see that man can no more feel, speak, or act for woman than could the old slaveholder for his slave. The fact is, women are in chains, and their servitude is all the more debasing because they do not realize it. O, to compel them to see and feel, and to give them the courage and conscience to speak and act for their own freedom, though they face the scorn and contempt of all the world for doing it!—From a Letter to a Friend

Ethical Means

The third means of persuasion, *ethos,* is perhaps the most difficult to describe. An ethical appeal is based on the character of the speaker. The audience are supposed to reason as follows: this is a good person speaking; thus his or her opinions must also be good.

Aristotle in *The Rhetoric* tells us that the character of the speaker is a means of persuasion when the speech is given in such a way as to make the speaker worthy of belief. I once asked a rhetorician how to teach ethical quality, and she replied, "How do you teach a man or woman to be good?" Being good, having ethical quality, isn't something you can pretend to be or have. All of us have heard a speaker or read a writer who was pretending to be better than he or she was. You know how short a time you listened to or read what was said.

You can be believable, however, and give your audience cause to trust you. One way is to allow your audience to follow your thoughts and give them evidence for your assertions. Stay as honest and faithful toward your subject as you can. Be as honest with your audience as you can as well. Express the truth as you see it for the moment. Permit your audience to see that given another time, another way of seeing, and new understandings which you cannot have now, you would be willing to see the truth in new ways.

In the following excerpt from Martin Luther King, Jr.'s letter to clergymen from the Birmingham jail, he tells them that he too favors negotiation and that given the particular set of circumstances, he sees nonviolent direct action as the quickest means to that common goal. He indicates that given other circumstances, he also would be against creating tension.

> You may well ask, "Why direct action? Why sit-ins, marches, and so forth? Isn't negotiation a better path?" You are quite right in calling for negotiation. Indeed, this is the very purpose of direct action. Nonviolent direct action seeks to create such a crisis and foster such a tension that a community which has constantly refused to negotiate is forced to confront the issue. It seeks so to dramatize the issue that it can no longer be ignored. My citing the creation of tension as part of the work of the nonviolent-resister may sound rather shocking. But I must confess that I am not afraid of the word "tension." I have earnestly opposed violent tension, but there is a type of constructive, nonviolent tension which is necessary for growth. Just as Socrates felt that it was necessary to create a tension in the mind so that individuals could rise from the bondage of myths and half-truths to the unfettered realm of creative analysis and objective appraisal, so must we see the need for nonviolent gadflies to create the kind of tension in society that will help men rise from the dark depths of prejudice and racism to the majestic heights of understanding and brotherhood.

Perhaps the best way to learn about ethical quality is through example. You can think of other good examples and will find others in the future. If you believe that ethical quality can be learned, if you believe that it exists, and if you search hard enough for it, plenty of evidence is available.

Exercise

1. Look again at the essay on handguns in Chapter 9. What means does Morrow use in trying to persuade his audience?
2. Bring to class some other examples of a writer using the ethical means of argument, showing that, given another way of understanding, the audience would be willing to see the truth in new ways.

The Successful Interview

Walking confidently into the reception area of the small business forms company, Ray Calvin announced who he was to the receptionist. "Ray Calvin," he said with a large smile. "I have an appointment with Mr. Starnes."

The receptionist returned his smile and replied, "Please have a seat. I'll call him." The receptionist approved of Ray Calvin. His expensive three-piece, pin-striped suit made him the most professional (and most interesting) man to pass her desk in a week.

Ralph Starnes, head of the small company, came into the reception area. His first impression of the man sitting there was of a friendly, confident young man who knew how to dress for an interview. "Ralph Starnes." The two shook hands. "Please come into my office."

"I'm very impressed with what I have read in your resume. You've been working for Apollo Printing. That's a big company. Why are you interested in joining such a small company as ours?"

With that, the interview began. Ray Calvin made a good impression on Starnes, the receptionist, the secretary—everyone. He was hired one week later. One month later Ralph Starnes fired Ray Calvin. He wasn't at all qualified for the sales job he had been hired to do.

A similar situation had happened twice before for different positions in the company. Ralph was beginning to doubt his ability to interview. He had worked hard to get where he was. He thought his experience with people had enabled him to recognize a good applicant when he saw one, but maybe it hadn't.

A few days after the firing of Ray Calvin, you and Ralph have lunch together. You work as a personnel director for a small agency and have been Ralph's friend for several years. In the course of the conversation, Ralph mentions that he just can't seem to conduct an interview that identifies good candidates for job openings. You and he chat for a while about how difficult interviewing is, and you say that you believe that there is an art to good interviewing.

As you start to leave the restaurant, Ralph asks a favor of

you: Would you be willing to sit in on an interview he is conducting next week and analyze what he is doing wrong? You agree, and the two of you set a time.

On Friday morning you arrive at Ralph's office about ten minutes before the new candidate for the sales position, Alice Adams, is to arrive. After the receptionist notifies Ralph that the applicant is there, Ralph goes out and shows her into the office. Ralph introduces you by name and lets Alice assume you have something to do with the company. She is twenty-eight, attractive, and conservatively dressed. As a matter of fact, you observe, she is more than attractive—she is beautiful. Ralph introduces you, and the interview begins.

STARNES: You have an impressive resume, Ms. Adams. You seem to have a good job at Quick Office Forms. Why are you changing jobs?

ADAMS: Well, I do have a good job there, and I'm very comfortable with my duties. But, you see, that's part of the problem. Because Quick is such a large company, it takes a long time there for your talents and hard work to pay off in job growth. I like challenges and working my way to the top. I think I can grow faster in a smaller company like yours.

STARNES: Well, there's certainly room for growth here. It's true that we're a small company, but I'm thinking big. This town is ready for another large business forms company, and I plan for us to be the one. I need someone who is progressive and innovative in her thinking. We've got to be better than the competition. We've got to show major companies that our business forms achieve the results they are looking for—and for a better price. I want someone who is aggressive—who is not afraid to go out and sign up some new customers. Do you think you could handle that?

ADAMS: Yes, I could. I really like that kind of challenge. When I saw your ad in the paper, I said, "That's the kind of job for me."

STARNES: Here's a brochure about what we've got available and a portfolio of some of the business forms we're proudest of that you might like to look at. (For the next five minutes Starnes and Adams look over the material. Adams is very enthusiastic about what she sees. Starnes is obviously flattered by her remarks. You've seen that look on his face before when a pretty woman walks into the room!)

ADAMS: You really have an impressive company.

STARNES: (Practically glowing) What do you do in your present job?

ADAMS: I handle the accounts in the southern part of town. We've got some big ones, too. Since I've been with the company, business is up 30%.

STARNES: (Visibly impressed) Good ! Who do you handle?

ADAMS: I handle Myers, Stanley, ABC . . .

STARNES: Those are the big ones. I need someone who can land the accounts of the big guys.

ADAMS: That's me.

STARNES: Is there anything else about our company you'd like to know?

ADAMS: You have a great reputation in town. I like that.

STARNES: What are some of your outside interests?

ADAMS: I like to run. Are you a runner?

STARNES: I never miss a day. (For the next ten minutes they talk about the benefits of running, the best kind of shoes, etc.)

STARNES: I've thoroughly enjoyed getting to know you. I think you may be just the kind of person I'm looking for. I'll be in touch.

As Alice Adams leaves, you make a mental note that you are impressed with her looks and personality, but that you know almost nothing about her abilities. You tell Starnes that you would like to take some time to analyze the interview. You will send him an analysis the day after. As you are leaving, Starnes calls out, "I was really impressed with her. I just may hire her."

Assignment 1
Write an analysis of the job interview that you have just observed, and make some suggestions to Starnes about interviewing techniques.

For class discussion
1. How specific were Starnes' questions? Which questions should have been more specific?
2. What questions did he fail to ask?
3. Did Adams deliberately evade any of Starnes' questions?
4. What persona should you adopt in writing your analysis?

Assignment 2
Just before the interview with Adams began, you asked Starnes to let you see a complete job description. He didn't have one. One of the things you know Starnes should be doing is writing a detailed job description before interviewing. The description would be given to candidates and would help

clarify the company's needs in his own mind. You suggest this to him, and he asks you to write one for him to use as a sample. Although you usually get paid for this kind of work, you don't mind doing it for a friend. Besides, maybe he'll give you a discount on office forms. Based upon what Starnes said he was looking for in the job interview and upon the following information Starnes provides you, write the job description.

> Position: Sales, business forms
> Qualifications: Experience in sales, preferably of paper-related products. Some knowledge of printing. Some minimal training will be provided.
> Salary: $18,000. Good retirement benefits.

For class discussion
1. What information should be included?
2. What requirements should be emphasized the most?
3. What image do you want to convey of Starnes' company? What persona would best convey this image?

Johnny Clifton

As you turned to leave your patient Mr. Thompson, you said "Good morning" to the small boy with intense, black eyes in the next bed. You were sure you noticed a flicker of recognition. Having only been at the hospital two weeks, you already know a great deal about nine-year-old Johnny Clifton. The other nurses said that Johnny was completely unresponsive. He had been severely brain-damaged in a car accident the year before, and he had not responded to any kind of physical treatment. Johnny was, in lay terms, a "vegetable." Noting, however, that flicker of recognition, you wondered why he was not receiving any program of mental stimulation.

One day while you were taking Mr. Thompson's temperature and Johnny was staring at you curiously, Dave Brown, one of the other nurses, came in to check on Johnny. You noticed that Johnny's eyes immediately became cold, and he transferred his stare to the corner of the room until Dave was gone. Your curiosity was aroused. This child definitely was *not* unresponsive.

Each day, thereafter, you made it a point to talk to Johnny as you came into the room. You worked out a system so that he could respond to you. Asking him to smile for "yes" and to frown for "no," you helped him manipulate his face into those positions. Soon with much effort, he responded with the signals on his own. Excited, you continued to widen the range of responses you could elicit from Johnny, and he pleased you by learning them quickly.

Trying to find something new each day to talk to Johnny about, you began to talk about some of the nurses that took care of Johnny. To your amazement, Johnny responded to their names with the signals for yes and no. To three names, in particular, Johnny's frown was quite apparent. You were surprised because these three were all efficient, caring, and concerned.

For the next several days, you made a special effort to observe the three nurses as they worked with Johnny. The thing that all three had in common was that they never talked to him. They did everything necessary for his physical comfort, but they did, in fact, treat him like a "vegetable."

You feel you have to do something to help these other nurses realize that Johnny *is* responsive. But you have a diplomatic problem. All three have been nurses in the hospital for several years, and you are brand new. All three are older and more experienced. All three pride themselves on the excellent care that they give to patients. Yet if you don't do something to bring his responses to their attention, Johnny might never be helped to develop to his fullest potential.

Assignment 1

You have decided that since Johnny is not your patient, a letter to your supervisor would be inappropriate as would be a report of your work to go in Johnny's file. You decide finally to talk the matter over with one of the more experienced nurses. She suggests that you write a report to Johnny's doctor. Write the report.

For class discussion

1. How will you describe your admittedly unscientific and unauthorized work with Johnny?
2. What tone will avoid any implication that the other nurses have not been doing their jobs?

Q and A

Ann Spain, the director of Student Life for the past four years at your college, has recently announced that she will be leaving at the end of the year to assume the same duties at a large southern university. You are a reporter for the *Daily Campus,* your school newspaper, and you have been asked by the news editor to interview Spain for Friday's issue. Your news editor hands you the following precis of information to be covered:

Spain is one of the few Black educators on campus, and she is also a woman. Find out if either of these facts has had any bearing on her leaving and also what she thinks about the local Affirmative Action program.

The university at large sees Spain's strengths and accomplishments as being her implementation of leadership workshops, programs for disabled students, and transfer orientation programs. See if she would list the same accomplishments and if she feels there are others.

The major incident concerning the Student Life office in Spain's term involved a student who was accidentally run over by a car driven by some drunk students at a fraternity party. Spain launched a massive campaign after that incident against alcohol abuse on campus. Get her perspective on the incident and find out how successful she thinks the campaign has been.

What are her plans for the new job?

You arrange for the interview with Spain, and she agrees to give you thirty minutes on Tuesday afternoon. When you arrive, your first impression is of a tall woman, about forty, and well-groomed. She also has the strongest, most compelling eyes you think you have ever seen. They are one of the first things about her you notice. She looks at you directly, and you sense complete honesty. At first you are somewhat embarrassed because she looks so tired; it's the end of a long day. You say you're sorry to impose upon her busy schedule. She smiles, visibly shakes off her tiredness, and tells you that she considers keeping the public informed one of her most important duties. You immediately feel more comfortable and ask her if she minds if you tape the interview. She consents.

After what you consider to be a successful interview, you return to your room and hurriedly transcribe the interview while it is still fresh in your mind. As you make the transcription, you jot down notes in the margin about other details you want to remember. Your transcription then looks like this:

Q: What is your opinion of the University's Affirmative Action Program?

A: Frankly, it's a joke. Oh sure, there are the token women and minority professors and administrators, but the program is moving backward instead of going forward. Did you know that there are fewer Blacks in full professorships and in administrative positions now than there were in 1973? The whole thing is disgraceful. *What a stupid first question! You've set her off on the wrong foot. What's she so mad about?*

Visible anger. Eyes flashing.

Q: Has this been a factor in your leaving?

A: Well, I have to admit it has played a part. *Calmer* But I will say that those Blacks who are on campus are very supportive of each other. To make matters worse, though, there is no real minority support in the surrounding community. There are times when I've felt very alone. But, I was brought here to do a job, and I believe that I've done it well. Let's talk about that. *Much calmer. Impatient to get on to other matters. She strikes a person as highly intelligent.*

Some evident pain. almost a vengeful tone.

Q: Sure. What is your overall idea of the function of a Student Life office?

A: A Student Life office ought to be thought of as a place for the enrichment of the lives of the students—not just a place to go when you've got a problem. It ought to make available to students an avenue for involvement and personal development.

Q: What changes have been made in the activities of the office since you've been here? Which ones do you consider most important?

A: Well, one of the programs I'm especially *almo* proud of is the disabled student program. I bet *swell* you didn't know that disabled students make *with* up 18 percent of the student body population. Before I came, nobody had given any thought *pride* to their needs. Our office has made a strong effort to see that access is provided to all buildings and activities. The blind facilities at the library have been expanded with more study rooms and more readers available. Let's see, another thing we've done is to introduce orientation programs for transfer students to help their adjustment to campus. In the past we only had orientation for beginning freshmen. I've had lots of positive comments about this program. A study we did last year shows more transfer students are staying here to finish their degrees than ever before.

Q: What about the . . .

again, the impatience with me.

A: Oh wait, before I forget, I also instituted student leadership workshops in the fall for all new appointed and elected campus leaders. Since then the program council has balanced its budget for the first time in five years. We have a more active student senate, and more students apply for leadership positions every year. But, pardon me, you were about to ask . . . ?

Q: What about the student with a problem— how does he or she get help?

A: We have a policy of "Drop in any time." No problem's too large, or too small.

Q: How well does that policy work? How many students with problems come in, on the average?

A: I help some twenty students a week. My secretary talks to and helps another ten or fifteen with problems that she can handle.

Q: There was the incident two years ago of a student getting run over by a couple of drunk students. After that you launched a campaign against alcohol abuse. How successful has that campaign been? *Fidgeting, uncomfortable.*

A: That incident was a real challenge for me, but there have been many such challenges during my service here that received far less publicity. I think you media people overplayed *Visible irritation.* that one. Anyway, yes it was a tragic occurrence. I felt determined that it wasn't going to happen again if I could help it. In our campaign we tried to get speakers from fraternities and sororities and other student organizations to make a stand against excessive drinking. We got the campus paper, your paper, to publicize the statistics concerning alcohol abuse on campus. I guess students will always be students, and I know there is still widespread heavy drinking, but at least there haven't been any more major incidents since then.

Obviously still pain left.

Q: How do you feel about leaving?

A: I do owe a debt to this university, and although I was very negative at the beginning of the interview, I have enjoyed my associations here. I think I've grown both professionally and personally. There are some people here I'll really miss—especially the students. *Honesty – her humility is genuine.*

Q: What are your plans for your new job?

A: I don't have any right now. It will be a huge job. I don't want to make any plans until I see the situation there first hand. My training and growth here have made that job possible.

Assignment 1

Because you were so impressed with Ann Spain, you decide to

capture the engaging quality of that interview in the story for the paper. Write the article about Ann Spain for publication.

For class discussion
1. What kind of detail could personalize the interview?
2. You, the reporter, want to bring your response to Ann Spain into the story. What should be your attitude toward the reader? How much of your response can you include and still keep the focus of the story on its subject, Ann Spain?
3. How do you feel about Ann Spain, both positive and negative feelings? Why do you feel this way?
4. How do you feel about women administrators? Black administrators? How do you think you *should* feel?

Assignment 2
Conduct an interview with a person on your own campus whom you find interesting. Write the interview in such a way that you capture the spirit of the interview and your own reaction to the person.

CHAPTER **11**

RESEARCHING A CASE

After you have read this chapter, you should be able to:

find information in available resources to aid in your cases;

take systematic and complete notes from your sources;

provide appropriate documentation in your writing to acknowledge the information from your sources.

In a number of cases, you have been asked to find information in other sources. You went to the library for information, interviewed other people, and made use of readily available resources. In other cases, too, you wondered what others had said about your topic. By this time, research is not new to you, and the researched case will be an extension of some things that you already know how to do. For years the research paper has been the bane of college students in the second semester of their freshman year. My own particular experience with the research paper resulted in "The Art of Bullfighting: Pros and Cons." Not especially inspiring, I know.

Doing the research for that paper worked me right out of a love for bullfighting and into an abhorrence of its violence. But I had the same fears all freshmen have. Where in the world do all those note cards come from? How will I avoid plagiarism? How many quotes are too many?

What I didn't seem to understand as I wrote my research

paper is that documentation of the sources you use as you write is not for the purpose of checking up on you. Instead, documentation makes it possible for your reader to retrace your steps and to have access to the same information that you used as you wrote the paper. An interested reader sometimes wants to pursue your subject in a fuller way than you have provided in your paper. Your footnotes and bibliography make it possible for the reader to do that.

If you think about research as being something that you have already been doing, then the researched case will be a natural step for you to take. Some of the pressure will be off for writing *the research paper!*

The case that follows this chapter asks you to make use of the information provided in this chapter about doing research.

The Comprehensive Bibliography

A starting place for almost any topic that you research is the reference room of your library, in general, and the shelves of encyclopedias, in particular. Read an article that talks about your subject in the encyclopedia. Beginning with an encyclopedia article provides you with two kinds of information. First, you will have a broad overview of your subject and the current information about it, and second, you may also find a bibliography containing the names of books about your subject that will give you a starting place.

Next go to the *card catalog*, an alphabetical card index of what is contained in your library. In card catalogs of most libraries, books are listed in three ways—by subject, by title, and by author. Libraries usually use the cards issued by the Library of Congress.

Knowing how to read the information found on the catalog card will save you time. An *author card* has the author's name appearing on the first line of the card. A book with more than one author will have cards under each of the authors' names. A *title card* will have the title of the book typed at the top of the card. A *subject card* will have assigned subject designations called Subject Headings typed at the top of the card. All three kinds of cards are filed alphabetically in the catalog, author's cards by last names, title cards by the first word of the title (excluding *the*, and *a* or *an*), and subject cards by the first word of the subject. Most libraries use the Library of Congress subject headings, and a two-volume book listing the subject headings can usually be found near the card catalog.

On the library card, you will find two kinds of information—a call number that helps you locate a specific book and bibliographic and descriptive information about the book. On the following page is an example of the different parts of the catalog card and a description of the information provided.

In addition to books on your topic, you will also want to consult periodicals for articles. A periodical is a publication issued on a continuous, regular basis (weekly, monthly, annually). Periodicals range from popular, general interest magazines to scholarly journals. To find periodical articles on your subject, consult *periodical indexes*. Periodical indexes list articles by subject and sometimes by author and note the issue of a periodical in which the article can be found.

The general index to popular magazines is the *Readers' Guide to Periodical Literature*. The *Readers' Guide* indexes the articles in over 160 general interest periodicals published in the United States since 1900.

The following are other *specialized periodical indexes:*

Applied Science and Technology Index. 1913 to date. Subject index to periodicals in aeronautics, chemistry, earth sciences, engineering, physics, and related subjects.

Art Index. 1930 to date. Author/subject index to periodicals in archaeology, architecture, art history, fine arts, and related subjects.

Bibliographic Index: A Cumulative Bibliography of Bibliographies. 1938 to date.

Biography Index: A Cumulative Index to Biographical Material in Books and Magazines. 1946/47 to date.

Business Periodicals Index. 1913 to date. A subject index to business and economics journals.

Education Index. 1929 to date. Author/subject index to education journals.

Humanities Index. 1974 to date. Author/subject index to scholarly periodicals dealing with archaeology and classical studies, area studies, folklore, history, language and litera-

The Call Number—serves as a
key to locating the book in the
library.

The Author—provides author's
name and sometimes birthdate.

Title—gives title of the book as it
appears on the title page.

Publication information—place
of publication, publisher, and
date of publication.

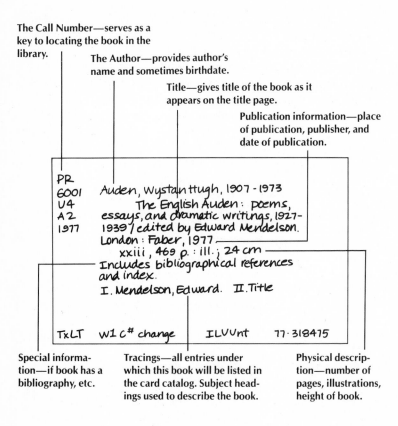

PR
6001
U4
A2
1977

Auden, Wystan Hugh, 1907 - 1973
    The English Auden : poems,
essays, and dramatic writings, 1927-
1939 / edited by Edward Mendelson.
London : Faber, 1977
    xxiii, 469 p. : ill. ; 24 cm
Includes bibliographical references
and index.
I. Mendelson, Edward.   II. Title

TxLT   W1 c# change   ILVUnt   77·318415

Special informa-
tion—if book has a
bibliography, etc.

Tracings—all entries under
which this book will be listed in
the card catalog. Subject headings used to describe the book.

Physical descrip-
tion—number of
pages, illustrations,
height of book.

ture, literary and political criticism, performing arts, philosophy, religion, and related subjects.

Modern Language Association of America. *International Bibliography of Books and Articles on the Modern Languages and Literatures.* 1921/22 to date. Index to scholarly periodicals dealing with literature, languages, linguistics, and literary theory.

Public Affairs Information Service Bulletin. 1915 to date. Articles relating to economic and social conditions, public administration, and international relations.

Social Sciences Index. 1974 to date. Author/subject index to periodicals in anthropology, sociology, psychology, and related fields.

For additional indexes, look in the card catalog under your subject for "Periodicals—Indexes."

Other sources that may be of use to you are as follows:
Newspapers

New York Times Index. 1913 to date.

Index to the Times. (London). 1907 to date.

Wall Street Journal Index. 1958 to date.

Washington Post Index. 1972 to date.

Contemporary Authors. 1962 to date. Biographical information on current authors.

Who's Who in America. Standard biographical entries on living Americans. Deceased persons are listed in *Who Was Who in America.*

Book Review Digest. 1905 to date. Short evaluative critiques.

Monthly Catalog of U.S. Government Publications. 1895 to date. Subject index to U.S. government publications.

As you find sources that may be of use to you, begin compiling a working, or comprehensive bibliography. You may include items in this list that you will not use later. Note cards are handy for this bibliography because if you put a single reference on a card, you can later discard the cards that are not useful to you. You should put the information on these cards in the same order that you will later use for your bibliography. Put the author's last name first, followed by his or her first name, and a period. Next put the title of the book, underline it, and place a period after it. Then comes the place of publication, followed by a colon. After the colon, put the name of the publisher, a comma, and the date of publication, followed by a period. Below is an example of a card for a book. Following that is an example of a card for a periodical. Notice that the form on the periodical card is the same as for a bibliography entry.

BF
175
L213

Wilden, Anthony.
The Language of the Self.
Baltimore: The Johns Hopkins
University Press, 1968.

①

Periodical

Bush, Douglas. "Polluting Our
Language." The American
Scholar, Spring 1972,
pp. 238 - 47.

⑦

Taking Notes

After you have identified what sources might be useful to you in your research, the next step is to take accurate and full notes on those sources. You should scan the book or article to see if it is, in fact, useful before you begin taking notes. After you have located useful material, take notes on 3-by-5 inch, 4-by-6 inch, or 5-by-8 inch cards. Keep your cards as consistent as possible. Provide accurate information that is clearly labeled so you won't have to return to your sources as you write the paper.

At the top of the card, put a heading that indicates a general area of information that the card includes. Using consistent headings will enable you to sort and categorize your cards after all notes have been taken. The categories can serve as a rough outline for the paper.

Under the heading place either the last name of the author of the book or article, or the call number to identify the source. Next note the page number.

On the card put notes about a single major point. List specific facts, paraphrase the words of the author, or jot down specific quotes that you might use, placing them in quotation marks. Use any shortened forms of note taking that you can devise to make your task easier.

Accurate notes will save you much time later. Even if you make copies of your sources, you will want to take notes on these sources. Taking notes helps you understand more clearly the information you are gathering. It also helps you begin to put ideas into your own words. If you just mark relevant passages on the copies instead of taking notes, you may find yourself simply stringing these passages together in your final paper, making only a few wording changes here and there. The result is a disjointed paper that contains many other people's ideas and none of your own. And despite the wording changes, such a paper is an instance of plagiarism.

Making an Outline

Because of the length of the usual research paper, you need to outline what you plan to do in order to manage so much material. A rough outline at this point will give you a guide to follow as you write your paper. If you stack your cards according to subject heading and then arrange those stacks in a logical order for the development of the information that you have, the stacks can provide a guide for your outline. You should follow standard outline form:

I. Primary idea
   A. Idea developing I
      1. Idea developing A
      2. Idea developing A
      3. Idea developing A
   B. Idea developing I
II. Second primary idea

This form should continue in the same fashion for as much information as you have.

As you write, keep your notecards and outline nearby, changing your outline whenever necessary as the paper develops.

Documentation

As you write, you should give credit to every source from which you have taken original information. If information is common property, you do not have to footnote it. But you must use footnotes after direct quotations and after statements of fact or opinion taken from sources and expressed in your words.

In the text after the part that needs to be documented, place a number slightly above the line. (Example: [1]) This number will be the same as the number beside the appropriate footnote at the bottom of the page or on a page at the end of the paper. The following form is used for footnotes.

Sample Footnotes—Books
A book with a single author

[1] George Henry Lewes, <u>The Life of Goethe</u> (New York: Ungar, 1965),
p. 28.

[2] <u>The Life of Goethe</u> (New York: Ungar, 1965), p. 73.

Use the second form if the author's full name is given in the text.

[3] Lewes, pp. 329-33.

Use this form for additional footnotes from the same book.

A modern reprint of an older edition

[4] Charlotte Mary Yonge, <u>The Heir of Redclyffe</u> (1853; rpt. New
York: Garland Pub., 1975), p. 348.

A book by two or more authors

[5] Charles F. Marden and Gladys Meyer, <u>Minorities in American
Society</u>, 4th ed. (New York: Van Nostrand, 1973), p. 92.

[6] Adolph Matz, Othel J. Curry, and George W. Frank, <u>Cost Accounting; Management's Operational Tool for Planning, Control and Analysis</u>,
3rd ed. (Cincinnati: Southwestern, 1962), p. 458.

A work in several volumes

[7] Gustavus A. Eisen, <u>Portraits of Washington</u> (New York: Robert
Hamilton and Assoc., 1932), I, 39.

A work in a series

[8] M.A.K. Halliday, "Descriptive Linguistics in Literary Study,"
<u>English Studies Today</u>, 3rd series, ed. G.I. Duthie (Edinburgh Universi-
ty Press, 1964), pp. 25-39.

A work in a Festschrift or a collection

[9] Thornton S. Graves, "Jonson in the Jest Books," in <u>The Manly
Anniversary Studies in Language and Literature</u> (Chicago: The University
of Chicago Press, 1923), 127-39.

A corporate author

[10] <u>Timber Resources for America's Future</u>, Forest Resource Report No. 14 (Washington D.C.: Forest Service, 1958), p. 43.

An anonymous (reference) work

[11] <u>Dictionary of Occupational Titles</u>, 4th ed. (Washington, D.C.: U.S. Department of Labor, 1980), p. 155.

An edition

[12] William Shakespeare, <u>Twelfth Night; or, What You Will</u>, ed. Morton Luce, 4th ed., rev. (London: Methuen, 1929), p. 27.

A translation

[13] Garcilaso de la Vega, el Inca, <u>Royal Commentaries of the Incas, and General History of Peru</u>, trans. Harold V. Livermore (Austin: University of Texas Press, 1966), p. 18.

Sample Footnotes—Articles

An article in a journal with continuous pagination throughout the annual volume

[14] Richard Liu and Loren Jung, "The Commuter Student and Student Satisfaction," <u>Research in Higher Education</u>, 12 (1980), 215-26.

[15] Liu and Jung, p. 217.

An article from a journal which pages each issue separately

[16] Ruth Silverman, "Communal Education: The Society of Brothers," <u>Young Children</u>, 35, No. 5 (1980), 15-19.

A piece from a weekly magazine

[17] Lance Morrow, "In Texas: The Uses of Yesterday," <u>Time</u>, 20 Oct. 1980, pp. 6-8.

A piece from a monthly magazine

[18] William Tucker, "The Wreck of the Auto Industry," <u>Harper's</u>, Nov. 1980, p. 45.

A piece from a daily newspaper

[19] John Koten, "Chrysler, Considering Further Cutbacks, Is Using a New Tough Standard to Decide," <u>The Wall Street Journal</u>, 27 Oct. 1980, p. 19, cols. 2-3.

An editorial

[20] Stephen Judy, "Editor's Page," <u>The English Journal</u>, 69, No. 5 (1980), p. 5.

An anonymous article

[21] "The Case for an Undervalued Stock Market," <u>Business Week</u>, 3 Nov. 1980, 95-96.

A letter to the editor

[22] Bernie Zilbergeld, "Letters," <u>Psychology Today</u>, 14, No. 6 (1980), p. 8.

A signed review

[23] Peter K. Manning, rev. of <u>Tropics of Discourse: Essays in Cultural Criticism</u>, by Hayden White, Contemporary Sociology, 9 (1980), 670-72.

Writing the Paper

Your next step will be to write the paper. Using your outline and notecards, pull together a rough draft. Paraphrase (restate or summarize) as much of the material from your sources as possible. When you do use a direct quotation, integrate it into the text of your paper. One way is to briefly explain the author's point, followed by a colon, and then the quote:

Hall believes that language is poorly suited to describe culture: "It is too linear, not comprehensive enough, too slow, too limited, too constrained, too unnatural, too much a product of its own evolution, and too artificial."[3]

Another way to integrate a quote is to write a sentence that the quote fits into:

Charles Goren argues that your opening bid in a bridge hand is "the first step in a campaign."[4]

As you write your first draft and after you finish it, read it over and make necessary revisions in wording, sentence structure, and organization. You may want to add new ideas and delete ideas that seem irrelevant. Finally, make your final draft and proofread it carefully, checking your spelling and punctuation.

The Bibliography

Your paper will be followed by a bibliography of the sources used in its writing. The form for a bibliography differs from the form for footnotes. A sample bibliography form follows, using the same sources as the sample footnotes.

Bibliography Form for Books

All entries should appear in alphabetical order by the author's last name. If the author is unknown, use the first significant word of the title.

A book with a single author

Lewes, George Henry. The Life of Goethe. New York: Ungar, 1965.

A modern reprint of an older edition

Yonge, Charlotte Mary. The Heir of Redclyffe. 1853; rpt. New York:

Garland Publishers, 1975.

A book by two or more authors

Marden, Charles F. and Gladys Meyer. Minorities in American Society.

4th ed. New York: Van Nostrand, 1973.

Matz, Adolph, Athel J. Curry, and George W. Frank. <u>Cost Accounting;</u>
<u>Management's Operational Tool for Planning, Control, and Analysis.</u>
3rd ed. Cincinnati: Southwestern, 1962.

A work in several volumes

Eisen, Gustavus A. <u>Portraits of Washington</u>. 5 vols. New York: Robert
Hamilton and Associates, 1932.

A work in a series

Halliday, M.A.K. "Descriptive Linguistics in Literary Study." <u>English</u>
<u>Studies Today</u>. 3rd series. ed., G.I. Duthie. Edinburgh:
Edinburgh University Press, 1964.

Anonymous reference work

<u>Dictionary of Occupational Titles</u>. 4th ed. Washington, D.C.: U.S.
Department of Labor, 1980.

Bibliography Form for Articles

Again, these should be listed in the bibliography in alphabetical order.

Article in a magazine

Morrow, Lance. "In Texas: The Uses of Yesterday." <u>Time</u>, 20 Oct. 1980,
pp. 6–8.

Anonymous article

"The Case for an Undervalued Stock Market." <u>Business Week</u>, 3 Nov.
1980, pp. 95–96.

Scholarly journal

Liu, Richard and Loren Jung. "The Commuter Student and Student Satisfaction." <u>Research in Higher Education</u>, 12 (1980), 215–26.

Newspaper article

Koten, John. "Chrysler, Considering Further Cutbacks, Is Using a New
Tough Standard to Decide." <u>The Wall Street Journal</u>, 27 Oct. 1980,
p. 19.

Foretelling the Future

As an employee of the Publications branch of the United States Department of Labor, you are involved in the preparation of a series of small pamphlets called *Looking to the Future*. The pamphlets are designed to help people make better career choices by acquainting them with the directions likely to be taken in the future in those careers. Some of the pamphlets are quite specific, such as "The Future in College Teaching." Others are much more general, such as "The Future of Broadcast Journalism." All of the pamphlets describe the present state of the field they are exploring, what can be expected in the immediate future, and a projection of the field ten to twenty years from now.

Assignment

You are in charge of one of the pamphlets. The information is your only concern. Someone else will do the design and layout. Choose an area that you would like to explore. It can be your own particular career choice, it can be another career that you are interested in, or it can be a more general area like home computers, farming the sea, space-mining, or television. Use your library and any other resources available to you such as interviews and brochures of companies to find out as much as you can about what is being predicted for both the immediate and long-range future for that area. If you choose a career option, explore what sorts of jobs will be possible in that area both in the next few years and in ten or twenty years from now.

If you choose a more general field, be sure to limit your topic so that you can handle it. For example, "Television of the Future" would be too large an area to cover in your pamphlet, but "Two-Way Cable Television for the Future" would not be too broad.

For class discussion

1. Other than your library, what sources of information might help you research your subject?
2. Who will the audience be for your pamphlet? What do they already know about the subject?
3. What is your purpose in the pamphlet?
4. What persona will be most appropriate for your audience and your purpose?

✧ MORE CASES

Rescuing the Past

You have always been interested in history, devouring history books when you were a kid and sitting for hours listening to the stories your grandmother told about when she was a little girl. You still remember the sketchy outlines of those stories, but you wish time and again you had been old enough to realize the importance of writing them down in all their fascinating detail.

In college you majored in business and never really had time for more than the required courses in history, but you never lost your interest. In fact, last winter you spent most of your evenings in the library researching your family history. Afterwards, you wrote up the history, mimeographed it for all the members of your family and sent it to them. They were delighted.

During the time that you worked in the library, you met a number of other people in the town who were interested in local history, and they encouraged you to join the Society for the Preservation of Local History. You have been a member for about a year now, and this will be your first year to participate in the Society's annual project.

In an effort to recover as much of the history of the area as possible, the Society members annually publish a monograph featuring oral histories told by older citizens and written up by the members. Each member is responsible for one oral history. This will give you a chance to do what you wish you had done as a child—record for the future those wonderful stories from the past.

Assignment 1
Choose an older person from whom you wish to obtain an oral history. Attempt to draw from that person a life story with

details, anecdotes, and incidents from the past that will acquaint modern readers with a sense of "how things were." Your first task is to create a questionnaire or outline that will keep the interview with that person in focus and elicit the kind of information that you are seeking.

For class discussion
1. What kinds of questions should your questionnaire include?
2. How personal should your questions be?
3. What are some logical classes of questions you could use?

Assignment 2
Conduct your oral history interview using your questions. You may tape record the interview if you wish, but be sure to set the recorder up in such a way that it will not distract the person you are interviewing. You should also take notes in order to get names spelled right, and to jot down the person's reactions, gestures, and expressions. Most people who do oral history have found that note taking, rather than being distracting, lends a sense of importance to the interview.

Assignment 3
Write up your oral history for the monograph. Preface the history with an introduction about the person you interviewed.

A Far-Out Case

"Beam me up, Scotty." "The force be with you." All of the memorable one-liners from the space shows you watched as a kid keep popping into your head as you contemplate the task before you. If eight years ago someone had told you what you would be doing today, you would have laughed and suggested that they check into the nearest funny farm. But here you are, a public relations employee for one of the first commercial ventures in outer space. You work for KREEP Mining Company. KREEP is an acronym for K (potassium), Rare Earth Elements, and P (phosphorus). These elements are found on the lunar surface, which also contains high concentrations of minor and trace elements, including thorium, and uranium. The headquarters where you work is on the space station Mother Lode. Workers are moved in and out on the space shuttle.

The curious thing about the whole venture is that the old frontier spirit seems to be gone from Americans. While the Western frontier fulfilled a creative vision, Americans are now resisting adventure. The truth is that you are having difficulties securing workers for your company. Your task is to write the text for a computer announcement that will encourage workers to come from earth to work for your company.

All kinds of workers are needed—office workers, engineers, miners, communication experts, and so on. On the lunar surface, versatility is much more important than brawn because of the absence of gravity. And although the space station has artificial gravity, living on it for the customary six-month term requires some adjustments. Your company is looking for workers who can do a number of tasks well. Strength is not as important as psychological health. People who take the jobs your company offers must be independent, adventurous, adaptable, and intelligent.

Assignment

Write the text for the job announcement. This case is different from the others in that you are free to use your imagination as much as you like. You are to classify the types of jobs available, write appropriate job descriptions, and invent the advantages of space station and lunar work. Feel free to use anything you can devise, or make use of anything you've seen in space movies or read about in science fiction. Somehow you've got to rekindle the adventurous spirit of Americans!

For class discussion

1. What are some of the possible advantages and disadvantages of this work that you should consider?
2. If Americans are no longer very adventurous, what should you emphasize to help them decide to work on the moon?

College Applicant

The time has finally arrived that seemed so long in coming. You are applying to the universities and colleges that you are interested in attending. The process is tedious—wading through several pages of fill-in-the-blank questionnaires for each college. But the application form for one college is completely different. After asking the usual questions—rank in class, grade-point average, courses completed—the application contains two additional questions that are to be written about at some length.

Assignment 1
The first question is as follows: "Describe your reading habits. What do you read for information? What do you read for pleasure? What is the last book you read? Keep your answer to 200 words, or less." Write your answer to the question.

For class discussion
1. Who will be the audience for your answer?
2. Knowing that the screening committee will be looking at thousands of applications, what might you include in your answer that will set you apart from all the rest?

Assignment 2
The second question is as follows: "Do you think it is better for a student to go immediately from high school into college, or do you think it is better for the student to break for a while and get some practical experience? Explain your answer." Write your answer to the question.

For class discussion
Consider the same questions for this assignment that you did for Assignment 1.

Art Museum Docent

Shortly after moving into the community where you now live, a friend invited you to the Brewster Art Museum on a Sunday afternoon. Although you had never regularly gone to art museums before, you discovered that you really enjoyed the experience. The Brewster Museum is primarily dedicated to American art and features exhibitions of both early American and more recent art. Although you never took art or art history courses in high school or college, you have become a regular Sunday afternoon visitor.

Your friend, a member of the local arts organization, called one day and asked you if you would be interested in being a docent at the museum. She said that many of the former docents had moved away, and the museum was in need of help. At first you protested, "I don't know anything about art; I just know what I like." But she persisted, saying that most docents did not know a great deal about art when they started, and that it was an excellent opportunity to learn more about art as you help others do the same. You finally agreed. She gave you the number of the person at the museum to call, and soon you found yourself signed up to be docent once a week on Saturday afternoons.

Your actual work as a docent would not begin for two months. In the meantime, on Saturday afternoons you attended a training session that prepared you briefly on what to say about each work of art. After your actual work began, you would continue to attend an hour training session on the two Saturday mornings before a new exhibit was to begin.

The training sessions concerned the current exhibition, American Landscapes. As Saturday draws near, you want to do more than just what is expected of you. You can make the tour more interesting if you can talk in more detail about at least one of the paintings on exhibit. You decide to learn about one painting each week so that eventually you will build up your knowledge about painting and about the museum as well.

One of your favorite paintings in the exhibit is Frederic Edwin Church's *Niagara.* About this painting, you had been handed the following blurb to memorize:

> In the era of Manifest Destiny, Niagara Falls became a symbol of that natural destiny. It was perhaps painted, photographed, and described more than any other spectacle on this continent. Frederic Edwin Church's painting *Niagara,* done in 1857, was perhaps the finest painting done by an American at that time. Notice particularly the feeling of motion and the mad rush of the falls.

You see that information you could find in the library would add much to this blurb, but of course you can't ask the people to stand in front of a painting for thirty minutes while you talk about it. You do think, though, that the tour would be more interesting if you give a five-minute talk about the painting. You check with the docent supervisor and discover that he is extremely pleased with your initiative.

Assignment 1
Go to the library and find additional information on this painting. Then write a five-minute talk using the material you found. Write the talk so that it would appeal to the audience you can expect to visit the museum on a Saturday afternoon.

For class discussion
1. What can you assume about your audience's knowledge of and attitude toward the painting?
2. What information is your audience most likely to be interested in?

Assignment 2
The docent director is so impressed with the good reports he has been receiving about your tours that he asks you to take special charge of a group of elementary school students coming through the museum next Saturday. The group will range in ages from nine to twelve. Vary your talk on *Niagara* to appeal to this young group.

For class discussion
1. What information are children of this age most likely to be interested in?
2. What changes in vocabulary and tone must you make in revising your talk for the children?

Assignment 3
Research another painting that is likely to be in the current exhibit, and prepare a five-minute talk for that painting.

Pollution and the Company Image

Each day as you drive home from Bond Chemicals where you work as a bookkeeper, you notice the waste pouring from the smokestack of the company's generating plant. You have long known that the company has not updated its devices needed to reduce the pollution. Probably because the economy in your small town is not exactly booming, no one has complained before. You know, however, that your company is interested in more than just profits; Jay Bond grew up in this town, and he wants his company to be a responsible member of the community. Checking around at work, you learn that no one in your company qualifies as an expert on environmental concerns. Because you are interested in moving up in the company ranks, you see an opportunity both to help the community where you live and to bring yourself to the attention of the company's executives.

Assignment 1
Collect all the information that you can on the effects of air pollution and devices to control plant emissions.

For class discussion
What are the possible sources for this kind of information?

Assignment 2
You are reluctant to approach the company president, but you are on good terms with Robert Little, the vice-president. You decide to start by making your information available to him. Write a background report covering the information on pollution laws and solutions that your company's executives need to know.

For class discussion
1. Should you include all of the information you found?
2. What tone will be most effective to achieve your goals?

Assignment 3
Obviously you can't just send the report to the vice-president without some explanation. Write a cover letter for the report that will explain why you collected the material.

For class discussion
1. What should the tone of this letter be?
2. How can you place the emphasis on your concern for the well-being of the company and the community?

Assignment 4
Apparently a few complaints from the community have come in, and your report was timely. The vice-president liked it and made it available to the president. Your hard work is paying off even sooner than you expected. The president called you in and told you that he was creating a new position, Director of

Community Relations, and that you seem to be the logical choice. There is one thing that he wants you to do right away. He asked you to write a press release for the local paper informing the community that the company is aware of the environmental problem and will take every step to correct it. This release should reveal your company as a good citizen of the community. Write the release.

For class discussion
1. How much technical detail should you use in describing the devices the company will install?
2. How will you explain the company's inactivity concerning pollution in the past?
3. How can you describe the effects of the devices in a way that will most enhance your company's image?

Let's Hear It for Women in Sports!

You are here at the university on a basketball scholarship, and you've never regretted your choice of universities. Having played on a basketball team since seventh grade, you made the All-State basketball team and received offers from three major universities in your state. This is your second year on the varsity team, and you love it. Right now half way into the season, your team, the women's basketball team, is leading the conference and has twice as good a record as the men's team.

Last night was your best night ever. You led in the number of baskets, and your team beat the second-best team in the conference with a score of 82–66. This morning after your first period math class, you hurried to the hall and picked up a copy of the campus newspaper. Turning to the sports page, you expected to see the team's victory in headlines. Instead, you saw a headline story about some big-deal high school football player who had accepted a bid from your school. Under that was a story about what a tough break it was that Tommy Bradshaw broke his thumb in the men's basketball game the night before and would have to be out for the season. The men's team lost again, placing them next to last in the conference. There, finally, about three-fourths of the way down the page was your team's story:

WOMEN'S TEAM WINS AGAIN

The women's basketball team did it again last night, outscoring the Eagles of Midwestern State 82–66. Completely controlling the second half, they tossed in 38 points in field goals and added 13 points in free throws.

Our Bears shot a scorching 78 percent in the second half as compared to 50 percent in the first half. They also dominated the boards, taking 60 of 90 rebounds.

Standouts for the team were guard Betty McRae and forward Sue Dickey. Betty McRae scored 20 points, 16 coming in the second half. Sue Dickey scored 18 points and pulled down 11 rebounds.

On Thursday the Bears take on the Terrifying Toads of Tahoka State.

You are irate. Who is this imbecile who writes for the sports page, and why can't women's sports get adequate and equal coverage?

Even after the passage of Title IX, equalizing funds for women's sports, the media, including your campus newspaper, shortchange women's sports events. For the past two years, you've been watching the ten o'clock television news coverage on the local station, reading the local city newspaper, and reading your campus newspaper, and there have never been any major stories about women's sports on campus. You've had enough.

Assignment 1
Write a letter protesting the inadequate coverage of women's sports by the media in your community. Write the letter in such a way that you can send copies of it to both the campus newspaper and to the city newspaper. Let the fact that you are angry show.

Assignment 2
You should have written that letter a long time ago. The response is overwhelming. Your letter was printed in both newspapers and has launched an ongoing debate in the editorial pages. Some letters have come from other women

athletes applauding your speaking out. Some have been from
male athletes also supporting your position. Others have been
from local fans expressing their support for the women's
athletic program on your campus. Still others from local fans
argued that additional coverage for the women's teams would
take away space from the more important (in their opinions)
men's sports. Here are a few samples:

Dear Editor:

Hurray for the letter by Betty McRae. Finally, a woman athlete
has been brave enough to speak out, and it's about time. We
women athletes are hardly the weaker sex. Women hold long-
distance swimming records for both sexes and often defeat men in
50-mile marathons.

Right now, women are making a name for Southern State in
this conference—a better name than the men's teams are making.
Let's give them our support, and let's see some good coverage.

Sue Brown, Women's Athletic Director, Southern State

Dear Editor:

In response to the letter by Betty McRae about the need for
better coverage of women's sports, I have this to say—Phooey!
Women will never be as good in sports as men. They're always
having babies or complaining that they can't play that day because
they don't feel well.

Don't give in to all this women's lib baloney. Keep on giving us
those football stories. That's the name of the game.

Name Withheld by Request

Dear Editor:

I read with interest the letter from Betty McRae. She makes a
good point about women's sports not receiving adequate coverage, but she doesn't tell the whole story. As a member of the men's
swim team, I'd like to protest too. All we ever see in the headlines
are the stories about football and basketball and baseball. Yet, this
year the men's swim team went to the regional championship. The
football team had a losing season, and the basketball team is in the
middle of one. Who's doing more for the glory of the school?

The swim team is discriminated against in every other way,
including scholarship sizes. Let's at least make amends with
adequate media coverage.

Tom Dodson, Men's Swim Team, Southern State

Dear Editor:

To Betty McRae—it's just not true. Women's sports get all the attention they deserve. A woman's place is in the home, not on the football field, anyway.

Lois Meddle

The last letter especially annoys you, and you want to make adequate reply. You contact the city newspaper sports editor, and he agrees to let you write an article for the city paper about the coverage of women's sports.

After a couple of weeks of amassing information, you have the following notes:

No women's sports writer on either campus newspaper or city newspaper. Information comes from the women's sports information office established in the summer of 1979. Men's sports information office established in 1948. Sports information office, both men's and women's, researches its own information and calls it in to the media.

Both papers claim to print everything they get.

Week-long survey revealed that in a 6-day period in October, the city newspaper printed 4 stories about Southern State's women's sports in a total of 42 pages devoted to sports—800 column inches.

The 4 stories amounted to 20 inches of column space. Not one story about women's sports ever printed on the first page of the sports section.

Campus newspaper in the same period had 5 stories about women's sports—32 column inches. Total of 400 column inches about sports. All stories printed close to the bottom of the pages.

During same 6-day period, on 10 P.M. news on Channel 11, only 1 story about women's sports broadcast, lasting 30 seconds. On 11 P.M. news on Channels 2, 4, and 7, no news about women's sports.

Using this information, write the article for the city newspaper.

For class discussion
1. What tone and approach will be most effective in convincing readers like Lois Meddle that you're right?
2. How can you best organize and present the hard data you've collected?

Assignment 3
The director of the women's sports information department saw your article and was impressed. She calls you and asks you to come over and talk to her about ideas for improving coverage. One idea you come up with is to provide biographical releases on famous women athletes. She asks you to choose your favorite woman athlete and write a release. Research the athlete and write the release.

For class discussion
1. What information can you provide about the athlete that will catch the media's interest and induce them to use the release you've provided?
2. What attitude toward your subject should you display in order to be most effective?

Assignment 4
Write a similar biographical release on one of the players on a women's sports team at your college.

Scientific Expedition

You love to travel, you love the "great outdoors," you're interested in science, you have some time, and you are eager to do something different. All of these factors contribute to your decision to volunteer for a scientific expedition you see advertised in *Watching Our Environment.* The expedition from Valdez, Alaska, northward to Prudhoe Bay, will try to determine the impact of the trans-Alaska pipeline on the indigenous mushrooms. Since even the tiny mushroom is vital to the balance of the ecology of the arctic, the expedition will determine the reduction in mushroom growth near the pipeline and the environmental damage of construction activities. All volunteers will collect samples, record data, and test soil.

The expedition will be in June. Evening temperatures may drop as low as 25 degrees F. Because all participants will pack their own gear and hike considerable distances, the ad says volunteers have to be able to endure hardships. Part of the application involves recounting an experience you've had that shows you can handle hardships.

Assignment
Describe such an experience.

For class discussion
1. How much background information should you include in your experience?
2. Would it be appropriate to describe an experience in which you've handled mental hardship if none of your experiences have involved much physical hardship?
3. How much detail should you include?
4. Who is your audience for this piece of writing?

Potboiler

At a party last week, you and two other friends were discussing the books you had recently read, and someone mentioned the enormous amount of money Jane Trueheart had received for her latest romance—*All My Dreams, All My Desires*. None of you had read the book, but you joked for a while about the formula of all of those books—a lonely, young heroine who is good-looking, competent, and rapidly moving upward in her profession meets an older, handsome hero, head of a corporation or creative genius of the century. The heroine falls in love, spends a great deal of time vacillating between marriage and career, and finally happily leaves her profession to become his devoted wife. For some zany reason, you suggest that you and your two friends should write a romance avoiding the formula and making your heroine much more realistic. If you could manage to capture reader interest, you just might make a fortune! Both of your friends say, "Let's do it," and you all agree to meet at your house Thursday night. Each of you agrees to bring along your ideas for one aspect of the novel.

Assignment 1
You are in charge of describing the setting of the romance.

You can choose any place you like. Write your fictional description.

For class discussion
1. What is the usual setting for romances?
2. What elements should the setting contain?

Assignment 2
Unfortunately, on Tuesday night one of your friends calls and says that she is just too busy to participate. You call your other friend and both of you decide to go on with the project. The friend who backed out was in charge of the character sketch of the heroine. Since your partner is hard at work on the character of the hero and since you have completed the setting, you agree to work on the heroine. You are interested in her character because it seems that in most of these books the heroine is presented as intellectually weak and easily intimidated, and you want to change all that. Write a description of your heroine.

For class discussion
What should such a description include?

A Daily Journal

You're a new college freshman, just returned from your first encounter with registration. Collapsed on your bed in your dorm room, you tiredly flip through the fliers on campus activities that were thrust on you. One of them manages to arouse your interest—the college's alumni magazine, *This Is Your Campus,* wants an incoming freshman to keep a journal of his or her reactions during the first ten days of classes. Interested students must apply to the magazine (the application blank is on the back of the flier); the student selected will keep the journal and write it up for publication. You were a dedicated staff writer for your high school newspaper, specializing in "reaction" pieces. You decide to apply for the chance to write this journal.

With the rush of buying books, meeting new friends, and

attending mixers, you completely forgot about the project until the call came today from the editor to say that because of your high school writing experience, you have been chosen to do the journal. The editor suggests that you be as honest and candid as possible. Since alumni from across the United States will be reading the journal, you still would like some sense of what those readers are like.

One thing that your high school journalism experience taught you is that a good reporter does homework. As you think about the project ahead of you, you settle upon two questions that you really ought to answer before you start the journal: (1) What are the alumni of my college like? (2) What do they share in common with me? Answering the second question, you feel, will help you have a sympathetic ear.

To answer the first question, you call the alumni office and ask the secretary if the office has available to the public any statistics about the alumni—their present occupations, their families, and their present interests. She informs you that she has nothing concise available for your use and suggests that you write to the alumni leaders in the larger cities. Of course, you will not have time to do that, so you turn to the next source that comes to your mind—past issues of *This Is Your Campus*—to see if there is anything useful in them. On the back two pages there is a section called "News from Alumni" which gives the year of graduation and short notes about recent accomplishments of alumni. Looking down one of these lists your eye lights on these entries:

1955—Bob Roberts has recently been named president of Texas Petroleum Bank in Houston.

1960—Jack Boyd won the highest award the American Red Cross gives to a person who saves a life for his rescue of Karen Pomeroy who had fallen out of her family's motorboat. Jack and his family live in Kansas City where he is the owner of a florist shop.

1971—Bob Drake and his wife Kathy (Phillips, '73) announce the birth of a son, Joseph Andrew, April 14.

1973—The Society of Historians gave its yearly Fred Parks Award to Dr. Beth Freeman for her book, *The Ouchita Women*. Dr. Freeman is associate professor of history at Central University.

Those entries make you realize that it is impossible to define specifically the type of alumni you will address. They engage in a wide variety of occupations and interests. What you do know about them, however, is that they are educated and that they have at some time in their lives shared similar experiences to the ones that you will encounter in the next ten days.

Assignment 1
Keep the journal for ten days. Don't be selective. Get down everything. You'll have time to go through and cull what is worth saving later. Write honestly and openly about your observations of these first ten days.

Assignment 2
Delete anything from your journal that you would not wish to appear in the published version, and edit that version for publication.

For class discussion
1. What kinds of experiences would alumni be most interested in, and why?
2. What sorts of items might appear in a daily journal that probably should be edited out for such a large readership as this?
3. What sort of persona would be appropriate here? How much of your own impressions should you include?

Mike Wallace Comes to Redgrove

You and Ted Garrett are the co-chairs for the program at the annual Chamber of Commerce awards banquet at Redgrove. Each year the Chamber puts quite a bit of money into the annual banquet to bring some prestige to the town and the Chamber. Enough money is available to bring in excellent speakers. This year is no exception.

The program chair usually presents a choice for speaker to the Chamber members who make the final decision. This year you and Ted are deadlocked over who will be your choice: he wants Dianne Feinstein, important San Francisco leader, and you want Mike Wallace of *CBS News*. Since you and Ted can't reach a decision, you decide to present two choices and let the Chamber make the decision for you. You will each attempt to persuade the members that your choice is the best for speaker.

Assignment 1
Because you can't really contact Mike Wallace's staff yet to get an advance biography, you have to rely on your own resources. Of course, you can make use of what you know about *60 Minutes* and Wallace's excellent exposures of wrong-doing in business and government, but that won't be enough for your presentation. You next turn to the public library, hoping to find there at least some press clippings about Wallace. You start by asking the librarian what she would suggest, and she sends you to a shelf you weren't aware of before—a shelf of collections of biography. There in *Current Biography, 1977,* you find all the information you will need. Using the notes from *Current Biography* (provided below) prepare your presentation for the Chamber that will persuade them to invite Mike Wallace to your awards banquet.
(Note: If you prefer, you may be Ted Garrett and make the presentation for Dianne Feinstein, using the same source.)

Wallace, Mike—broadcast journalist, CBS News, 524 W. 57th St., New York City, N.Y. 10019.

Biographical information

Born May 9, 1918, Brookline, Mass. Given name: Myron Leon Wallace. Parents: Frank Wallace, wholesale grocer and later, insurance broker, and Zina Sharfman Wallace. Frank Wallace, immigrant around turn of century from Russia—name originally Wallik, mistaken for Wallace by immigration official.

Education: Brookline High School—B- average, public speaking, dramatic society, school newspaper, tennis team. 1935—enrolled at University of Michigan in Ann Arbor. Intended to become English teacher. Worked way through school: waited on tables, washed dishes, part-time work for National Youth Administration. B.A.—1939.

Marital status and family

Married Lorraine Périgord, a painter (third marriage for him).
Two sons by first marriage: Peter (killed mountain-climb-
ing in Greece, 1962) and Christopher (broadcast journalist).
Two stepchildren, Anthony and Pauline.

Career

1939—continuity writer and rip-and-read announcer for
WOOD WASH, Grand Rapids, Michigan, radio station

1940—Detroit. Narrator, announcer, and actor, radio series,
Lone Ranger and *The Green Hornet.*

1941—*Chicago Sun,* broadcaster. Acted in *The Crime Files of
Flamond.* Announced *Ma Perkins, Road of Life,* and *The Guiding
Light.*

1943—communications officer, Navy. 1946—honorable discharge, lieutenant junior grade.

1946—*Chicago Sun's* air edition broadcaster. Moderator, *Famous
Names,* quiz program. Announcer—*Curtain Time, Fact or Fiction,* and *Sky King.* Interviews from Balinese Room of the
Blackstone Hotel. Commercials for *Super Circus,* televised
children's show.

Late 40's—divorced first wife, Norma Kaphan Wallace. Married actress, Buff Cobb, 1949. Teamed up for *Mike and Buff,*
90-minute talk show from Chez Paree. CBS—moved show
to New York City, nationally televised. Ended 1954 with
their divorce.

1950's—hosted *All Around the Town, There's One in Every Family,
I'll Buy That, The Big Surprise, On a Sunday Afternoon,* and *Adventure.* Radio: *Stagestruck,* documentary series about Broadway,
and co-anchor with Margaret Truman and later, Virginia
Graham, *Weekday.*

October, 1954—Broadway debut in *Reclining Figure.*

1955—With Ted Yates, Jr., organized news department for
WABD-TV, New York, and began broadcasting nightly
news. *Night Beat*—1956, weeknightly talk show—WABD-
TV. Guests—Ethel Waters, Dame Sybil Thorndike, Will
Rogers, Jr., novelist, Philip Wylie, etc.

1957—ABC bought show—*The Mike Wallace Interview:* Gloria
Swanson; Senator Wayne Morse; racketeer, Mickey Co-
hen; and the Grand Wizard of the Ku Klux Klan.

1960—anchored Westinghouse Broadcasting Company's 1960 election coverage. Hosted *PM East-PM West*, talk show like *Tonight*. Left after few months to do script consultation and narration for David Wolper's *Biography*, public affairs series.

1963—CBS News special correspondent. *CBS Morning News with Mike Wallace*. Also anchored *CBS Mid-Day News*. *Mike Wallace at Large*, weekly radio program. Stand-up reporter on *CBS Evening News*. Questioner on *Face the Nation*.

1968—*60 Minutes*: John Mitchell, H. L. Hunt, Eldridge Cleaver, two American soldiers from My Lai incident. Recent stories: Medicaid fraud, child abuse, busing, nuclear power plants safety, Nazism, press junkets, prisoner rehabilitation.

Awards

A number of journalism awards, including:
Carr Van Anda Award, Ohio University
Alfred I. DuPont-Columbia University Award
Sigma Delta Chi's award
Handful of Emmys.

Quotes

Repeatedly insists he doesn't "pry for the sake of prying" and tries to encourage "a reasonable exchange of ideas."
Often quotes judicial opinion written by Supreme Court Justice William O. Douglas: "The function of free speech under our system of government is to invoke dispute. It may indeed best serve its high purpose when it induces a condition of unrest, creates dissatisfaction with conditions as they are, or even stirs people to anger."

For class discussion
1. How much of the above information would be relevant to your purpose?
2. How should you include personal observations in your presentation?

Assignment 2
The Chamber has decided to invite Mike Wallace this year and Dianne Feinstein next year. Wallace accepted your invitation to come, and you are to write the press release, announcing

that he will be the speaker for the Annual Awards Banquet, January 21, Grand Ballroom, Hinton Hotel. Include as much of the information that you found for your first presentation as seems necessary and useful.

For class discussion
1. What does your audience already know about Mike Wallace?
2. What information about him have you found out that they might not know and might be interested in?
3. What attitude toward your subject might you take that would attract publicity for your banquet?

Assignment 3
As co-chair of the program and as last year's recipient of the "Most Promising Young Business Person" award, you have been selected to introduce Mike Wallace at the banquet. (Ted will have his day next year.) You will be allowed five minutes. As you write your introduction, remember that the Chamber members have heard most of the biographical information before; therefore, you may want to enliven it with personal observations of the *60 Minutes* program, additional information from other articles about Mike Wallace, and additional quotes that you can find.

Movie Critic

From the time you were old enough to sit upright in a chair, you've been a movie freak. Throughout your childhood, Saturday afternoons were spent with a box of popcorn, a candy bar, your best friend Jackie, and a good movie. And you never outgrew your passion. No more than two or three major films escape you during a year. In fact, some weekends you go to as many as three movies.

Knowing your passion for films, Reverend Wilson from your church called two weeks ago and asked if you would be interested in writing a feature article on movies for your church paper each month. His idea is that while G and R ratings are easily understood, the members of the church

would like more guidance about whether they should take
their children to see the movies rated PG. He asked you to
discuss two or three movies each month, evaluating how
suitable they would be for children under twelve. You are glad
to do the article because it gives you one more reason to go to
the movies.

Assignment
Write your first article, evaluating two or three films with a
PG rating.

For class discussion
1. Who will be your audience for this writing?
2. How would you classify the article—informative? persuasive? expressive?
3. Should you give a summary of the movies you evaluate?
4. How can you define "suitable for children under twelve"?
5. What evidence should you give to support your judgment?
6. Should you state your evaluation at the beginning of the
   section on each film, or at the end, or in both places?
7. What other areas besides sex and violence ought to be
   considered in evaluating the suitability of a film for children
   under twelve?

Registration Madness

For the last three semesters you have earned some extra
money by working at the registration office. Your duties have
varied, but every time you observed the same bewildered look
on the faces of the incoming freshmen. They wander around
the registration area trying to find the proper place to go and
taking twice as long as everyone else to register. You have
witnessed some of these poor, lost souls crumple into a corner
chair and just sit for a while until they build up enough
confidence to go back out into the melee. You must have
answered the same question a hundred times, "What am I
supposed to do with all this stuff once I've gotten all the classes
I need?"

You belong to a Welcome Week committee that plans first

week activities on campus to welcome new students. This summer as the committee planned the Welcome Week activities, you made the suggestion that one really useful service your committee could provide would be to make registration easier for beginning freshmen. The committee liked your suggestion, and after some discussion decided to provide two registration services—a booth for answering questions (to be staffed by members of the Welcome Week committee) and a pamphlet of registration guidelines to be sent to new freshmen at the end of the summer.

Since the project is your idea, you, of course, have been asked to draw up the registration guidelines to be mailed out. You guess the first place to look is at what the freshmen now receive—the undergraduate catalogue. As you turn to the section called "Registration," your feelings as a bewildered freshman come back to you. You've never read a worse piece of gobbledygook anywhere. No wonder those poor freshmen have no idea what to expect! You decide to translate all that bureaucratic jargon into some human language for the freshmen. This revised information, along with some tips on how to get through registration gracefully, or at least with your sanity, will constitute the pamphlet you send out.

Assignment 1
Revise the passage about "Registration" from the undergraduate catalogue, keeping in mind that the audience to whom you are writing will be unfamiliar with many of the procedures and terms that you will be using.

Registration
A registration period commences each semester and summer term during which time a student completes the formal procedure of becoming officially enrolled in the University. This registration takes place in the Old Main Auditorium. Prior to the period of registration at the beginning of each semester or summer term, every student who has completed the appropriate admission procedures up to that point in time will be notified of the acceptance of his or her admission to the University and will be furnished with the appropriate materials which will be needed by the student during the actual registration procedures.

The aforementioned materials will include a letter from the

academic dean with instructions appropriate to the designation of the student. In addition to this letter, a packet of computer-prepared registration materials will be mailed to the permanent home address that has been provided to the registrar's office in the initial admission procedures. In this packet of materials will be found either on the Verification card or on the reverse side of the official Permit to Register the appropriate day and hour for the student to appear at Old Main to complete his or her admission procedures and to become officially enrolled in the University. Additional instructions will be provided in this packet through the office of the Registrar, and these should be examined with utmost care.

Students must take upon themselves the responsibility of arriving on campus sufficiently early to provide adequate time to confer with their departmental advisors and to receive approval by the advisor of their proposed course schedule. Freshmen will have been advised by their departmental advisors at the orientation session of their choice attended during the summer prior to enrollment in the University.

The registration packets will be mailed up until approximately three weeks prior to the day on which registration will occur. Students being accepted for admission subsequent to that time will have to take upon themselves the responsibility of obtaining registration materials in person at the Registrar's office.

The priority basis for establishing the time of a student's registration is the accumulated hours taken and passed by the student combined with the total number of grade points acquired by the student. These figures will be calculated after the spring semester and will determine the student's priority number for the following two designated fall and spring registration periods. For example, the achievement of 80 hours for credit for courses taken in conjunction with the achievement of 210 grade points will result in a combined number of 290 for registration procedures. Freshmen will be assigned a registration number on the basis of a lottery system. This system results in an equal opportunity for all incoming freshmen to receive a registration number of high priority or of low priority.

Each student will be known officially to the University through a matriculation number based upon the student's personal Social Security number. This number will be requested as the means of classifying the student's academic records during the time that the student is officially enrolled in the University and at all other times in the future. A student without a matriculation number at the time of registration will encumber the registration procedure since he or she will have to proceed from registration to the office of the Registrar in the administration building to be assigned an alternate number to be used in place of the Social Security number. It is advisable that any student who plans to register at the University should proceed immediately to the post office or Social Security office in his or her community in order to apply for a Social Security number. This procedure should be initiated at least five weeks prior to the registration date established by the University. The entire procedure takes approximately three weeks to be executed.

Upon arrival at the registration situation at the time designated on the student's Verification card or on the reverse side of the Permit to Register card, a student will present to the admissions officer the following materials: Verification card, Permit to Register, Social Security identification card, and schedule card appropriately stamped by the student's departmental advisor. Failure to present any of these materials will result in the student's being barred from admittance to the registration procedure and will result in a severe delay of the registration process both for the student and for the University.

Students should receive a class card for each course designated on their schedules. These can be obtained upon request from the sectionizer at each of the so-designated tables located throughout the registration hall. Each student is responsible for checking to see that he or she has obtained the proper class registration cards before proceeding to the final check desk in order to obtain admittance to the business office area where enrollment fees will be paid. Should a student fail to make a proper check of his or her cards and thereby secure the improper enrollment card for a particular course, he or she will be required to pay the designated cost to officially drop the inappropriate course and to add the appropriate course resulting in additional time wasted and in additional expense both on the part of the University and of the student.

Students who have received all of the appropriately designated class cards and have satisfied themselves as to the correctness of their registration to this point should proceed immediately to the check station and then to the appropriate hallway to pay tuition and fees. Students must pay their fees during the process of registration itself. Students who fail for whatever reason to pay the tuition or fees at this point in time will be cancelled from the University enrollment and will have to complete the official registration through the Registrar's office at a later time during registration week with the additional charges accrued for this special handling.

Students are responsible for correct entries on their registration materials. Mistakes are costly to the University and to the individual student.

Every student who plans to operate a vehicle while on campus must obtain the appropriate parking permit from the office of Traffic and Safety. Failure to display a valid parking permit will result in the towing of the automobile or other vehicle at the expense of the owner.

Parking permit fees may be paid at the time of registration at the designated table situated at the exit door of the registration hall.

For class discussion
1. How could this material best be organized?
2. What information needs to be stressed most?
3. How can all the details be presented in a memorable way?

Assignment 2
Now that the registration procedures are written in human language, compose an unofficial guide to registration for the new freshman that will include tips about things you wish you had known before you registered for the first time. Keep in mind that the person reading this guide will not have registered before, so use only those terms that will be familiar or give an adequate explanation for any unfamiliar terms. Also, keep in mind that this guide will be sent out from the Welcome Week committee—make the tone of the tips as warm and friendly as possible.

For class discussion
1. What do incoming freshmen need to know most?
2. How will you organize the tips?
3. How can you make the pamphlet sound warm and friendly?

Assignment 3
Look up the description of registration procedures in your college's catalogue. If you feel it could be improved, revise it, and send your revision to the office in charge of producing the

catalogue, along with a letter explaining why you're recommending the changes.

Pet Tales

As a recent graduate in advertising with a specialty in writing copy, you have been hired by your city's health department to work in the advertising office. It is hardly the job you dreamed of, but it will be good experience. Your first assignment has actually turned into a lot of fun. The department is disturbed by the large number of reports of pet abuse they have received. Since in most homes where there is a pet, there are also children, your employer has decided to conduct a campaign for better pet care aimed at those children.

First on the list is to make a film about pet care entitled "Pet Tales." A number of pet stories will be featured about live animals that have been abused and about their recoveries and new homes. The film, then, will end with some specific information concerning taking care of pets. The emphasis will be on dogs and cats.

Assignment 1
You are working on the first story about pet abuse. First, work out the details of the story. What kind of animal will be featured? What are the circumstances of the animal's abuse? What led to the animal's recovery? Use your imagination to describe the story, but work to make the story one that might have happened.

Assignment 2
Your next task is to work out the exact words that the narrator will say in the film to tell your animal abuse story. If it helps you as you write, make marginal notes about what will be happening on the screen as the narrator speaks.

For class discussion
1. What attitude should your narrator take toward the story?
2. What tone should he or she use?

Assignment 3
Before you write the script for the other dog and cat abuse stories, you decide to work on the informative section. Decide on some categories to be covered in taking care of pets. (Example: Feeding Your Dog or Cat) Make a list of the questions to be answered in each category.

Assignment 4
Choose one of your categories and do the necessary research on the topic from pamphlets, encyclopedias, dog and cat books, and any other sources you can find.

Assignment 5
Write the exact words of the narrator for the informative section of the film.

Save the Brewery!

For years now you have watched your middle-sized town participate in what you consider deplorable acts. First, the railroad station built in the middle of the last century was torn down to make room for a multi-storied downtown parking garage. Next, the two wonderful Victorian houses remaining atop Hancock Hill were torn down and replaced with an insurance building. But the latest proposal before the city planning commission seems to be the worst of all. In the central-city district (one that is rapidly declining) stands a Romanesque brewery built at the turn of the century. The sandstone central office building with high ceilings and ornate moldings is surrounded by four brick warehouses. The structures have been occupied recently by a variety of businesses ranging from auto repair to adult books. Now there is a proposal before the commission to tear down the brewery and replace it with a towering office complex. This time you are angry enough about the proposal to try to do something about it. There is to be a meeting next week of the commission, and anyone interested in or concerned about the project has been invited to speak.

Assignment 1
This case asks you to make use of everything that you have learned about writing. From your library and from any local projects of this nature, gather as much information as you can about the rehabilitation of old structures. You will need information about possible tourist interest, construction time, rehabilitation costs as compared to the costs of new structures, energy use in older buildings as compared to use in new structures, and any federal incentives that might be available for rehabilitation. Make use of one or a variety of attitudes toward your subject and your audience. Use any combination you wish of the means of persuasion: logical, emotional, ethical. Use any of the patterns of thought that seem useful as you explore your subject. Your goal is to convince the commission not to tear down the brewery. Give it all you've got!

For class discussion
1. What are the ranges of attitudes toward subject and audience that are possible in this piece of writing?
2. How could logical means be used? How could emotional means be used? How could ethical means be used?
3. What patterns of thought (classification, cause-effect, comparison, syllogistic reasoning) would be useful in writing this plea?

Assignment 2
Find a building in your own town or city that has been neglected and seems to have possibilities. Research the building's history if you can. Discover all you can about it—when it was built, who was the architect, what it has been used for in the past, and so on. Devise a possible plan for the building's rehabilitation. Write a proposal exploring the building's value and its possibilities, and send your proposal to your city's planning commission.

You Make a Case for It!

This time it's your turn. You are to write the last case in this book, and give it to one of your fellow students to work through. By now, you are an expert on cases. You have seen how they create fictional situations that approximate realistic writing circumstances. Create such a fictional situation and the writing assignments for it. Be sure you give your audience all the information they will need for doing the case—factual information and details, information about the audience for the writing, and any information you want to include about the attitude to be used. Have fun, and try to create a case that you would like to write about.

A Brief Guide to Correctness

Sometimes making correct choices in usage, punctuation, and grammar probably isn't very important. If you are writing in your diary, and you will be the only one to see that diary, it doesn't matter much if you misspell a word or forget a comma where one is normally needed. But if you intend for your writing to be read by another audience, then correct choices become very important. Correct choices permit you to communicate accurately with your reader. They permit your reader to follow your thoughts without annoying hesitations.

This guide is not intended to be complete. Instead, it is a ready reference for the most important problems you will encounter. All of the finer points of grammar can be obtained from a good handbook.

Sentence Problems

Fragments
A fragment occurs when what is punctuated as a sentence is not a complete sentence. While professional writers sometimes use fragments for special effects in their writing (see the

Thoreau passage, p. 200), unnecessary fragments should not appear in edited prose.

A fragment is often a subordinate clause without an independent clause:

> I am going to the movie Saturday night. *If I can get my work done in time.* (fragment)

> I am going to the movie Saturday night if I can get my work done in time. (correct)

A fragment may contain a verbal rather than a verb:

> The early morning fog obscured the pedestrians. *The boys standing on the corner.* (fragment)

> The early morning fog obscured the pedestrians and hid the boys standing on the corner. (correct)

Comma splice or comma fault
A comma cannot be used to link two independent clauses:

> He was my favorite teacher in high school, he was calm and patient. (incorrect)

The comma splice or comma fault can be remedied in one of three ways:

1. with a comma and a coordinate conjunction—

> He was my favorite teacher in high school, **for** he was calm and patient.

2. with a semi-colon if the two ideas are closely related—

> He was my favorite teacher in high school; he was calm and patient.

3. with end punctuation—

> He was my favorite teacher in high school. He was calm and patient.

Run-on sentences

The run-on sentence is the result of omitting punctuation between two independent clauses not joined by a conjunction.

> School had started it was the beginning of the new semester. (incorrect)

It can be remedied in one of the three ways used for the comma splice:

> School had started, and it was the beginning of the new semester.
>
> School had started; it was the beginning of the new semester.
>
> School had started. It was the beginning of the new semester.

Misplaced or ambiguous modifiers

Modifiers should refer clearly to the words they modify and placed as close to those words as possible:

> The choir was singing while I was listening in a very high key. (incorrect)
>
> The choir was singing in a very high key while I was listening.

An ambiguous modifier is one placed between two words either of which could, with sense, be modified:

> The choir that had been singing loudly left the room. (incorrect— did the choir sing loudly or leave loudly?)
>
> After the choir had been singing loudly, they left the room.
>
> The choir that had been singing left the room loudly.

Almost, only, nearly, hardly, and other adverbs should refer clearly to the words they modify:

> I only received three new books.

This sentence has two possible meanings:

> Only I received three new books.
>
> I received only three new books.

Dangling modifiers

Dangling modifiers have nothing to modify in the sentence:

> Cheering the team onward, the stadium was filled to capacity. (incorrect—there is nothing in the sentence that can cheer.)

> Cheering the team onward, the crowd filled the stadium to capacity.

Punctuation and Capitalization

End punctuation

End punctuation is the mark used at the end of a sentence—a period, question mark, or exclamation mark.

A *period* is used after a declarative sentence, an imperative sentence, or an indirect question:

> Declarative: The student put the door stop down as he left.

> Imperative: Close the door when you go out.

> Indirect question: He asked if I would help with the interviewing.

A period is also used after polite requests, particularly in business letters:

> Will you please send me a new seed catalogue.

Periods are generally used after abbreviations:

> *Dr., Mr., Ph.D.,* P.M.

A *question mark* is used after a direct question:

> Who is in charge here?

An *exclamation mark* is used after a sentence showing strong feeling:

> How beautiful!
> A car's coming!

Commas

Commas are used to mark grammatical units.

1. A comma is used to separate independent clauses when they are joined by *and, but, or, nor, for, so,* and *yet:*

> He said he was not prejudiced, but then he made a highly prejudiced remark.

2. Commas are used to separate words, phrases, and clauses in a series:

> He bought nails, screws, and washers.

> I ordered a large hamburger without onions, an order of French fries, and a chocolate shake.

> She asked me to stay, she showed me the letter, and then she began to cry.

3. A comma is used after a long introductory subordinate clause, a long introductory modifying phrase, or two or more introductory prepositional phrases:

> If I were going to be at the game, I would certainly carry an umbrella.

> Running with abandon across the sand, she stepped on a piece of glass.

4. A comma is used to separate contrasting elements:

> He was lazy, not sick.

5. A comma is used to separate two or more equivalent adjectives that modify the same noun. The test is generally to see if the sentence makes sense with *and* between the adjectives:

> She was wearing blue denim jeans. (*And* sounds strange.)

> He had on a shabby, ill-fitting overcoat.

6. Commas are used *both before and after* nonrestrictive modifiers, subordinate phrases and clauses that are not

necessary to the meaning of the term they modify, and appositives:

> The ticket money, which is the first money we have earned this year, will be used to throw a party for the club.
>
> Joseph Heller, author of *Catch-22,* will be our speaker at the creative writing convocation.

7. A comma is used to separate words in direct address:

> Will you come, Jordon?
>
> He is the one, sir, whom I think you should appoint.

8. Commas are used to set off items in dates, geographical place names, and addresses and titles after names:

> October 14, 1957, is his date of birth.
>
> Dallas, Texas, has become famous on TV recently.
>
> The boy's address is 568 Second Avenue, Jamestown, Virginia.
>
> Bill Robinson, Ph.D., is the speaker for the luncheon.

9. Commas are used to separate parenthetical elements from the rest of the sentence:

> I didn't know, however, that he is your brother.

10. A comma is used after *yes* and *no:*

> Yes, I will do it for you.

11. Commas are used to prevent the misreading of a sentence:

> However, I moved his arm, and the pain was still there.
>
> However I moved his arm, the pain was still there.

12. A comma is used to separate an independent clause from a dependent question:

> You will come to the party, won't you?

13. Commas are used to separate expressions like *he said* or *she answered* from the sentence of direct quotation:

> "I have an earache," she complained, "but I guess I'll come to class anyway." (Note that commas and periods are placed *inside* quotation marks.)

Semi-colons

Semi-colons are used sparingly, and you should know their specific purposes.

1. A semi-colon is used between two independent clauses that are closely related in thought and are not joined by a coordinate conjunction:

> Rachel rode her bicycle around the block; then she crossed the street.

2. A semi-colon is used between independent clauses joined by a coordinate conjunction when the clauses are excessively long or have internal punctuation:

> I have been to Los Angeles, California, which is perhaps one of my favorite cities in the whole world; but I don't think I'll be going back until I have a longer vacation, a hopeless dream now.

3. Use a semi-colon to separate the elements of a series if there are commas within those elements:

> This summer on vacation we went to Santa Fe, New Mexico; Tucson, Arizona; and San Francisco, California.

Colons

Colons indicate that what is to follow will explain what went before.

1. A colon is used to introduce a formal list when a complete statement precedes the colon:

> Make sure you have everything needed for the barbecue: salt, pepper, barbecue sauce, tongs, charcoal, smoker, a brisket.

2. A colon is used between two independent clauses when the second clause explains or amplifies the first:

There is only one way to pass your tests: you have to know the right answers.

3. A colon introduces a long, formal quotation, especially if the quotation contains more than one sentence:

George Eliot used an interesting description in *Adam Bede:* "He was like a cock who thought the sun had risen to hear him crow."

4. A colon is used between hours and minutes—8:30 P.M.; between chapter and verse from the Bible—Mark 2:9; and after a formal salutation in a letter—Dear Mr. President:

Dashes
1. Dashes are used to indicate a break in the thought of a sentence, to introduce an abrupt shift, or to set off elements for emphasis:

The test was too hard for the students—or, for that matter, anyone—and they all failed.

The room was filled with eerie shadows—but that story is too long to tell tonight.

2. Dashes are used to set off parenthetic elements that have internal punctuation:

The three hostesses—Allison, Margaret, and Sylvia—were filled with excitement about the party.

Quotation marks
1. Quotation marks are used to set off direct quotations:

"I can't work these math problems," Josh said, "but I'm not going to quit trying."

You should indent every time there is a change of speaker in a dialogue:

"I know you don't like the food in the cafeteria," the nutritionist told the students.
"That's putting it mildly," they replied.

Use single quotation marks for a quotation within a quotation:

"Could you believe her innocence when she asked, 'Do you have a large budget?'" the director asked the supervisor.

2. Quotation marks are used for titles of short stories, essays, articles, songs, speeches, poems, and short plays:

Her favorite poem is "Dover Beach."

3. Commas and periods are always placed inside quotation marks. Semi-colons and colons are placed outside. If a question mark or an exclamation mark applies to the quoted material, it should be inside the quotation marks; if it applies to the whole sentence it should be outside:

"I am eager to be on my way," she replied, "since this is the start of a brand new career."

I know he liked the poem "Stopping by Woods on a Snowy Evening."

We asked, "May we bring our own tape recorders?"

Did you reply, "Of course, you may"?

Parentheses
Parentheses are used to enclose incidental remarks, additional details or examples, and figures used in enumeration:

I was confused (perhaps I should say I was terrified), and I left the movie before its end.

The convention (March 3-6) will be held in New York City.

I see the problems with the apartment as (1) high electrical bills, (2) inadequate air conditioning, and (3) torn carpets.

Brackets
Brackets are used to enclose an insertion into quoted material when that insertion did not appear in the original.

"Thousands of Japanese lost their homes in this tragic event from our history [the Japanese internment in World War II]."

Ellipses

An ellipsis is a mark of three spaced periods indicating that something has been omitted from quoted material. If the omitted material comes at the end of a sentence, the end period is retained and is followed by three additional periods:

> At first he determined to fling himself heart and soul into his work ... then he saw how great an influence women exert in social life, and suddenly made up his mind to go out into this world to seek a protectress there.—Balzac, *Pére Goriot*

Italics

In printed works words are emphasized by italics, slanted type. To indicate italics when writing or typing, underline the words.

1. Italics are used for emphasis:

> I *can* get the book finished by the deadline.

2. Italics are used for names of newspapers, books, and magazines:

> *Pamela* is a book filled with letters written by Pamela herself.

3. Italics are used for foreign words:

> She asked the gentleman what *hoy* meant in Spanish.

4. Italics are used for words used as words:

> You have too many *but*'s in that sentence.

Capitalization

1. The first word of a sentence, of a direct quotation, or of a line of poetry (except in some modern poetry) is capitalized:

> My apartment is unbearably hot today.

> The woman asked, "Did you see my glasses?"

> It was many and many a year ago,
> In a kingdom by the sea,

That a maiden there lived whom you may know
>By the name of Annabel Lee.
>—Edgar Allan Poe, "Annabel Lee"

2. Names of proper nouns and adjectives derived from proper nouns are capitalized:

Washington, Spanish, Monday, Thanksgiving, Uncle Fred, President Truman

3. All words are capitalized in the title of books, poems, songs, short stories, works of art, essays, and chapters (except articles, prepositions, and conjunctions):

The Sound and the Fury, "I Have a Dream," "On First Looking into Chapman's *Homer.*"

(The first word of a title is always capitalized.)
4. *North, south, east,* and *west* are capitalized when they refer to a specific region of the country:

I come from the East.

Apostrophes
Apostrophes are used to form contractions, to show possession, and to form a few plurals.
1. An apostrophe is used to form the possessive of most singular nouns, plural nouns, and indefinite pronouns:

the bus' seats	oxen's yoke	everyone's favorite
Don's book	trees' leaves	girls' locker room

No apostrophe is used in *his, hers, ours, theirs, its,* and *yours* used for possession.
2. An apostrophe is used in a contraction to take the place of the letters left out:

doesn't	I'm
they're	it's
you're	

3. An apostrophe is used to form the plurals of letters, numbers, and words used as words:

> Don't forget to make your *e*'s and *i*'s clearly.
>
> Have you studied your *2*'s in your flash cards?
>
> Count the *and*'s in your sentences.

Hyphens

If you are unsure whether to use a hyphen, look in your dictionary.

1. Hyphens connect several words being used as a single expression:

> sister-in-law, editor-in-chief

2. Hyphens are used to keep parts of words distinct:

> anti-nuclear, semi-professional

3. When two words act as a single modifier before a word, a hyphen is used:

> That article will have far-reaching consequences.
>
> This declaration is a well-written document.

If the modifiers come after the verb, the hyphen is not used:

> This document is well written.

4. A hyphen is used to avoid awkward spelling:

> The door was bolted to prevent re-entry by the thieves.

5. A hyphen is used to prevent confusion:

> I am going to re-cover my wingback chair.

6. A hyphen is used at the end of a line of writing when the whole word will not fit on the line. Divide words only between syllables.

Chapter Two

From "For Freedom of Speech" by Archibald Cox, a speech given at a teach-in on Indochina sponsored by Young Americans for Freedom and Harvard Young Republicans on March 26, 1971. Cited in *The Eloquence of Protest,* ed. by Harrison Salisbury. Boston: Houghton Mifflin Company, 1972. Reprinted by permission of Professor Cox.

Reprinted with permission from "Photochemistry of Organic Ions in the Gas Phase" by B. S. Freiser and J. L. Beauchamp in the *Journal of the American Chemical Society,* No. 11, 1976. Copyright © 1976 American Chemical Society.

Specified excerpts from pp. 81 and 91-92 in *Why We Can't Wait* by Martin Luther King, Jr. Copyright © 1963 by Martin Luther King, Jr. Reprinted by permission of Harper & Row, Publishers, Inc.

From "A Defense of Shyness" in *Small Talk* by Harold George Nicolson, 1937. Reprinted by permission of Harcourt Brace Jovanovich, Inc. and literary executor to the author.

From "Weatherstripping Windows" and "How to Fight Inflation at Home" in *McCall's* Magazine, September 1979. Copyright © 1979 The McCall Publishing Company. Reprinted by permission.

From "Dietary Fiber? The Medical Profession Demurs" from *The Medical Letter on Drugs and Therapeutics.* Cited in *Nutrition Today* Magazine, January/February 1976. Reprinted by permission of The Medical Letter, Inc.

Chapter Three

From "Problem-Solving, Composing, and Liberal Education" by Richard Larson, *College English,* March 1972. Copyright © 1972 by National Council of Teachers of English. Reprinted by permission of the publisher and the author.

Excerpt from "The Welcome Wears Thin" in *Time,* Vol. 116, No. 9, September 1, 1980, Copyright Time Inc. 1980. Reprinted by permission from *Time,* The Weekly Newsmagazine.

From *Teaching as a Conserving Activity* by Neil Postman. Copyright © 1979 by Neil Postman. Originally published in *Atlantic* as "Order in the Classroom." Reprinted by permission of Delacorte Press.

Chapter Four

Specified excerpt from p. 202 in "Once More to the Lake" from *Essays of E. B. White* by E. B. White. Copyright 1941 by E. B. White. Reprinted by permission of Harper & Row, Publishers, Inc.

Chapter Nine

Chapter Ten

More Cases